MADE IN CHINA

MADE IN CHINA

A Prisoner, an SOS Letter,
and the Hidden Cost of
America's Cheap Goods

AMELIA PANG

ALGONQUIN BOOKS OF CHAPEL HILL 2021

Published by
ALGONQUIN BOOKS OF CHAPEL HILL
Post Office Box 2225
Chapel Hill, North Carolina 27515-2225

a division of
WORKMAN PUBLISHING
225 Varick Street
New York, New York 10014

Library of Congress Cataloging-in-Publication Data
Names: Pang, Amelia, [date]– author.
Title: Made in China : a prisoner, an SOS letter, and the hidden cost of
    America's cheap goods / Amelia Pang.
Description: Chapel Hill, North Carolina : Algonquin Books of Chapel Hill, 2021. |
    Includes bibliographical references. | Summary: "After an Oregon mother finds
    an SOS letter in a box of Halloween decorations, a story unfolds about the man
    who wrote it: a Chinese political prisoner, sentenced without trial to work grueling
    hours at a 'reeducation' camp—manufacturing the products sold in our own big-
    box stores"—Provided by publisher.
Identifiers: LCCN 2020034508 | ISBN 9781616209179 (hardcover) |
    ISBN 9781643751139 (ebook)
Subjects: LCSH: Manufacturing industries—China—Social aspects. | Costs,
    Industrial—China—Social aspects. | Work environment—China. |
    Political prisoners—China.
Classification: LCC HD9736.C62 P36 2021 | DDC 331.11/732—dc23
LC record available at https://lccn.loc.gov/2020034508

10 9 8 7 6 5 4 3 2 1
First Edition

For those buried in unmarked graves, waiting for wotou

CONTENTS

ʮʮʮ

MADE IN CHINA

A Message from the Graveyard

It was a slow Sunday afternoon in October 2012, and Julie Keith was thinking of going to the store to buy decorations. Her daughter, Katie, was turning five, and they were getting ready for the birthday party next weekend. Katie had asked for a Halloween-themed celebration. They already had some decorations, although Julie could not remember what exactly.

She made her way outside to the storage shed to sort through what was there. She was a forty-two-year-old mother of two, of average height, with brown eyes and straight golden-brown hair. Her three-bedroom house sat at the end of a quiet cul-de-sac in Damascus, Oregon, a suburb of Portland. She opened the shed, filled with the detritus of suburban life: suitcases, pool toys, Christmas lights. Inside, nestled on a corner shelf, was something that she had forgotten was there: decorative gravestones. A relative, who had purchased the package on clearance from Kmart a few days after Halloween in 2010, had passed it on to her.

Julie brushed off the dust and read the words on the unopened package: TOTALLY GHOUL—RICHLY DETAILED GRAVEYARD KIT HAS AUTHENTIC LOOK, WEIGHT AND FEEL! The product included four headstones, a "bloody cloth," and black velvet roses.

It was perfect for not only Katie's party, but also Halloween. Julie lived in an upper-middle-class neighborhood that attracted hundreds of trick-or-treaters, and her front yard, with its big slope, was a fine spot for a fake graveyard. She carried all her Halloween decorations back inside the house.

As the rays of late afternoon sun scattered through the living room skylights, Julie and Katie sat in the entryway, tearing open dusty cellophane. Julie pulled out the foam headstones. She did not notice that a piece of onionskin paper, folded in eighths, had drifted out of the box. It landed on the floor with the packaging waste.

Julie had grown up in Oregon City, a rural community that was once the final destination of the Oregon Trail. During her childhood in the 1970s, it was still small, with less than fifteen thousand souls. Her father repaired and sold fire extinguishers. Her mother taught ballet from their basement. They owned one acre adjacent to a pasture filled with hay bales, where Julie would chase her friends.

In high school, Julie was not a part of the cool crowd, but she also was not a nerd. She was, in every sense of the word, normal.

By the time she turned eighteen, she was ready to leave Oregon City, but she didn't wander far. She attended Portland State, fifteen miles away from her hometown. She graduated with a degree in sociology and psychology. She didn't know what to do with it. For the next ten years, she worked as a retail buyer for the local NBA team, the Trail Blazers, choosing which souvenirs to stock. She later worked in ground service for Alaska Airlines, driving baggage carts back and forth and enjoying free flights to Hawaii, Mexico, and Germany, before settling down as an assistant to the director of operations at Goodwill's corporate office in Portland.

It was then that Julie, at thirty-four, married her boyfriend of one year, Chris Keith, a kind and burly guy with deep-set brown eyes.

Chris was a self-made man who had worked his way up from electrician to foreman to general foreman. He enjoyed hunting and loved retelling a story about the time he saved his company $500,000. They had an outdoor wedding in a friend's backyard. Julie gave birth to their first child a year later.

"Mommy, what's this?" Katie asked, picking up the paper and unfolding it.

It was a note, handwritten in blue ink. The writing was neat. But the letter was filled with crossed-out words and broken English. The author had added a few Asian characters in parentheses. It looked like an early draft of something.

Julie froze as she read the message.

> *If you occassionally buy this product, please kindly resend this letter to the World Human Right Organization. Thousands people here who are under the persicuton of the Chinese Communist Party Government will thank and remember you forever.*

She was bewildered. *Is this a prank?* she thought. She kept reading.

> *This product produced by Unit 8, Department 2, Mashanjia Labour Camp, Shenyang, Liaoning, China. (中國, 遼寧,瀋陽,馬 三家勞動教養院二所八大隊) People who work here, have to work 15 hours a day with out Saturday, Sunday break and any holidays, otherwise, they will suffer torturement (酷刑折磨), beat and rude remark (打罵體罰虐待), ~~no~~ nearly no payment (10 yuan/1 month). People who work here, suffer punishment ~~nearly~~ 1~3 years averagelly, but without Court*

Sentence (unlaw punishment) (非法勞教). Many of them are Falun gong practitioner, who are totally innocent people only because they have different believe to CCPG (中共政府), they often suffer more punishment than others.

A mixture of terror and disbelief shot up Julie's spine as she understood the gravity of what she was holding: It was an SOS letter from the person who made her decorative gravestones. The letter had slipped past armed guards at a Chinese gulag, eluded managers at all stages of the supply chain, and traveled more than five thousand miles across the Pacific Ocean before landing on Julie's forest-green rug.

She stood there, stunned. She had heard of Chinese sweatshops, but she did not realize that forced-labor camps still existed. She rushed to her laptop to Google "Masanjia," clicking on the first link, a Wikipedia entry.

She read that Masanjia labor camp was established in 1956 and expanded in 1999 to make room for the followers of a newly banned spiritual movement called Falun Gong. She did another Google search, this time clicking on IMAGES. Disfigured bodies with purple, swollen faces appeared on her screen.

What could she, a nonprofit administrative assistant, do about this? She felt sick as she tried to formulate a plan.

Who do I even call?

It's Sunday . . . No offices are open.

Time seemed to slow down. Katie's muted singsong voice hummed in the background as Julie posted about her discovery on Facebook, attaching a picture of the letter.

"I found this in a box of Halloween decorations that I just opened," she wrote. "Someone in a Chinese labor camp asking for help. I am going to do as they asked, I will turn this over to a Human Rights Organization . . ."

She wanted to stop everything to read more about modern labor camps. But this was the only time she had to prepare for the birthday party next weekend. She returned to sorting decorations in a daze.

It's been two years since this package was purchased.

When was this undated letter written?

Two years ago? Five years ago? Ten years ago?

Little did Julie know, the letter that had landed in her home was one of many SOS messages written by various prisoners across China, which would emerge from stores like Kmart, Walmart, and even Saks Fifth Avenue. Consumers found notes inside a set of cupcake boxes, tucked in the zipper compartment of a purse, and hidden inside a paper shopping bag made in China. News outlets such as the *New York Times*, the *New Yorker*, and the BBC would report on at least seven different Chinese SOS letters found in products between 2012 and 2019.

The first well-documented case had occurred in 1994, when a Chinese American human rights activist named Harry Wu got hold of a letter from a man trapped at a forced-labor quarry in the province of Guangdong. The man was Chen Pokong, a prominent pro-democracy organizer, and he had signed the letter with his real name. A flurry of international condemnation—including a US congressional hearing—ensued. The exposure eventually helped Chen leave the labor camp and immigrate to the United States.

But what could Julie, an ordinary American, do for a nameless Chinese prisoner? As she cooked dinner for her family that night, she felt entirely alone. Then she heard the pull and thud of the door. The clunk of a dropped bag. The screech of chair legs. Chris was home from a hunting trip.

"You're never going to believe what I found in this box," Julie said, pointing toward the packaging that still littered the floor. "It's been sitting in our shed for years!"

Chris read the letter but remained quiet for some time.

"It's probably fake," he finally said.

"Well, I think it's real," she said. "I'm going to take it to work to have my coworker translate the Chinese parts to see if it says anything else. He's from China."

"Okay," he said gently. "You do that." Although Chris was worried that Julie was falling for a hoax, he did not want to start an argument.

The conversation shifted to concerns about the family data plan. But the words in the letter kept running in the back of Julie's mind: *People who work here have to work fifteen hours a day . . . Otherwise, they will suffer torture . . .*

The alarm clock went off at five fifteen in the morning. Julie rolled out of bed. As she waited for the coffee to brew, she snuck in a few minutes to check the comments on her Facebook post. "What about contacting the news and do our part in educating the masses?" her friend Vikki had written.

The idea of talking to journalists felt intimidating to Julie. It sounded like something one needed training to do. But she was relieved people were taking her seriously. It reaffirmed her will to do something. She just wasn't sure yet what she needed to do.

She arrived at work at eight and spent the next few hours answering phone calls, consoling customers upset about their expired store credits, and handling invoices. She also told a few coworkers about the letter. "I didn't realize things were that bad in China," one person said. "I'm going to try to avoid 'Made in China' stuff now."

Many of them offered to help in whatever way they could. Heartened by the support from her colleagues, Julie decided to call human rights organizations. The only one she had heard of was Amnesty International, so she started with that.

"Thank you for calling Amnesty International," a recorded voice said. "This call may be recorded for quality assurance. Please hold for the next available operator." Bland music dragged on for several minutes. An unenthusiastic operator greeted her, put her on hold, and transferred her call. Julie was put on hold again before being sent to someone's voicemail.

A few coworkers helped her look up more organizations to call. Julie left messages for Human Rights Watch, the United Nations Human Rights Council, and Anti-Slavery International. A friend of a friend sent her the phone number of the head of the East Asia office of Amnesty International, allowing a morsel of hope. But that call also ended with a voicemail.

When Julie told Chris later that night about her progress, he was not enthused.

"The Chinese government must not like you doing this. What if they send a sniper to our house?" he said in a half-joking, half-not voice.

A few days passed without anyone calling Julie back. With no fresh news, her coworkers returned their focus to work. She considered moving on too as doubts overtook her.

Is this letter real, or is Chris right—is it a hoax?

Are the organizations not interested because this sounds fake?

Am I naive for believing in it so much?

Later that week, Julie bumped into the person she'd been waiting to see—Robert, a middle-aged Chinese maintenance worker, who only came to her building on certain days. Robert, who was taking English as second language classes, could read Chinese. She showed him the crinkled letter.

"The Chinese words say the same thing as the English," he said, seeming unfazed by its content.

Since China's state-controlled media doesn't use the term "forced labor," instead reframing it as merely manufacturing work criminals do to pay their debt to society, the system may sound reasonable to many Chinese people. If they have not been through it themselves, they might not realize how deadly the working conditions are, or that *anyone* can be arbitrarily marked as a criminal.

Julie was disappointed the Chinese words did not reveal new clues. She was running out of ideas, but she wondered if it would help to spread the word to more coworkers.

"Look what I found in something I got from Kmart," Julie said to Goodwill's public relations manager. "It's like a message in a bottle. Maybe you can publish this in the employee newsletter."

The PR manager's eyes turned serious as she read the note.

"Oh, Julie," she said. "I think it's much bigger than that." She paused. "I have some contacts with the *Oregonian*. Are you willing to talk to the press?"

Julie hesitated; her instinct was to say no. But she felt a growing guilt, and fear, that if the letter *was* real, then too much time had already elapsed. Why did she wait two years to open that package?

"Sure . . . I'll talk to the *Oregonian*," Julie said.

A young reporter came the next day. The woman's youth—her untarnished skin, and bright eyes—struck Julie. She wondered if this journalist was fresh out of college. When the reporter had finished the interview, she promised to be in touch soon.

But after the initial adrenaline from talking to the media died out, the waves of guilt returned. Julie could not put it to rest; there had to be something else she could do. She kept talking about it, asking friends and coworkers for ideas and advice. Then someone suggested reaching out to Immigration and Customs Enforcement (ICE). She thought this was a long shot. But she gave the agency a call anyway.

As it turns out, ICE and Customs and Border Protection (CBP) are the primary agencies responsible for preventing forced-labor products from entering US markets. And later that week, two men dressed in business-casual attire arrived in her office lobby. Julie led them to a conference room and sat the agents down beneath a sprawling map of Goodwill locations. Then she handed them the Totally Ghoul box, along with the mysterious letter.

"Where did you buy this product?" one ICE agent asked.

"How long ago?" the other asked.

She did her best to give detailed answers.

Still more questions: "Was the package opened before you bought it? Could it have been possible for someone to slip in the letter at Kmart?"

"No," Julie said. "The package was completely sealed in cellophane."

The interview ended after thirty minutes.

"We'll write a report and send it to our headquarters in DC for further investigation," an agent said.

"Wait," Julie said. "What else should I be doing? I've been contacting human rights organizations—"

"That's probably the best route to go."

After meeting with Julie, ICE made a formal request to the Chinese government to visit Masanjia Reeducation Through Labor Camp in November 2012. But China refused to cooperate. At the time, the Masanjia case was one of twelve pending investigations involving Chinese forced-labor facilities that were likely exporting to the

United States. To date, China has not allowed US officials to visit any of these sites. In the end, the US government could not issue a detention order for Totally Ghoul decorations without more proof that they came from a labor camp. "One piece of evidence is generally not enough," a Customs and Border Protection official later told me over the phone.

For the next two months, Julie waited in the dark. ICE never updated her on the results of its investigation. There was also no word from any human rights organizations or the reporter. She assumed that the *Oregonian* had forgotten about her, or that maybe they didn't believe the letter was real.

Knowing her husband's stance on the note's authenticity, she rarely shared her frustrations with him. She cracked open a golden ale as she watched *The Amazing Race*, but her thoughts kept drifting to that faceless prisoner.

Is it a man or a woman?

Young or old?

How did this person end up in a labor camp?

Is he or she still alive?

1: The Brink of Death

ᒡᒡᒡ

Shenyang, China, 2009, three years
before the letter was discovered

Sun Yi lay on a stretcher in a barren white room. His mouth was parched. A steel gag had kept it pried open for more than twenty-four hours. Sun, a forty-two-year-old man with pensive eyes and a small frame, listened for noises in the hallway.

Silence. The other detainees, who worked fifteen- to twenty-hour shifts, were downstairs laboring in workshops, where they produced diodes, Halloween decorations, and disposable underwear, all of which was exported from China to the United States and Europe.

Sun looked around. His vision was blurry without his glasses—he strained to focus on the three iron bunk beds, where other prisoners were sometimes chained and starved.

He heard a metallic click. Someone was unlocking the door. The noise startled Sun, and his body jerked, causing the cuffs around his wrists and ankles to dig deeper into his skin.

A nurse wearing a bloodstained white dress entered the room, followed by two sullen colleagues. One carried a bowl of lumpy, heavily salted cornmeal. Another held tubes used for force-feeding.

The nurses rubbed talcum powder on their hands and put on white plastic gloves before organizing the tubes, some bottles, and a stethoscope.

Finally, one of the nurses broke the silence. "Are you going to cooperate this time?" Her voice was gentle and unsure, as if she did not want to be there.

Sun was too frail to talk. Unable to clench his hands into a fist, his fingers twitched as he prepared to resist the next round of torture.

Sun was afraid of death. He had been ever since he was ten years old, when he came home after school and saw his paternal grandmother sitting at the bottom of their shared bunk bed. An illiterate, brittle woman with soft eyes and a tense jaw, she was staring at some creased papers. A fortune-teller had once told her she had a blessed face, that her life would get better as she aged. The fortune-teller was wrong.

"Will you read this for me?" she asked, standing up to hand him the papers.

Sun's father, an engineer who designed petroleum extraction equipment, had warned him earlier that day to not read for her if she asked.

"Please read this to me," she said.

Sun hesitated before taking the papers.

It was her medical diagnosis. She had coronary heart disease; the major blood vessels in her heart were close to rupturing.

"What does it say?" she asked.

"I don't know," Sun lied. "I don't recognize a lot of these words."

He walked over to his reading desk by the window and listened to the raindrops clatter on the gravel outside. It startled him, the imminence of death. He blinked back tears. *Grandmother will be gone soon*, he thought. *Everyone eventually dies. One day I will die too.*

He wanted to run to his mother, but she wouldn't be home from her administrative job for several hours. Both his parents worked six days a week at the petroleum equipment manufacturing plant to earn a combined income of 70 yuan (roughly $137) a month. It was 1976, and the Cultural Revolution was reeling to an end. Everyone was poor, except for a few government officials.

Sun leaned closer to the window to hide his moist eyes. *What a difficult life Grandmother has lived.*

Her husband's gambling addiction had bankrupted the family's small food-processing factory. Then he got lung disease and passed away abruptly one night, leaving Sun's grandmother to feed two children on a maid's salary. Against all odds, Sun's father won a scholarship from the China University of Petroleum in Beijing. He graduated with a degree in geophysics exploration. But the proletariat class was slightly better off than the educated class at the time; he would have earned a higher wage as an assembly-line worker.

Sun grew up during a time of immense human suffering. Between 1958 and 1962, before he was born, as many as forty-five million people died from starvation and state-sponsored violence during the failed Great Leap Forward, when Mao Zedong, chairman of the Chinese Communist Party, tried to create rapid industrialization by forcing farmers into mass collectives. A combination of political violence, disorganization, and unrealistic pressures had led to widespread food shortages. In the following years, many of the refugee farmers migrated from the province of Henan, a largely agricultural region, to the area around Sun's home village, near the city of Taiyuan, which had more industries bolstering its economy. He used to save kitchen scraps for the famine refugees.

Sun was living with his maternal grandmother. His parents, like most able-bodied adults at the time, had to work so much to make ends meet that they could not care for their children. Sun would not live with them until he started school.

One night in the village, when it felt like it was below 20 degrees Fahrenheit, Sun followed the refugees to a half-built structure where they slept. It was a thatched, doorless cottage, made of mud and bricks and held up by a single wooden post. Sun saw a group of skeletal people huddling on the floor as an icy wind pierced the shack. He was particularly disturbed to see a rail-thin toddler girl among them. He ran home and begged his maternal grandmother to sell their family's copper spoons so they could donate money to the refugees.

"The spoons are antiques, but they won't sell for much money right now. Plus, we need them for our daily use," his grandmother said. "How about you give them some leftovers tomorrow morning?"

He sprinted to the doorless cottage early the next morning, carrying sticky rice cakes. But the cottage was empty. He scampered outside, running a little way in different directions. He could not find any trace of them. He carried the sticky rice home, wondering if the little girl would survive the winter.

A few years later, Sun looked over at his dying paternal grandmother on the bunk bed as she knitted and muttered Buddhist scriptures. He watched her needles crisscross above the blue plaid bedsheet.

Although it was dangerous to openly embrace religion during the Cultural Revolution, Sun's paternal grandmother held on to her faith. She would secretly burn incense at Mount Wutai, a cluster of sacred peaks of which the tallest transcended ten thousand feet. She would watch the trickle of smoke rise into the air and vanish. According to legend, the bodhisattva of wisdom—an enlightened being who has deferred paradise to help others—resided in these mountains and sometimes appeared in the form of colorful clouds. The lush forest, filled with poplar, fir, and willow trees, induced introspection.

Sun could tell that whenever his grandmother returned from Mount Wutai, she was at peace with the way her life had unfolded.

She was one of the few who dared to return to Mount Wutai. She never took Sun. It was too dangerous. But she taught him Buddhist scriptures at home. He didn't understand what the words meant at first, or why she held on to them so dearly.

Then, one summer, it began to make sense. Before the start of the fifth grade, Sun read *Journey to the West*, a classical Chinese novel chronicling the adventures of a monk on a pilgrimage to retrieve holy scriptures from India. In the beginning, Sun would stop to look up new words. But the story was so thrilling, and it spoke to him so deeply, that he started skipping over unfamiliar vocabulary. He finished all one hundred chapters in just two months.

Sun felt especially inspired when he learned that the tales were based on true events. In AD 629, a scholarly monk named Xuanzang had indeed embarked on a journey to India by foot, to collect Buddhist texts and bring them back to China. After completing the seventeen-year round trip, the monk spent the rest of his life translating the thirteen hundred manuscripts he had transported.

Journey to the West triggered something in Sun. He began pondering the meaning of life. Yearning for a part of his culture that was now forbidden, he wanted to go on a spiritual journey of his own. But where could a person find spirituality in modern China?

It was years later, on one early winter morning in 1998, when Sun would come across a group of Falun Gong followers meditating in a Beijing park.

The Falun Gong movement, also known as Falun Dafa, founded in 1992 by Li Hongzhi, a former government clerk, is based on a set of standing and sitting qigong exercises. Qigong is a slow-moving Chinese healing art with a four-thousand-year-old history. Inspired by Buddhist traditions, Li combined his meditative exercises with a moral code. Followers study Li's writings on spirituality, which center on the ideas that the mind and body are connected, that morality and meditation can elevate a person's plane of consciousness, and that this elevation can in turn resolve personal issues and even illnesses. They believe traditional qigong theories that state that illnesses are caused by blocked energy channels and karma, and that by practicing qigong exercises and living a moral life, one can eliminate karma and heal disease.

While Falun Gong has some religious characteristics, drawing on Buddhist, Taoist, and ancient folk teachings, it does not have clergy or a formal conversion process. It also does not have places of worship, although before the Chinese government banned the practice in 1999, there were regional Falun Dafa Associations, whose volunteers organized group exercises in parks.

Li Hongzhi introduced the practice during a critical period in Chinese history—a time when people in China were finally allowed to search for spirituality and meaning again after several traumatic decades of repression.

The political upheaval began in 1966 with the decade-long Cultural Revolution. Chairman Mao Zedong's Red Guards, a paramilitary group that consisted mostly of college and high school students, carried out mass killings to help Mao solidify his control over the country's Communist Party. The Red Guards annihilated anything and anyone that represented pre-Communist China's "four olds," which the party vaguely defined as old ideas, old customs, old habits, and old culture. All religious activities were banned, and the Red Guards desecrated temples. They ransacked libraries, shops, and private homes, torturing and killing traditional authority figures, such as their former teachers and principals. As schools and universities shut down, more than sixteen million young people were sent to the countryside to do hard labor on farms. In theory, this was supposed to help integrate these young people with the working class.

In the end, the Cultural Revolution killed millions and mangled China's economy. This is why modern mainland Chinese ideals tend to place higher value on social stability than human rights. The last thing people want is another revolution.

After Mao died in 1976, one of his successors, Deng Xiaoping, carried out sweeping social and economic reforms, such as relegalizing private business and reopening China to foreign trade and investments. Deng set forth a series of policies that would eventually transform China from an impoverished nation into the world's second-largest economy. His reforms also lifted the ban on religion, and a qigong resurgence ensued. Thousands of practices like Falun Gong formed throughout the 1980s and '90s, filling China's spiritual void.

But unlike many other qigong groups, Falun Gong made its exercise music, meditation instruction videos, and texts available for free on the internet. It became the most popular meditation practice, attracting seventy million followers in China at its peak, in the mid- to late 1990s.

The Chinese government initially supported Falun Gong and gave it favorable media coverage. In 1995, the Chinese Communist Party (CCP) invited the practice's founder, Li, to give a talk on meditation at the Chinese embassy in Paris. But relations between Falun Gong and the party started to strain in 1996, when the group left the state-run China Qigong Scientific Research Society after a dispute over fees. The stated goal of the society was to conduct studies on the effects of qigong, but more importantly, it gave the party full control over member semireligious groups.

The Chinese regime often uses a co-opt strategy to manage dissent. People with influence outside the government, such as celebrities, union leaders, and priests, have to join the party. If the party cannot convince a potential threat to support the ruling coalition, that threat has to be eliminated. So when Falun Gong distanced itself from the government qigong association, it was problematic for the party. A group with seventy million followers was now outside its control. If Falun Gong felt inclined to launch a democracy movement, it could potentially topple the regime. It was then that anti–Falun Gong propaganda—"dangerous cult," "evil cult"—began to flood state-run news networks.

It was a predictable response. The modern Chinese political system was, after all, designed to prevent a second mass democracy movement. Starting in the early 1980s, economic reforms had allowed a portion of the Chinese population—many of whom were party leaders—to quickly grow massive amounts of wealth. As China's income disparity widened, aggrieved college students, workers, and intellectuals began calling for political reforms, which included democratic elections and freedom of the press. In the spring of 1989, as many as one million people gathered at Tiananmen Square to protest the party's corruption. The authoritarian regime ended the six-week protest with a massacre.

Ever since then, the CCP has been steadily increasing its domestic security, to stamp out any flicker of organizing that could ignite political unrest. And that included uprooting Falun Gong before it could leverage its power to become a threat.

Even when Falun Gong is discussed in the media outside China, it is often with some derision. This is partially due to the party's propaganda. The main criticisms of Falun Gong are that its practitioners often refuse medical treatment and that its code of beliefs trends conservative. Falun Gong members are generally not supportive of LGBT rights or abortion. They are also not supposed to drink, use recreational drugs, or engage in premarital sex.

Overall, though, the Falun Gong community both inside and outside China is a microcosm of religion—there are fundamentalists, moderates, and those who meditate but do not care for the practice's code of beliefs.

It's true that the more fundamentalist followers of the practice will refuse medical treatment. This is the criticism that the Chinese government has homed in on. According to the party, the ban on Falun Gong is protecting people from engaging in superstitious behaviors that could endanger their lives.

But more moderate Falun Gong followers often do not take a literal interpretation of this concept; they do not believe meditation can fully cure illnesses and are very willing to seek medical attention when qigong exercises fail to improve their ailments. Plus, the Chinese government did not create programs to help people leave what was supposedly a life-threatening cult. Instead, the CCP put them in prisons and labor camps.

Regardless of the nuances of Falun Gong's beliefs and practices, many of its followers in China have entered a new category of their own: political dissidents. What began as advocacy for freedom of religion would morph into a sprawling underground resistance movement, and by 2013, Amnesty International would estimate that Falun Gong detainees made up a third to almost 100 percent of the population of some labor camps in China. Initially an apolitical meditation group, Falun Gong would react to its slander and repression by morphing into one of the Chinese Communist Party's loudest and most organized critics.

• • •

I first heard about the Kmart SOS letter in the US press in 2013. Sun was not the first to send a message from a Chinese gulag, but the fact that he was a religious dissident imprisoned for his beliefs and political activism, rather than a violent criminal, made his letter harder to forget.

I had always wondered what happened to the authors of notes like these. By a stroke of luck, a human rights advocate reached out to me three years later, in 2016. She saw I had written an article about Chinese forced laborers manufacturing Christmas lights. She was in touch with Sun. She wanted to get his story told.

As a journalist with a personal connection to Falun Gong (my Chinese mother is a Falun Gong practitioner), I was familiar with the group's battles with the Chinese government. Although I am not a Falun Gong member myself, I used to write for the *Epoch Times*, a US-based Chinese dissident news organization that was staffed mostly by Falun Gong followers. More significantly, I felt that Sun's fight for freedom and his subsequent imprisonment were emblematic of a much broader human rights issue, which extends beyond Falun Gong. As China veers toward an increasingly dystopian future, the efforts of resistors like Sun become ever more important.

Over the course of three years, I immersed myself in Sun's story and the accounts of other labor camp survivors. As I spoke with the wholesalers who serve as middlemen between labor camps and big international retailers, the people who audit Chinese factories for multinational corporations, and the sales managers at the factories who respond to US consumer demands, it became clear this was more than a story about Chinese human rights. This was about unfettered globalization and overconsumption.

There is a darker side to China's rags-to-riches transformation—and our own pleasure in the cheap products that we consume daily.

During our endless search for the newest trends for the lowest prices, we become complicit in the forced-labor industry. Chinese manufacturers often believe they have no choice but to secretly outsource to gulags, because they cannot meet the global consumer demand for budget prices and the latest trends. Studies have shown it is precisely brands' demands for lower prices, faster production, and fulfillment of unanticipated orders that compel factories to illegally subcontract work to places like labor camps.

And to what end? The trajectory for so many types of low-priced merchandise, and their raw materials, is a bleak one from labor camps to landfills. According to one study, about 60 percent of all clothing manufactured around the world is discarded within a few years of production. That is equivalent to one garbage truck full of clothes arriving at a landfill every second. And landfills are running out of space at a rapid pace as nonbiodegradable materials like cheap synthetic textiles and foam decorations can take decades to hundreds of years to decompose. In fact, China's largest landfill—which is the size of one hundred soccer fields piled some fifty stories high—became full a quarter of a century ahead of schedule.

This is unsustainable from both a land use and a climate perspective. Landfills release an enormous amount of carbon emissions into the atmosphere—on top of the manufacturing sector's already-extensive carbon footprint.

It is crucial that China, the world's largest producer of greenhouse gases, reduce its carbon emissions. About 25 percent of those emissions come from the manufacturing of products for export—but this estimate is based only on factories that corporations and the Chinese government are officially tracking. In other words, this data fails to cover the massive unknown number of forced-labor facilities and other substandard factories that these manufacturers are illegally sourcing from.

The key to curbing an imminent climate catastrophe is to have accurate tracking of emissions and energy policies that cover all emissions sources. Without measurable, reportable, and verifiable statistics, countries like China cannot assess if they are on track to meet their emissions targets.

Despite the dire circumstances, there is hope for change. A global anti-sweatshop campaign against the sportswear company Nike in the 1990s ultimately forced many brands not only to begin auditing their factories but also to share those audit reports with the public—a level of transparency that was previously unfathomable. And now, as the ongoing climate crisis worsens, we are living at a time in history where people care more about sustainable and ethical consumption than they ever have before. This is especially true of millennials and members of Generation Z. Whether it's supporting companies that have reduced their carbon footprint or ones that appear to have ethical factory conditions, we are seeing a new willingness among consumers to select, or reject, brands for the express purpose of making a positive impact in the world.

Transparency, sustainability, and ethical sourcing have become hot marketing buzzwords in recent years. In 2014, CDP, a nonprofit that conducts environmental research for businesses and governments, found that companies on the S&P 500 index with a sustainability mission outperformed businesses without one. Corporations with an active plan for curbing climate change saw an 18 percent higher return on investment than companies with no such initiatives. And companies who disclosed their emissions data saw a 67 percent higher return than those who did not.

But are these companies' sourcing practices truly transparent, sustainable, and ethical? This question can't be answered without addressing the laogai (reform through labor) industry.

Inspired by Soviet gulags, China's first labor camps opened in the 1930s. China's laogai system remains the largest forced-labor system in operation today. It includes a vast network of prisons, camps, and various extralegal detention centers. These modern labor camps often have innocuous labels, such as drug detox centers or pretrial detention centers, which disguise the fact that they are forced-labor factories.

In these camps, millions of emaciated people must work fifteen to twenty hours a day, seven days a week. Many also undergo political indoctrination and torture. According to survivors, the guards torture the detainees and deprive them of sleep if they fail to meet production quotas. When there is a spike in demand, they sometimes force detainees to stay up around the clock until they finish the work.

Unlike inmates in prisons, reeducation through labor (RTL) detainees do not have trials or access to lawyers. Instead, they recieve informal sentences of up to four years from public security bureaus. When their terms are up, some detainees receive sentence extensions. Some are also transferred to other types of forced-labor facilities upon release. Many die in the camps, from torture and lack of medical care.

Sun was imprisoned in Masanjia RTL Camp, which first opened in the late 1950s. It was expanded in 1999 to make room for the sudden influx of Falun Gong captives, when the government began cracking down on the group. The Chinese economy flourished as millions of forced laborers made products for global corporations in the Chinese forced-labor network—a labor force that became equivalent to at least 25 percent of the US manufacturing sector by 2014, comprising three to five million people. And that figure is still growing. It does not include the emerging reeducation camps in the region of Xinjiang, which are currently estimated to detain 1.5 to 3 million people alone. It is unclear what percentage of those detainees are currently forced to labor.

The laogai industry is an open secret among Chinese factories. If they are ever desperate to fill a last-minute order, they know they can turn to gulags for cheap and fast production. According to Dan Cui, an apparel factory owner in the city of Guangzhou, it is well-known that factories illegally subcontract some of their work to Chinese prisons and various detention centers. When I asked her on LinkedIn if she knew any suppliers that sourced from labor camps, she said, "This is not [a] secret. Yes, some companies do like this way." But she insisted her manufacturer has never sourced from a forced-labor facility. And she would not reveal the names of suppliers that did.

The chains on the door rattled. A man with a white mask covering half his face walked into Sun's torture room. His name was Dr. Xu. He was a "barefoot doctor," a rural villager with some basic medical training. As he took over the force-feeding procedure, the look in his eyes showed Sun the doctor had a conscience. But he also wasn't looking for trouble. He had to earn a living. Without pause, he inserted a white plastic tube into Sun's dry and inflamed nose. Dr. Xu did not squirt lubricant into Sun's nostril before inserting the tube. He had been told to make the procedure as painful as possible.

With his four limbs tied, Sun could only resist by shaking his head. He struggled with such force that blood dripped from his nose.

Dr. Xu removed the bright-red tube, rubbing oil on it this time before reinserting. It slipped in easily, causing Sun's body to lurch forward. His eyes watered as he felt an urge to vomit. A guard closed his own eyes before reaching over to press Sun's head down.

The tube was slicing down his throat now. Doctors at Guantanamo Bay, who also force-feed prisoners, would stop at this point to take an x-ray or test with a dose of water to ensure that the tube was following the correct course. If a tube was inserted in the wrong spot, it could cause a collapsed lung, pneumonia, or even death. They did not bother with x-rays at Masanjia.

Sun felt an unbearable agony followed by a sharp puncture. The tube had reached his stomach.

Dr. Xu picked up the stethoscope and listened to Sun's abdomen. He surmised that the tube was in the right place.

The doctor felt the soy milk container with the back of his hand. The procedure had taken longer than he expected. The milk was already cool. According to Chinese custom, one should never consume cold drinks. He left the room to reheat the liquid, leaving behind an uncomfortable silence. Perhaps this was the only kindness Dr. Xu could show.

When Dr. Xu returned, he injected the soy milk into the tube with a syringe. Sun winced as warm fluid poured into his body. He was startled by a strange ecstasy as his muscles contracted and relaxed. His stomach, no longer his own, was eager to accept the milk he did not want. But as the liquid entered his digestive system, Sun's body went into shock. A fishy sweetness gurgled in his throat; he threw up.

Sun closed his eyes and tried to forget where he was. He thought of his wife—her oval face, her soft jawline, and how her eyes curved upward. He thought of the first time he saw her—at a dance in southwest China. It had been the fall of 1994, and Sun was beginning his English studies in the city of Chongqing. He was new in town, and he was the only northerner. He remembered noticing how her dark, wavy hair fell past her shoulders, and that she wasn't as dressed up as the other girls. Her beauty was quiet. He liked that about her. She was the last thought on his mind before he lost consciousness.

Sun woke up shivering. It was the middle of the night, and the window was open. Feng Jun, an inmate-guard assigned to watch Sun at night, was watching him intently.

The official title for these inmates who are also guards is *si fang*, which means "four prevention." They were supposed to prevent four things: suicides, escapes, uprisings, and other subversive acts. But they were really there to assist the other guards with brutality. Prisoners with a violent past were often selected to become si fang. In return, they received benefits such as a reduced sentence and access to clean drinking water.

"You can fall asleep with the gag on?" Feng said, sneering. "I must report it to your division's labor captain tomorrow. The mouth gag clearly isn't working."

Sun felt something warm near his face. It smelled spicy. Feng was eating a bowl of instant noodles. Without a word, he scattered garlic chili powder into Sun's open mouth, which a forced feeding gag kept pried open.

Sun erupted in hacking coughs. When they quieted, Feng rubbed chili powder across his eyes and nostrils. Trying his best to not give the inmate-guard a reaction, Sun held his breath.

Looking around, Feng grabbed a horseradish sauce from the cart that a guard had brought in earlier to assist with force-feeding torture. He smeared the green paste across Sun's eyelids. As Sun screamed, Feng drizzled the rest of the horseradish onto his instant noodles. Sun squeezed his eyes shut as a messy mixture of tears and mucus streamed down his face.

It was a long time before the stinging diminished. Sun opened his eyes and stared blankly at the white ceiling. A cold draft burned against his bare skin, and it occurred to him it was winter. He remembered the letters he'd written.

It's been a long time. I guess no one received any of the SOS messages I wrote.

Did my English not make sense?

Maybe people just didn't notice the letters and threw them all away with the packaging.

He lingered on these thoughts. He lay motionless on the stretcher as bloody mucus hardened on his face.

2: Laogai Nation

ᔥᔥᔥ

Historically, systemic forced labor was not unique to China. Unpaid labor has made many empires wealthy throughout the centuries. Slavery was central to the Roman Empire's economy, and Britain's booming sugar plantations in the West Indies were built on the backs of African chattel slaves. In the United States, it was the slave-produced cotton industry that led to the nation's transformation into the world's largest industrial power. As Cornell University historian Edward Baptist details in his book *The Half Has Never Been Told*, "Cotton was the most important raw material of the industrial revolution that created our modern world economy."

And in the world's second-largest economy, China, forced labor stretches back several centuries. For hundreds of years, Chinese emperors have forced unpaid workers to build public projects, such as the Great Wall, the Grand Canal, and a system of national roads. During the first half of the Ming dynasty (roughly AD 1368 to 1506), the government forced unpaid corvée workers to manufacture silk fabrics. But it was the Chinese Communist Party that began brainwashing political prisoners and placing them in permanent labor camps.

After China's final imperial dynasty collapsed in 1912, the country fell into an anarchic period, when regional warlords fought one another for control of the country. A small band of Chinese Communists formed a political party in the early 1920s, and they initially collaborated with a larger group, the Nationalists, to form a military alliance to defeat the warlords.

Then, in 1927, Chiang Kai-shek, the military leader of the Nationalist Party, betrayed the Communists, purging anyone with Communist affiliations and killing thousands. As the surviving Communists went underground, Chiang Kai-shek reunified most of China under a Nationalist government the following year.

The Chinese Communists began fighting a civil war against the Nationalists, which would last through most of the 1930s, relying on guerrilla warfare to take over and establish military bases in rural regions. Whenever the Communists overtook new territories, they would capture landlords and redistribute the land to peasants. They forced some of their early political enemies—including those landlords, as well as farmers who were more well-off than others—to labor in makeshift factories inspired by Soviet gulags. There, forced laborers manufactured goods for the CCP's military. These were the first laogai camps.

When Japan invaded China in 1937, the Communists and the Nationalists were forced to put a moratorium on their civil war as they united to fight the Japanese. This allowed the Communist Party, whose numbers had been declining after heavy military losses, to stabilize and recruit new members.

After the Japanese surrendered in 1945, the civil war between the Communists and the Nationalists resumed. The Communist Party was much larger than its foe now. The Nationalists suffered a military defeat in 1949, which forced the remaining members of the Nationalist government to retreat to the island of Taiwan. Newly empowered, the Communists took over mainland China's municipal prisons, transforming some of them into wool and textile plants, where forced laborers made pants, hats, and gloves for Communist officials.

Forced labor went on to play an important role in rebuilding China's war-torn economy. The detainees were mostly wealthy people who had been stripped of their land and savings in the Communist turnover, as well as anyone who had ties to the Nationalists. Liu Shaoqi, a top-ranking CCP member who would shortly become the third most powerful man in China, remarked at a national public security meeting in 1951: "The [laogai workers] make up a labor force numbering in the hundreds of thousands to millions, which is equal to the entire labor force of Bulgaria. These criminals do not need insurance or wages. They can do many different types of jobs and can form a giant enterprise. After all, the Soviet Union used criminals to construct several canals. These prisoners are economically and politically useful, that is the reason we keep them alive."

By June 1952, there were over six hundred laogai farms and more than two hundred laogai mines, as well as various railroad construction projects that relied heavily on forced labor.

Then in 1956, a movement called the Hundred Flowers Campaign was put in place. The Chinese Communist Party, claiming it was open to democratic reforms, asked for constructive criticism from citizens. The policy was supposed to "let a hundred flowers bloom, and a hundred schools of thought contend." This was before the Cultural Revolution; there was still a sense of hope that the new ruling party could improve people's lives. And so intellectuals such as writers, academics, and students began speaking out against their impoverished living conditions and the corrupt party officials who looted money from the working class.

The party received millions of disapproving letters. The volume and severity of the complaints might have scared Chairman Mao. Or perhaps he had always intended to use this policy to lure out critics of his regime. Either way, in 1957 Mao launched a movement that became known as the Anti-Rightist Campaign, which sent hundreds and thousands of intellectuals into reeducation through labor camps.

Ai Qing, the father of dissident artist Ai Weiwei, was one of those intellectuals. In 1957, the year of Ai Weiwei's birth, Ai Qing and his family were exiled to a remote part of China. For his reeducation, Ai Qing, a famous poet who had once advised Mao on literary policies, was consigned to cleaning public toilets and dragging heavy construction stones. Ai Weiwei spent his entire childhood living in squalor, including in a pit house that had been built for livestock. His father attempted suicide several times.

Meanwhile in Xinjiang, there was *hashar*, a program that forced disenfranchised Turkic people to work in agricultural and public works programs without payment. Although this began in preindustrial China, Turkic people between the ages of eighteen and sixty-five are still required to work in these programs for weeks at a time, several times per year, in some areas of Xinjiang today. The state does not give hashar laborers food or housing. Many report sleeping outside and eating instant noodles for days. Injured hashar workers not only have to pay their own medical expenses, they also have to search for a family member to cover their missed hours. If they are unable to find anyone, they have to pay a fine.

Although Nikita Khrushchev, then-secretary of the Communist Party of the Soviet Union, began dismantling Soviet gulags after Premier Joseph Stalin's death in 1953, the Chinese did not follow suit after Chairman Mao Zedong's death in 1976. Instead, his successors built more laogai camps, as they continued to imprison anyone vaguely defined as "enemies of the people." And these camps have only expanded since, as some periods of major economic growth have been connected to a surge in labor camps.

One particularly powerful catalyst for the proliferation of laogai camps was the US decision to establish formal diplomatic relations with the Chinese Communist Party. When the Communist Party took over mainland China in 1949, the United States initially refused to acknowledge it as a legitimate government. It was the beginning of the Cold War, after all. For the next thirty years, the United States still recognized the loser of the Chinese Civil War, the Nationalist government in Taiwan, as China's sole legal representative. But after months of secret negotiations, at the end of 1978, President Jimmy Carter announced he would acknowledge the CCP.

This was a big moment for the laogai industry. US trade with mainland China had been limited since 1950, when the United States imposed a trade embargo after China began giving North Korea military assistance during the Korean War. But when President Carter restored full diplomatic relations, the United States became China's second-largest importer.

The laogai industry's production value was worth 1.7 billion yuan in 1958. Between 1978 and 1980—during and after the restoration of trade relations with the United States—laogai facilities produced a heaping 14 billion yuan worth of products, with a net profit of 2 billion yuan. And the profits only increased from there.

In 2013, Peng Daiming, a former deputy administrator of Masanjia, admitted to a Chinese magazine called *Lens* that this single camp's five thousand prisoners could generate nearly 100 million yuan (almost $15 million) a year. And Masanjia was only one out of at least a thousand camps and prisons—all of which had been filling with new waves of laboring dissidents and petty criminals as the original landlords and political prisoners perished.

In 2008, the public security bureau sentenced a twenty-year-old named Wang Dong—without trial—to one year in Masanjia for "premeditated robbery" because he had a fruit knife at a bus stop. The same year, when a high school student from the province of Sichuan ran away from home and was caught in Beijing without a valid residential ID card, the police charged him with "premeditated robbery" as well. He, too, received a one-year sentence to Masanjia. The punishments may have been disproportionate to the tenuous crimes they were accused of, but that didn't matter. What mattered was that labor camps had enough workers to fill production quotas.

People currently imprisoned in laogai camps can be divided into roughly seven categories: political prisoners; those who practice forbidden religions; ethnic minorities; petitioners; migrant workers; juvenile offenders; and adult criminals, a category that includes petty criminals and sex workers.

The political prisoners are intellectuals, activists, journalists, and others who express opposition to one-party rule. According to the Paris-based NGO Reporters Without Borders, as of October 2019, China held the highest number of journalists behind bars of any country in the world.

While most prisoners in China are likely incarcerated for normal nonpolitical crimes, there is no reliable data on this. Most of the information about the laogai system comes from the accounts of survivors—and from a Washington, DC–based human rights NGO called the Laogai Research Foundation. The NGO was cofounded in 1992 by Harry Wu, who survived nineteen years in Chinese gulags.

Wu and his researchers spent years chronicling the system by posing as prospective buyers of laogai products. They called the camps, tracked their online advertisements, and, at great risk to themselves, personally visited laogai factories. The Laogai Research Foundation eventually identified more than fourteen hundred operating camps and prisons.

But when Wu passed away abruptly in 2016, at age seventy-nine, the organization was effectively shuttered. Since his death, there have been significantly fewer people documenting the camps and their partnerships with transnational brands. Every now and then, a journalist will find a connection between a labor camp and a big company. But there are no longer any active organizations dedicated to this research.

Another reason there is no reliable data on what percentage of laogai prisoners fall under each category: dissidents often receive flagrantly false charges. Environmental activists have been arrested for prostitution; activist artist Ai Weiwei was detained for economic crimes; Ai's lawyer received a twelve-year sentence for supposed financial fraud. What we do know: China's pervasive facial-recognition surveillance cameras—of which there are expected to be 2.76 billion by 2022—do not allow dissent to go unnoticed for long. The authorities detain almost all activists at some point and require them to labor in these facilities. It is an efficient way for the government to quarantine dissidents while simultaneously boosting the national economy.

The religious population in labor camps includes Christians, Muslims, and Tibetan Buddhists. Their crime is worshipping outside of state-sanctioned churches, mosques, and temples. And among adherents of unsanctioned religions, there are followers of Falun Gong. Although some of these people are imprisoned only for practicing forbidden religions, many of them, like the majority of imprisoned Falun Gong practitioners, had taken on activist roles in response to religious suppression, so they may also be considered political prisoners.

The ethnic minorities include groups such as Tibetans, Uyghurs, and Kazakhs. The government is trying to force these people to reject their languages, cultures, and faiths to assimilate to a Han Chinese political identity.

The petitioners are people who repeatedly travel to Beijing to seek redress for grievances, such as land seizure, demolition, wage theft, and other social issues. This petitioning is part of the formal system for voicing complaints to the government, but when too many petitioners gather in the capital, the government believes they pose a risk for revolution. Petitioners are often detained as soon as they arrive in the city.

The migrant workers are rural villagers who migrate to cities to earn a living, but who have been caught without the official documents that permit them to work in those cities.

As for juvenile offenders, many of them are impoverished rural children. There are an estimated two hundred thousand to three hundred thousand juveniles working in Chinese detention centers, although it is difficult to verify. In 2019, I called the Shanghai Juvenile Detention Center in Songjiang District, which manufactures stationery, radio parts, toys, and electronic components, to ask if they could export to my fake company in Canada. The person who answered the phone said they could, before giving me the extension for the sales manager. When I talked to the sales manager, however, he was more cautious.

"Who told you that? How did you hear about that?" he asked.

"A friend said he had a good experience buying from you," I said. But unable to name anyone he knew, I gave myself away.

"We don't make products here," he said. There was a palpable tension in his voice. "We have never made products here. This is a detention center."

Sun was a religious dissident, and his longest stretch of imprisonment began in 2008 in Masanjia. During his time there, the camp held predominantly petty criminals, underground Christians, and Falun Gong followers. More than a decade later, these groups of people are still subject to forced labor. But the camps are even worse for ethnic minorities, particularly in Xinjiang. Bordering Afghanistan and Pakistan, the region is home to several indigenous Turkic Muslim minorities, predominantly Uyghurs, followed by Kazakhs. It is also, according to a 2009 report by Amnesty International, "the only area of China where the general population (non-prisoners) is systematically subject to a government policy of forced labour."

Although the Chinese government claims it eliminated hashar policies decades ago, human rights organizations and the United States' Congressional-Executive Commission on China continue to document the system's persistence. And while Turkic people have been subjected to forced labor in agricultural and public works projects under hashar for years, now, in the reeducation camps that China calls "vocational training centers," they must also labor in factories for little or no payment.

In Xinjiang, Turkic people have long lived as second-class citizens. But in recent years, small and sometimes violent protests have begun to erupt in the region in response to worsening inequality. In turn, the Chinese government has increased its spending to transform the region into an unprecedented high-tech police state, with artificial intelligence facial-recognition cameras that monitor ethnic minorities at checkpoints throughout Xinjiang.

The Jamestown Foundation, a DC-based NGO that informs policy makers about trends in totalitarian countries, found that, between 2016 and 2017, China raised its spending on domestic security in Xinjiang by 92.8 percent—from 30.05 billion yuan to 57.95 billion yuan. That figure is almost 1,000 percent higher than the budget in 2007. The US Department of Defense affirmed that in 2019, political reeducation camps in the region held as many as three million central Asian Muslims.

One reason most captive Muslims in China appear to be kept alive, for now, at least, is their utility as forced laborers. And consumers around the world are allowing the Chinese government to profit from this forced labor by buying products made at these camps. In October 2018, a state-run news channel broadcast the supposed success of a camp's vocational training program. The footage featured Turkic men dressed in lemon yellow and Turkic women in crimson red, sewing clothing with their heads bowed at Hetian Taida Apparel Co. Two months later, the Associated Press (AP) broke the story that Badger Sportswear, a US company that makes uniforms for high school and college sports teams, had been sourcing some merchandise from a Hetian Taida factory located inside a reeducation camp.

Wu Hongbo, Hetian Taida's chairman, admitted that the apparel company had a factory inside the camp's compound and confirmed that its workers included reeducation detainees, but he attempted to portray the camp as a vocational training center. "We're making our contribution to eradicating poverty," Wu told AP.

When AP journalists tried to visit the compound, they found barbed wire, surveillance cameras, and dozens of armed guards patrolling the area. The reporters saw not just one factory, but more than thirty facilities inside, which included warehouses, workshops, and dorms. After the exposé, Badger Sportswear stopped sourcing from Xinjiang entirely.

Badger Sportswear is far from the only Western company to have sourced from China's labor camps. In recent years, camp survivors have revealed that Chinese forced laborers have made a wide range of products for export: disposable chopsticks, children's toys, cheap clothing. Most of these products are subcontracted out to prisons by their manufacturers' official factories. As one example, a labor camp survivor reported spotting H&M logos in a manufacturing facility in Shanghai's Qingpu Prison, and H&M has an official factory, called A CAP Ltd., only an eleven-minute drive away. (An H&M spokesperson told me its internal investigations could not confirm whether the prisoner's "claims are accurate or not.")

On a reporting trip to China, I visited the factory and struck up a conversation with two workers leaving at the end of a shift. They told me that the factory subcontracted a large portion of its work, although they weren't sure who did the work.

While the proximity suggests A CAP might have been the H&M factory outsourcing to Qingpu Prison, it could have easily been a much more remote factory. When I followed trucks that left these labor camps, they sometimes drove to manufacturers as far as ninety minutes away. *Financial Times* journalist Yuan Yang reported a similar situation in 2018, when she followed a truck from a detention center in the province of Jiangsu to a garlic manufacturer two hours away.

H&M has about 19 factories in Shanghai and nearly 140 more in surrounding provinces. Almost all of these factories are a ninety-minute drive or less from prisons, pretrial detention centers, or drug detox centers.

What's more, Chinese prison products are not limited to cheap goods. High-end products are often outsourced as well. A photograph in a November 2016 article promoting a local politician's visit to a drug detox center in the city of Meizhou, in Guangdong, revealed a stack of flattened American Girl boxes inside the facility. In the picture, the *i* in "Girl" is dotted with a star, just like in some versions of the doll brand's official logo.

When I asked an American Girl spokesperson if the company has any suppliers in or near Guangdong that could be sourcing from a drug detox center, I was told that the company was beginning an investigation. Over the course of a year, I sent several follow-up emails, with questions about the company's sourcing practices and the results of the investigation. The American Girl spokesperson never answered any of those questions.

While there are no precise figures on exactly how much of the world's second-largest economy relies on forced labor, Jeffrey Fiedler, a commissioner with the US-China Economic and Security Review Commission and cofounder of Laogai Research Foundation, told me he thinks estimates are irrelevant. "Clearly, forced-labor products are a small percentage of the total economy," he said, since there are far more regular factories in China than labor camps. "That was never the issue for us. The issue is not the size of the system versus the economy, but the existence of the system itself."

3: Who Was Sun Yi?

It didn't seem like the baby would live. His wrinkled body had sharp features, lacking fat. It was October 9, 1966, the beginning of the Cultural Revolution. Lingyu held her newborn close to keep the heat from escaping his thin body. Her smile was wide and contagious. The infant had large, searching eyes and high-arching eyebrows that gave him a surprised expression. They wrapped him in layers of clothing to protect him from the cold world, and named him Sun Yi. His name meant "perseverance." Sun was going to be a survivor.

The grandparents, aunts, and uncles were ecstatic; an exalted magic stayed in the air after they brought him home.

Lingyu had been starving throughout her pregnancy. She had also been sick for a while. The coughing, sneezing, and fatigue continued after the birth; less than a week later, the child became sick as well, his breathing coming in rasps. A doctor diagnosed Sun with bronchitis. He went on to have frequent bouts of illness throughout his childhood—fevers, excessive sweating, a tonsil inflammation that made it painful to eat. He often woke up to find his bedsheets cold and wet from perspiration.

Sun spent his first seven years with his maternal grandmother in the village near Taiyuan, where cluttered rows of small mud-brick homes extended over the hills. The village did not offer many jobs, so the able-bodied left to work in cities, leaving older folks and children behind. The petroleum equipment factory where Sun's parents worked was nearly seven hours away.

The villagers searched for sparks of joy to distract themselves from their numbing hunger. Sun would amuse people by doing impressions of elders. He'd mimic the slow, stiff cadence of their gaits, their deep and loud sighs. A group of seniors often gathered around Sun on sluggish afternoons, laughing at how a small child could sound so old. Sun would ask them questions about life after his little performances. The old people always had time to answer, rousing in him a deep and lasting curiosity.

Most of the kids in his village had wild childhoods. It was not hard to escape the gazes of bone-weary elders. An older child often led a group of little ones around; they inhaled the thick dust of dirt roads as they ventured a mile or two from home. They played hide-and-seek in scratchy cornfields and made secret treks to nearby communes, left over from one of Mao's policies of the late 1950s, to watch war propaganda films.

"When you get older and you make money, what will you buy for Grandmother?" an aunt asked Sun one day.

"A submachine gun," Sun said.

The cinematic images of high-intensity battle from the commune films mesmerized the children. One of his friends carved a wooden gun. They pretended they were soldiers, dividing themselves into little battalions.

When it was time to begin elementary school at age seven, Sun left Taiyuan to join his parents in the city of Xi'an. This was the age when rural children typically reunited with urban parents. For the most part, there had never been good schools in the countryside.

Sun's father was a smoker who did not treat himself to brand-name cigarettes; instead, he saved his change to purchase books for his son. He bought several volumes in a series called One Hundred Thousand Whys. The books gave detailed scientific explanations of how things worked in various fields—from farming to astronomy, to marine biology.

Sun felt a gnawing wanderlust after reading the books. The sea, in particular, consumed his imagination. He had never seen it; Taiyuan and Xi'an were landlocked. He envisioned himself standing alone in front of the water, maybe running his hands through the sand. He dreamed of becoming a boat captain.

Although the Chinese Communist Party had, in the name of equality, eliminated school entrance exams in 1966, it had reinstated the tests by the time Sun entered middle school in 1978. He got into a competitive one, the Xi'an #85 Middle School. The school, which divided each grade into six classes based on test scores, admitted Sun into its elite class.

Lingyu, who had dropped out of high school to work at a vegetable-processing company after her father died, made sure they splurged on extra study books for Sun. She would go over the problems with him night after night. Winning multiple math competitions, Sun rose as the school's academic star.

As a teenager, Sun's remarkable grades got him into the highly coveted Communist Youth League, a government-run group for high-achieving young people. It was a big deal to him at the time, because it was a breeding ground for China's elites. The students in the league paid a small membership fee, and for the most part they learned about patriotism, but the whole experience felt superficial to Sun; he did not know anyone who actually cared about socialist ideals. Instead, young people mostly joined because it was a gateway to formal CCP membership, which had a notoriously arduous application process. Joining the party meant access to more career opportunities, as well as political and corporate leadership positions.

As a teenager, Sun preferred to spend his time watching movies in the dusty yard of a dorm for construction workers. It was not unusual for companies to provide dorms and other amenities for employees, and they sometimes offered entertainment. Once, he saw a film about the solar system, examining how the Earth came to be after the melting and cooling of magma. The existential questions that had plagued Sun as a young child had never gone away, and a heavy feeling unfurled in his chest as the film reminded him of the vastness of the cosmos: From the beginning of time until now, human history was a mere speck in the history of space. Against all odds, a life is born, and then shortly after birth it dies.

Sun had trouble falling asleep that night. Feeling a profound sadness, he wondered if there was a purpose to his short time on Earth, if there was a higher plan for him. "The past is magma. The future will probably be magma. Our lives briefly exist in between these two states," he later recounted. "I felt sad knowing that our lives are so small. We have so little control, in the larger context of things. I wanted to somehow feel integrated with the universe . . . I could only hope *Journey to the West* was a true story . . . that there would be an end to the cycles of suffering. One can have a better life after death."

Sun's father taught him to look for answers in history. Xi'an, which had been an imperial capital, was home to the Stele Forest—a museum filled with three thousand inscribed stone slabs, also known as steles, and sculptures from ancient times. Religious and historical texts were recorded on the stone pillars, including one engraved in the handwriting of Emperor Kangxi, the longest-reigning monarch in Chinese history.

Sun loved walking through that museum. One of the buildings was once a Confucian temple, its roofs designed with curves to repel evil spirits. He would spend hours reading the dynastic histories etched onto each tablet, often bringing a writing utensil and paper to press against the slabs and trace the ancient words. One of his favorite steles displayed the Confucian proverb "If you have self-restraint and moral principles, you will go undefeated."

Sun could not wait to leave Xi'an. He envisioned himself traveling the world, like a modern-day Ferdinand Magellan.

Sun was one of the few who scored high enough on the college entrance exam to pick his school. For most students, their scores picked for them. He was admitted early, at sixteen, to Dalian University of Technology, which he chose because it was near the Yellow Sea. He wanted to learn how to build boats, but that program had limited openings; the Chinese government assigned quotas for majors based on regional economic needs. The school gave him, instead, a slot in the submarine engine design program.

Still, Sun was enthralled by Dalian. "I was very lucky to be admitted," he said. On his first night, he went to the sea. He stood on the rocks, in the darkness. He breathed in the salt-laden air. He wanted to spend the rest of his days there.

It was the early 1980s, soon after the Cultural Revolution had ended, and before the next intellectual clampdown. It was a lively time to be in college. He read the German philosopher Georg Wilhelm Friedrich Hegel's writings on consciousness. He also turned to science for answers to his questions about the universe.

In Dalian, Sun survived on corn-flour cakes and steamed buns. He could afford to spend only one yuan (about 16 cents) a day, and he often skipped meals to buy books. Sometimes he stole books. His parents sent Sun half of their meager income every month, leaving just enough for the rest of the family to survive on.

Sun didn't tell his parents, but he developed a severe case of rhinitis during this time. A steady stream of mucus seeped from his nose, causing him to wake up as frequently as every half hour throughout the night. He took a Chinese herb called ephedra to help clear his nose, but it didn't always work.

With the qigong movement blooming, Sun experimented with a practice called Dove Qigong. It required lengthy squatting poses, which he found painful, but the classes were free. He would have preferred to study a more popular qigong practice called Zhong Gong, but the group charged way more than he could afford.

Sun was doing better when his father surprised him by visiting. How happy Sun was to see his familiar long face and kind eyes. His father treated him to grilled chicken even though their family could not afford to eat meat at home. Then he took Sun to the mall to buy a tape recorder: he wanted Sun to learn English.

As Sun's father approached the counter to pay for the recorder, he pulled 100 yuan (about $15) from a secret pocket sewn into his underwear. The overly cautious quirk struck Sun at once as embarrassing and deeply moving. His father had saved two months' worth of wages for him.

"It was the last time I saw my father," Sun said. "He went back home, got sick, and died a few months later." His death caused Sun to spiral into depression. After fifty years of hardship, the essence of his father's being has vanished. Just like that. He concluded that human existence might have no intrinsic meaning.

Sun graduated from college in 1987. He took an entry-level position at the China National Petroleum Corporation in Beijing, where he worked for seven years before listening to his parents' advice: if he wanted a promotion, he would need to improve his English. So he took a foreign-language aptitude exam. He scored high, and his company paid for a three-month English course in Chongqing.

The southern city was known for its river port, as well as for numbing chili peppers and abandoned factories. During the Japanese invasion in the 1930s and '40s, it had been a defense industrial base, teeming with ammunition plants and arsenals hidden in hillside caves. By the time Sun arrived in the fall of 1994, most of the factories had shuttered. An acidic stench wafted through the city, which dumped its trash into the Jialing and Yangtze Rivers.

Sun was a northerner; the locals spoke a Sichuanese dialect with a heavy southern drawl that he struggled to understand, making it hard for him to form human connections. Instead, Sun spent his free time memorizing vocabulary words and practicing his British accent. It distracted him from loneliness.

One weekend, he decided to go dancing. The airy, melancholic pop music of Teresa Teng resonated through the dance hall, putting the crowd in a sentimental mood. The lyrics centered on romance rather than revolution, which was a departure from the political propaganda songs that Sun's generation had grown up with.

He saw, from across the room, a young woman who was less dressed up than the others around her. Her quiet demeanor struck him as genuine. He approached her and said hello. To his great surprise, she responded in a northern accent. Her name was May. She had grown up near the Qin Mountains in north-central China.

The connection was instant, almost startling. They exchanged some light banter. They both could not believe they had found another northerner. With the dialect barrier gone, Sun felt like he was talking to an old friend.

"What are you doing in Chongqing?" he asked.

"I'm taking night classes at the Southwest Aerospace Workers University," she said, "across the street from this dance hall."

Like Sun, May had already graduated from college. She was taking a few technical classes to advance her accounting career.

As the night came to a close, May and Sun agreed to look for each other at the next weekend's dance.

The forlorn mood Sun had been in since arriving in Chongqing lifted. He caught himself thinking about her in class. Sun found her at the next dance, and the next. They began meeting up to watch action movies, May's favorite kind of film.

They visited tourist sites together. The area was picturesque; there were looming mountains and dense forests near the edges of the city. During boat rides past the towering cliffs of the Three Gorges, Sun revealed to May his innermost thoughts. He felt understood when he was with her. They stayed up many nights talking to each other about life and fate. Listening to her voice with rapture, he had to remind himself he wasn't going to be in Chongqing for much longer. Although he was trying not to, he was falling for her.

One early evening, May and Sun lingered by a dock. The faint outline of a mountain was visible in the hazy horizon. They stood in front of the spot where the Jialing and Yangtze Rivers connected. The two rivers—one green, one brown—touched but did not mix. Sun noticed a look in May's eyes. As local merchants called out prices for boat rides, he leaned in to kiss her. She kissed him back. It was at that moment he was certain he loved her.

Before Sun knew it, his three months in Chongqing had passed; it was time for him to return to Beijing. He wanted to marry May. But the job market was competitive in the national capital. One needed connections to find work; he would likely have to support her for a while, and his entry-level salary wasn't high enough to do that. It didn't seem practical for them to continue the relationship.

The breakup was quick, but the pain lingered. He wrote her a poem before leaving:

> *The Chongqing rivers know our desires*
> *Song and dance late at night*
> *The second rainbow has arrived*
> *The other end of the world is within reach*
> *Rain and wind linger into the night*
> *Lights, intoxicated, on the pagoda*
> *I yearn to hear the words in your heart*
> *I cannot help but yearn*
> *Pacing back and forth, I hesitate*
> *Sadness fills the space*
> *Incense of the heart, I pray*
> *The sea turns into a field of mulberry*

In Beijing, Sun's physical and emotional condition declined. He was often light-headed and dizzy. His vision blurred whenever he stared at a computer screen for more than ten minutes. It looked like the words on the monitor had grown hair.

What's more, his work environment itself was unstable. A new manager seemed to arrive every month. The frequent shake-ups kept morale low as coworkers formed factions. It was more difficult for Sun to navigate office politics than to master technical skills. He wondered if his position was as unstable as his managers'.

The coldness of corporate culture left Sun dispirited. He soon realized it didn't matter how many skills he acquired or how hard he worked; what mattered were his *guanxi*, his connections. And what connections could Sun give his boss in exchange for a promotion? Nothing. He did not come from a powerful family.

Like that, two years passed and he was still missing May. At the time, China's state-owned businesses provided housing for their employees. Sun learned that his company could not allocate him an apartment of his own if he remained unmarried. This was the excuse he was waiting for: a sign that he should find May.

He took a thirteen-hour train ride to her hometown, Baoji, a city in a valley by the Wei River. The waterway had been an ancient cradle of Chinese civilization, and it was surrounded by the Qin Mountains' cloud-covered peaks—a sacred Taoist site where a few Taoist hermits were still rumored to live. Sun wondered if the hermits were really there.

He got off the train. He was nervous, not knowing how she would react. Did she resent him? Was she seeing someone?

May opened the door.

"Hello," he said, laughing. He was unable to contain his excitement.

"Sun Yi . . . hello," she said. Her eyes lit up.

Sun was relieved to find out that May was still single. They sat down to catch up. Her parents, who had spent their lives working in a military factory, wanted her to find an affluent partner. But she had rejected the dates they'd arranged because she still had feelings for Sun.

"I don't have a lot. But will you marry me?" Sun asked.

She looked at him, this man who—as her parents had pointed out—had ailing health and little money.

"I would love that," she said.

To her parents' dismay, they applied for a marriage license the next day. Dressed in their best outfits, they took a photo in front of a red backdrop before submitting their application to a Civil Affairs Bureau clerk.

It was an emotionally charged wait. China had a bureaucratic household registration system called *hukou*. Since Sun and May were not from the same town, nor were they planning to live in either of their hometowns, it was possible the government could deny their marriage application. They would leave for Beijing together if they got the marriage license. They would go their separate ways forever if they did not.

After three days, the province of Shaanxi granted them the marriage license. They laughed as they received two marriage certificate booklets that looked like red passports; it meant they were legally married. Sun rushed to buy May a ring.

They arrived in Beijing with nearly nothing. Sun was living in a male dormitory that his company had provided. Although it was not allowed, May moved in with him as they waited for couples housing. By chance, Sun's roommates had moved out. They were alone for the time being.

In love, they did not need much. They took evening walks around Beijing, their fingers intertwined. They savored the piquant taste of Beijing's *jianbing*, a thin rolled pancake stuffed with scallions, chili sauce, and wonton strips. They thought they would always live like this.

But it took May several months to find work. Sun took on odd jobs on top of his engineering work—doing sales for a cousin's cigarette company and working part-time as a tour guide. As he stayed up late to memorize tour scripts, his health declined further. It became hard for him to walk up the four flights of stairs to their apartment. He was bloated no matter how little he ate. After a doctor diagnosed him with an enlarged spleen, he became scared. "My father also had bloating symptoms before he died," Sun said.

He was only in his early thirties, but headaches and blurred vision continued to plague him. He attempted the Dove Qigong exercises again. They didn't help. Desperate to try anything that could improve his health, he started waking up to jog before dawn.

It was winter 1998. The cold air stung his lungs. On his third morning out, he noticed human shadows in the park. He got closer and saw that people were meditating. Many were elderly. "How strange," he recalled thinking.

The meditation music consisted of hollow rings of a temple block. It soothed him when he jogged past. Sun completed a circle around his neighborhood and ran back. The old people were still sitting cross-legged, deep in trance. They reminded him of his grandmother when she returned home from Mount Wutai.

On one dark morning, a meditator opened her eyes as Sun jogged by. He seized the chance to talk to her.

And so it began. After obtaining a collection of the group's main teachings from an elderly Falun Gong follower, he read everything. The books reminded him of his childhood conversations with his grandmother. There were some esoteric parts he didn't understand— something about energy channels, and a spiritual phase called the "mysterious pass." But the theories about reincarnation spoke to him deeply. Suffering suddenly had a purpose: It resolved bad karma; it was a cleansing before the next life.

He liked that Falun Gong's belief system revolved around the surrender of self-interest, offering a refreshing alternative to China's intensifying commercialism. Sun had come of age at a time when people were breaking away from the recent decades' socialist ideals and traditional village lives, and chasing cars, houses, and luxury brands. Deng Xiaoping, the Chinese leader who reformed the country after Mao, once had said something along the lines of: "To get rich is glorious." While China's so-called "economic miracle" dramatically improved living standards, it also placed so much emphasis on material goods that many people were left searching for a deeper sense of fulfillment.

Falun Gong seemed to answer Sun's lifelong existential questions. The objective of the practice was to reach enlightenment, a release from the cycle of rebirth. Its beliefs centered on the idea that a person's life began not on Earth but somewhere else in the firmament—not necessarily a heaven, but a higher plane in another dimension of space—and that people who lived moral lives could return to their origin. This gave Sun a sense of purpose. Like the characters in *Journey to the West*, he felt he was finally embarking on a spiritual journey of his own.

After Sun began meditating, his rhinitis, headaches, and blurry vision lessened. Perhaps it was a coincidence, but Sun believed it was the result of the qigong exercises. During this time, his primary allegiance shifted from the Chinese Communist Party to his meditation practice.

This was still in 1998, only two years after Falun Gong's withdrawal from the China Qigong Scientific Research Society. At the time, Falun Gong was receiving some negative press coverage—and, more significantly, its books had just been banned. As a result, the meditators responded boldly, organizing protests and demanding retractions or corrections of articles that criticized the group as superstitious and anti-science. They coordinated around three hundred demonstrations from 1996 to 1999, many of which successfully achieved retractions.

In 1997, the Ministry of Public Security conducted two studies to determine if Falun Gong was heretical, against the party. Both studies concluded Falun Gong was not—at least not yet. A year later, the government launched a third investigation. This time, under-cover police officers infiltrated the Falun Gong network to gain intel-ligence. The investigators were supposed to try harder to prove it was a dangerous cult.

4: Rebel Meditators

Everything can be taken from a man but one thing: the last of the human freedoms—to choose one's attitude in any given set of circumstances, to choose one's own way.
—VIKTOR E. FRANKL

The silence was deafening—no shouts, no megaphones, no banners. There was a still a chill in the spring air as people began assembling at seven in the morning. Throughout the next sixteen hours, a crowd of ten thousand Falun Gong protestors gathered outside the Chinese Communist Party's central headquarters, a fifteen-hundred-acre rectangular compound in Beijing, called Zhongnanhai. Fearing a bloodbath was coming, cyclists hurried by as paramilitary officers in green caps gathered across the street.

Whatever issues some people may have with Falun Gong's beliefs, it is hard to deny that this protest was an unthinkable act of courage.

Civil disobedience has always been dangerous in China. But it was more risky during some periods than others. This demonstration, on April 25, 1999, occurred at an acutely sensitive time and place. It was less than six weeks before the tenth anniversary of the Tiananmen Square massacre, when student-led democracy movement protests ended with an estimated ten thousand people gunned down in one night.

Yet there they were: a motley mass of Falun Gong followers—elderly folks in tennis shoes, yuppies in suits—quietly standing by in the surrounding streets where tanks had crushed student activists a decade earlier. It was the largest protest since then.

Some people sat reading in the dirt. Others stood on the sidewalk next to Fuyou Street's newly leafed trees. Soft music wafted from another part of the block, inspiring a number of demonstrators to meditate.

The protest was primarily sparked by the recent arrests of practitioners in Tianjin, a city seventy-five miles away. A theoretical physicist named He Zuoxiu had published an anti-qigong article in the Tianjin Normal University's *Young Reader* magazine earlier that month, which criticized Falun Gong as superstitious, pseudoscientific, and harmful, and alleged that Falun Gong had caused a postgraduate student to develop schizophrenia. He Zuoxiu was, incidentally, the brother-in-law of a top public security official named Luo Gan, and a member of the CCP's Politburo Standing Committee. And the magazine—like all publications in China—was run by the state.

Interpreting the article as a smear, an estimated six thousand Falun Gong adherents staged nonviolent protests at the university and the Tianjin municipal offices. Riot police arrived, attacking and arresting forty-five practitioners. The police informed the remaining demonstrators that the central authorities in Beijing had sent them.

That was why Sun stood in the crowd that day at Zhongnanhai. He had been involved with Falun Gong for a little over a year. The Zhongnanhai protest marked a turning point for many practitioners: a departure from political apathy.

Although Sun was steadfast about his faith and meditation, slivers of doubt may have crept into his mind during the protest. He had a lot to lose. He had recently been promoted to an intermediate management position at his company, where he oversaw the health and safety of workers. May had found an accounting job and they finally had an apartment of their own.

As the crowd grew larger by the hour, China's then-president, Jiang Zemin, was resting after breakfast. He may have felt annoyed to receive an urgent call on a Sunday morning. He must have been shocked when Luo Gan, the secretary for legal and political affairs, informed him a mass rally was taking place at that very moment in front of the party's central headquarters.

The president told him to engage the demonstrators in dialogue.

At eight thirty that morning, Premier Zhu Rongji, the party's second-in-command, came out of the compound.

"I have already made an official announcement about your problem," the premier said to the gathered group, trying to disperse the gathering.

"We haven't received it," a practitioner said.

Scanning the crowd of thousands, the premier motioned at a few random protestors to follow him inside.

In the compound, the Falun Gong representatives met with the deputy director of appeals and one of the premier's top aides. The dialogue carried on for six hours.

"We demand the release of the practitioners who were arrested in Tianjin," a protestor said.

"We demand a safe environment to practice Falun Gong meditation."

"We demand the right to publish Falun Gong literature."

Luo, the official who had initially notified President Jiang of the protest, slipped into the room to help persuade the demonstrators to leave, assuring them that the regime supported their meditation.

But many protestors remained outside the compound until eleven o'clock that night. The thousands of meditators had limited their food and drink intake over the sixteen-hour protest to avoid inundating public restrooms, and as the crowd dispersed, they also picked up their trash, leaving the street litter-free.

Their mindfulness didn't make a difference. The party felt threatened by Falun Gong's ability to organize. On June 10, 1999, a month and a half after the Zhongnanhai protest, the Chinese government formed a security agency called the 610 Office, named after the date. Its sole mission was to orchestrate a nationwide campaign to crush the Falun Gong movement.

Arrests began two days before the government officially announced that Falun Gong had been banned. The surprise move was an attempt to destabilize Falun Gong leadership. According to UCLA political science professor James W. Tong's book, *Revenge of the Forbidden City: The Suppression of the Falungong in China, 1999–2005,* some Chinese media initially reported that local Falun Gong organizers in twenty-two cities were arrested before the July 20 announcement of the ban. A mass arrest of Falun Gong adherents followed.

Over the next few years, surveillance grew, and labor camps across China expanded to make room for the influx of detainees. Many in these camps pledged to cut off ties with Falun Gong. Some would leave the group for good, while others would rejoin, underground, after getting out of prison. Others searched for opportunities to leave China, whether through tourism visas or family-based immigration, and those who succeeded sought asylum.

Some of the Falun Gong followers who remained in China were able to carry on undetected, meditating only in their private homes. But many became more brazen. Ultimately, the Chinese regime's efforts to eradicate Falun Gong backfired as practitioners began to organize against the CCP.

During the first years of the persecution, they pulled off some especially imaginative and harrowing feats. Pulitzer Prize–winning journalist Ian Johnson once described the early years of the Falun Gong resistance in China as "arguably the most sustained challenge to authority in 50 years of Communist rule."

In response to anti–Falun Gong propaganda pervading state-run media, a team of Falun Gong computer engineers outside China released an internet censorship circumvention software called Freegate in 2002. It used proxy servers to breach the Great Firewall, the technology that enforces China's highly censored version of the internet. Over the next ten years, the Freegate software would spread to Iran, North Korea, Syria, and Vietnam, helping democracy activists in those countries access censored social media, such as Facebook and Twitter, and other sites containing criticisms of their governments. In 2009, the *New York Times* credited Falun Gong's proxy service as one of the tools that allowed Iranian activists to coordinate postelection protests—which helped launch Iran's pro-democracy movement.

Falun Gong's Freegate introduction made some headway in bolstering freedom of information in China. But a year earlier, in 2001, an event had occurred that effectively turned many Chinese people against Falun Gong. That January, a video was broadcast of five people setting themselves on fire as they meditated in Tiananmen Square. Two of the self-immolators—a woman and her twelve-year-old daughter—burned to death. The state-run Chinese media said the self-immolators were Falun Gong followers, and that the promise of heavenly paradise had driven them to suicide.

But when Philip P. Pan, a journalist then writing for the *Washington Post*, visited the hometown of the two dead self-immolators to investigate, a neighbor told Pan the woman had been an exotic dancer at a nightclub. This sounded strange. Why would an exotic dancer be willing to set herself on fire for such a conservative group? Other neighbors described her as a violent person with mental illness. None had ever heard her talk about Falun Gong.

Falun Gong followers claim the self-immolation was part of a smear campaign: the Chinese regime was so threatened by the Falun

Gong movement that the party felt it needed to resort to extreme measures to escalate its propaganda.

As dubious as it sounds, this theory is not out of the question. A retired party official, whom I know but cannot name without endangering his safety, told me he was in charge of "managing religion" in one province in the early 2000s. He also said the central government had warned officials in his position that Falun Gong was a major threat to the stability of the party, and that they had to focus on eradicating the group at all costs.

Despite the loss of public support, Falun Gong followers in China stepped up their efforts. In 2004, members formed an underground initiative called Tuidang, which translates to "withdraw from the party." Using secret printing presses, they printed literature that countered the state's narrative of the group and distributed those materials by hand. Through mass emails, snail mail, faxes, and automated phone calls, Falun Gong activists inside and outside China collected Chinese citizens' renunciations of the Chinese Communist Party. Although Tuidang never led to any real changes in the political system, it offered an avenue for Chinese nationals to voice their grievances against the regime.

By 2018, the movement claimed to have collected renunciations of the party from three hundred million people. In theory, that means three hundred million people have withdrawn from the three official party organizations—the Youth League, the Young Pioneers, and the Communist Party itself—but there is no way to verify this number. Some have questioned the credibility of the information, considering how competitive it is to gain party membership in the first place, and how cumbersome the yearlong application process is.

There is evidence that the Tuidang movement was effective enough to at least raise concerns for the Chinese government. A 2010 statement on the Chinese government's China Anti-Cult Association web page showed the party saw the elimination of Falun Gong as a kind of litmus test for the stability of the regime: "The competition against Falun Gong is the principal means of competition for the hearts and minds of the masses . . . Whether or not we perform the education and conversion work well is a test of the Party's advanced nature and ability to govern."

Sun covertly worked for the Tuidang movement by providing tech support. He helped improve the security and anonymity of calls. But as Sun and May's apartment became cluttered with phone cards, SIM cards, and old cell phones, their relationship grew strained.

She resented that Falun Gong seemed to be worth more to him than anything else. "Why do you have to do this?" she would ask him, over and over.

Their lives had already been shattered by his devotion to the practice—a few years earlier, on an afternoon in March 2001.

Most people at work knew Sun was a Falun Gong practitioner, and when a coworker heard that their employer was cooperating with the local police department to send Sun to a "transformation center," an extralegal detention facility where Falun Gong followers were tortured, that coworker warned him. Sun went into hiding just as police officers raided their apartment.

Although the company had no incentive to protect Sun, they sent him a written guarantee that they would not report him to the police if he returned to work. Sun was too trusting. He went back the following week. Two months later, police officers arrived at his office and dragged him away. He was tortured for three days before they released him.

After his company's betrayal, Sun was unemployed, allowing him more time to focus on subversive work. Always on the run, he carried nothing with him but a small bag of toiletries. He never slept in one location for more than a few days. Suspecting his cell phone was tapped, he made calls from phones borrowed from strangers. He avoided GPS tracking by only turning his phone on briefly while he was on moving trains. That was how he texted May every night to let her know he was safe, usually with just one emoji.

But Sun could not evade the surveillance cameras forever. After nearly a year, he was arrested during a citywide sweep of dissidents in Beijing. The regime wanted to create a facade of citizen satisfaction with the government before the convening of the Sixteenth National Congress of the Communist Party of China in November 2002. The police did not need arrest warrants during important political events like this, which were considered sensitive periods. The international press reported on the disappearances of a handful of famous dissidents during this time, but it was unclear how many little-known activists like Sun were arrested.

The police tortured Sun at the Shijingshan District Detention Center for a month before they permitted May to bail him out. Rail-thin, he no longer looked human. He cried when their eyes met. Unable to walk by himself, he leaned on her as they left the gray gated building.

Their future in China was bleak. It was possible for dissidents to find refuge if they made it to Hong Kong, however, so when Sun's health improved after seven months, he quietly left for Guangzhou, a southern city that he thought he could escape from. May planned to follow later. But not long after his arrival in Guangzhou, a security guard caught Sun with Falun Gong flyers on the manicured lawns of Jinan University. He was arrested and sentenced, without trial, to two years in Guangzhou No. 1 Reeducation Through Labor Camp.

The camp's alternate business name was Chini Stone Quarry. Detainees primarily extracted limestone. During the period when

Sun was imprisoned, the quarry extracted three hundred thousand tons of stone a year. It also exported cement and, of all things, artificial flowers.

Although the primary value of laogais comes from the free labor of those imprisoned there, the central government also gives camps considerable bonuses for the successful "reeducations" of dissidents. Prisoners are considered reeducated if they verbally admit guilt and error during self-criticism sessions, sign a guarantee (*baozhengshu*) stating that they have changed their offending thoughts, and demonstrate overall submissiveness to authority. The transformation rate of political attitudes directly affects the guards' salaries, bonuses, and promotions.

"The state paid the labor camp ten thousand yuan [around $1,458] a month for each Falun Gong practitioner they accepted to undergo ideological reform . . . We became goods in their trade," a labor camp survivor later said.

The centrally devised system of quotas and financial incentives sometimes made it more profitable for labor camps to torture prisoners than to work them. The camp could not receive their hefty bonuses unless they could document significant changes in political or religious attitudes, and it was easier to extract those things through torture. Sun, who immediately protested his incarceration by waging a hunger strike, was one of many prisoners who never worked a day at the Guangzhou camp. It was a serious act of defiance. Not wanting Sun to influence other detainees, camp officials sent him to a hospital to undergo force-feeding.

The camp notified Sun's mother that her son was in the hospital. They wanted her to visit him and weaken his will. Worried sick, Lingyu rode the train from Xi'an to Guangzhou to see him. It was an eighteen-hour ride and the longest distance she had ever traveled. She was lost the moment she arrived. She tried to ask for directions, but the locals spoke Cantonese, a dialect quite different from Mandarin. She wandered around the city, a dizzying blend of ancient temples and futuristic skyscrapers. She received directions from several people before she could understand where the hospital was.

As Lingyu walked into Sun's ward, camera flashes blinded her. The labor camp was holding a media event to capture Sun's renunciation of Falun Gong for television. Clutching her travel bag, she ran to his bed.

"Why are your feet so swollen?" Lingyu asked. She cried as she touched his legs. "It looks like you have no ankles." She turned to the guards and screamed, "What did you do to my son? How can you treat my son like this?"

"We have healed his psychological wounds," a guard said.

"You need to go," Sun told his mother, his face twisting as he watched the old woman cry. "They are using you to try to make me eat, in order to keep me here longer."

Lingyu had no choice. She returned home by herself.

To avoid taking responsibility if he died, the camp released Sun on bail a few days later, at the end of July 2003. His successful hunger strike ended after forty-two days.

Back in Beijing, Sun tried to ease himself into an unremarkable life. A friend gave him a job at an export company. It could well have been sourcing from prison labor. But Sun, who had not yet experienced forced labor himself, did not think to ask.

He did, though, remain in touch with the underground Falun Gong network. He knew it was safer to fade quietly into the background; May begged him to stay safe. But he may have felt guilty about living a normal life when fellow practitioners were dying.

One day, someone from that network asked him to join a bold initiative: they were going to hijack China's television signals.

Over the years, Falun Gong followers had disrupted local and national television and radio broadcasts in several cities. The most notable hacking to date had occurred in March 2002, when a small band of underground meditators with limited technical experience had interrupted all eight channels of the city of Changchun's municipal cable TV network for nearly one hour during prime time. After a brief blackout, banners appeared on the screen that read FALUN DAFA IS GOOD. Then two videos played. One showed Falun Gong members protesting outside China, suggesting that the group had not been extinguished. Another video showed a frame-by-frame analysis of inconsistencies in the self-immolation footage (for example, the meditating self-immolator was not crossing his legs in the lotus position). The Falun Gong hackers may have been replacing the party's propaganda with its own, but they managed to show an estimated three hundred thousand households an opposing view.

Of course, they achieved this at a cost. Those responsible—Zhou Runjun, fifty-one; Liang Zhenxing, thirty-eight; Liu Haibo, thirty-four; Hou Ming-kai, thirty-two; Liu Chengjun, thirty-two; and a twenty-six-year-old named Lei Ming, whom they called Little Brother—were all later tortured to death.

And when a Chinese American citizen named Charles Lee traveled to China to join a similar signal-disrupting initiative in 2003, the police arrested him upon arrival. The government had long been monitoring his contacts. For the next three years, Lee would assemble Christmas lights and Homer Simpson slippers between force-feeding sessions.

Sun contemplated these arrests and deaths, which he had read about on Falun Gong's online samizdat, Minghui. But to him, it felt just as dangerous to live in a society with access to only one viewpoint. In 2004, a year after his release from Guangzhou, he decided to work for the project. "We need to inform people," Sun said. "That is the main purpose."

Sun rode the train at night, traveling nearly six hours to the province of Shanxi. There, he retrieved electronic parts that another practitioner had smuggled in from overseas.

He took the train back on the same night to deliver the equipment to hackers in Beijing, and would return to work the next morning as usual. The authorities caught on after his sixth trip. They arrested him at work.

Between 1999 and 2008, the police arrested Sun twelve times for participating in the underground Falun Gong movement. Each time, he was detained for periods lasting from a few days to ten months. In most cases, he forced his way out through hunger strikes. The hunger was so debilitating he sometimes felt a desire to eat the bricks on the walls of his cell, but he was never willing to sign a pledge to cut ties with Falun Gong.

He thought he had experienced it all. Little did he know, his life would take a darker turn on one February evening in 2008.

He told May he was leaving for a few days. She was disappointed he would choose to go away during the week of Chinese New Year. Her parents had been pressuring her to divorce him, and she was considering it. She was realistic; she did not think his sacrifice could lead to a freer China.

"Don't tell me what you'll be doing," she said. "I'll be more afraid if I know."

"I'll be back in two days," he said.

For a long time, she would not know what happened to him that night.

The air was bitter and dry as firecrackers crackled through the city. Sun had been meeting with two other Falun Gong followers—Lu Daqing, forty-two, and Tian Guide, forty-four. They were working as a team to surreptitiously install satellite dishes for New Tang Dynasty Television, Falun Gong's New York–based dissident television network. But on that late evening, they were meeting for another reason. They passed the snow-covered vehicles parked on the street, and quietly ascended the stairs to a secret printing press in the Tongzhou District of Beijing.

Sun unlocked the paint-chipped door. He was at one of roughly two hundred thousand autonomous underground printing houses popping up throughout China. From rented spaces in office buildings and from living rooms in private homes, dissidents used proxy servers to connect to censored Falun Gong websites, from which they downloaded and printed flyers and books that not only countered the state's account of the group, but also the party's narrative of its own history. The book they distributed, *Nine Commentaries on the Communist Party*, detail various deadly political campaigns left out of Chinese textbooks.

Preparing to deliver the materials to another city, Sun and his two friends loaded a car with two printers and dozens of copies of the *Nine Commentaries*. As they returned to carry more materials downstairs, police officers emerged from all four sides of the courtyard. Sun and his friends were sentenced, without trial, to two and a half years of hard labor.

When they arrived at a reeducation through labor camp in Beijing's Daxing District, they were told this was the place they wanted to be. "We can't use electric batons in Beijing, because there is oversight here," a guard said to them. "The guards at Masanjia use electric batons."

Since the camp was packed with detainees and Sun did not have a Beijing residence card, Sun knew that he would likely be sold to a more remote labor camp, and he knew that he could end up at Masanjia. Always needing newcomers to fill the emptying workshops, Masanjia paid 800 yuan (about $120) per prisoner. Sun had heard that since Masanjia was for repeat offenders, the facility prioritized changing behavioral patterns—through any means necessary. The camp was infamous for having high suicide rates and a number of deaths that went unaccounted for.

"I'd be on good behavior if I were you," the guard said to Sun. "If you improve your behavior, we'll send you to Mongolia instead."

After two weeks in the Beijing labor camp, the guards dragged Sun, Tian, and several other prisoners outside. Their hands were cuffed to each other. One detainee sobbed as they walked through the yard. Armed guards stood on both sides of the road as they got on an unmarked bus. The authorities were selling them from one camp to another, like slaves.

The bus's window curtains were drawn; they sat in darkness as they lurched through the city's stop-and-go traffic. Through a slit between the curtains, Sun glimpsed traces of civilization: people driving in cars, a woman calling someone on a cell phone, perhaps a loved one. He wondered when he would see his wife again.

His eyes sharpened with fear as he saw a road sign affirming they were heading northeast. He looked over at Tian. They were definitely going to Masanjia. Sun sat in silence as his new reality sank in, and he wondered: *Am I going to make it out alive this time?*

5: Entering Masanjia

To a passerby who didn't know what it was, Masanjia Reeducation Through Labor Camp may have looked beautiful. It lay in the middle of a remote verdant grassland in the province of Liaoning, sprawling across eleven hundred acres of orchards and fields. The banality of some of the buildings, surrounded by power lines and lacking barbed wire, made it hard to imagine the torture inside. The camp's alternate business name was Masanjia Xinsheng Farm; *Xinsheng* means "new life."

The sound of a coach bus arriving disturbed the quiet April evening. Exhaust diffused into the air as the unmarked vehicle entered the gate—disappearing into the place where China's undesirable citizens were transmuted into different people.

The bus drove to the end of a long road before shutting down the engine. As Sun, Tian, and the other prisoners got off, si fang surrounded them. These inmate-guards were dressed in camouflage uniforms and red armbands, and gripping batons. They told the prisoners to squat in lines and wait.

As Sun's thigh muscles strained, he noticed the crows. There were crows circling the darkening sky, crows perched on rooftops, crows searching for dead flesh. Masanjia opened in 1957 on top of a wasteland filled with thorns and graves. Even in 2008, dead inmates were still buried on-site.

"Get up. Line up to go upstairs. Keep your heads down," a si fang said. To prevent them from planning escapes, prisoners were forbidden from looking at their surroundings.

Sun was unable to discern if the batons were electric or wooden; he was afraid to raise his eyes from the ground. One prisoner near him dared to look up, and an inmate-guard whacked the man's head with a baton. A muted scream rang through the desolate field.

The new prisoners were led upstairs to the third floor, where a sign by the entrance read UNIT SIX. A CONFINED AREA.

Standing near a window, Sun stole a glance outside: a yard, a military parade ground, and beyond the towering walls, endless wilderness.

A guard waved his baton at Sun. "Head down!" he shouted. "No looking out the window."

Later that night, more than thirty inmates crammed into a large cell containing a number of twin metal bed frames. They were to sleep on the bare frames, without mattresses, pillows or blankets. Until that moment, Sun had expected each man to get a bed of his own. It was how they had slept in previous detention centers and labor camps. But a si fang claimed two bed frames for himself. The rest of the detainees squeezed onto six twin beds pushed together, cursing and elbowing each other for the edges, which offered slightly more space. Like sardines packed in a can, the men lay next to each other in alternating positions, feet to faces.

Sun climbed onto a spot in the middle of the beds near his friend Tian. He winced as the cold metal dug into his skin. He moved slowly, adjusting his limbs to search for a comfortable position. The inmate next to Sun pushed back to reclaim his space.

"It's too cold in here," a detainee said.

The si fang walked over to the person who complained. Without a word, he bashed him with the baton. A silence fell upon the cell.

After a while, Sun turned to whisper to Tian. This was their first chance to talk to each other since the arrest.

"I guess our contact's landlord must have tipped off the police," Tian said.

"He must have gone into the apartment and seen the printers," Sun replied.

"I wonder where Daqi is," Tian said.

"Daqi is from Beijing, so hopefully he can stay in the Beijing Inmate Transfer Bureau," Sun said.

"Shut up!" the inmate-guard yelled. "No more talking."

Throughout the night, a roving searchlight glared through the gated window. It kept waking Sun up. Trying to ignore the musty odor of feet on either side of him, he turned his face toward the ceiling and thought of May. A deep sadness spread in him. How was she doing? How would she react once she found out he had been transferred to such a remote camp? There was no way to communicate with her or his family.

A guard took Sun and a few other prisoners to use a dark, smelly bathroom. Sun had lost his space when he returned. He tried squeezing into a gap between two men but couldn't fit his whole body. He remained sitting the latter half of the night, listening to his stomach growl and watching a foot poke into someone's mouth. His eyelids grew heavy.

Not long after Sun dozed off, the guards began shouting. "Get up!"

It was still dark outside as the dozens of men rushed into the narrow bathroom.

"You have five minutes," a guard said.

There weren't enough faucets for everyone. Sun pushed his way toward a sink, where he managed to wet his towel with some brown water. He smelled something rotten as he raised the towel to dab his face. It felt sandy. The five minutes were up.

They ran outside to do morning exercises. The guards beat those who lingered in the bathroom. As he ran laps around the yard, Sun gripped the waist of his beltless pants to keep them up. He looked at the horizon—the camp wall silhouetted against a reddening sun— unaware that this would be his last time outdoors for two and a half years.

In a canteen that smelled like chemicals, each prisoner received a bowl of soup and a lump of steamed corn flour, called tava. The tava had an acidic taste, leaving an unpleasant tingling in Sun's teeth. Decomposing greens, specks of dirt, and blades of grass floated in his soup. Sun waited for the sediment to settle before sticking his spoon in.

"There's rat urine in our food," Tian said. "I used to drive tractors. I know what rat urine smells like."

"The conditions are better now," an older detainee said. "We used to only have two meals a day."

After breakfast, the guards shuffled them off to produce decorative paper mushrooms.

In the last two RTL camps, Sun had started a hunger strike immediately and never got a chance to work. But at Masanjia, he figured he should avoid challenging the status quo.

He was appalled to learn they had to work at least fifteen hours every day, and would only receive 10 yuan [about $1.50] a month for the labor. Still, he tried to be optimistic. Perhaps life would be more interesting in this camp, laboring instead of starving. At least he would have something to do.

As blue and purple mushrooms gradually filled the workshop, he realized the job involved far more than just doing origami. He had to rub the abrasive paper for a long time before it showed the first fuzz of softness, a sign it was ready to fold. The repetitive creasing motions numbed his mind. His fingers, chafed raw from rubbing, stiffened with pain.

"May I have some water?" Sun asked a guard. They were allowed to drink water at previous labor camps.

"You have enough water to drink when you go to the toilet six times a day," a guard said.

The only access the prisoners had to drinking water was the sinks in the bathroom. As others urinated next to them in rust-stained toilets, they stuck their mouths under the grimy faucets, their dry tongues desperate for any drop of liquid, even this water tasting of sand.

"There used to be a duck farm near here," another inmate told Sun. "That's what makes the water stink."

Back in the workshop, Sun heard a guard say the paper mushrooms were going to be exported to Europe, so they should take pride in their work. They were contributing to the glorious Chinese economy.

For decades, it has been well-documented that Masanjia and other camps like it are exporting. In Washington, DC, Harry Wu's Laogai Research Foundation put together a database of Chinese labor camps and their alternate names. In 2008, the foundation examined listings on Dun & Bradstreet, a business database company that helps brands connect with suppliers, and found more than 250 labor camps represented in over three hundred commercial listings. Sixty-five of these suppliers openly had the word "Prison" in their names. The labor camps listed in the database produced more than seventy different products, including clothing, electronics, and ceramics. According to Dun & Bradstreet, nearly 90 percent of Fortune 500 companies use its databases.

In its earliest days, the foundation began investigating the Masanjia region after receiving a tip about the city of Shenyang. The 1989 edition of the *Liaoning Economic and Statistical Yearbook*, a government report on economic growth in the province, issued to attract Chinese investors, contained a photograph of a Western businessman visiting a Shenyang prison's rubber processing plant. According to the caption, the man was a representative from Dow Chemical, a US company. "In the early years, they published a lot of stuff. They just didn't think anybody read Chinese," recalled foundation cofounder Jeffrey Fiedler.

Through phone calls and on-site visits, the foundation uncovered that Masanjia was an expansive forced-labor town, home to a conglomeration of prisons, whose inmates had undergone trials, and camps, whose detainees had not. The laogai facilities in Masanjia produced dozens of products, from scented soaps to waterproof paint and insulated pipes.

The laogai factories were mostly state-owned enterprises managed by the Prison Administration Bureau, but some were so lucrative that they had received and accepted private offers to form joint ventures. Others, managed by prison officials who lacked business acumen, struggled. In 1998, the central government attempted to address this predicament by cutting taxes for prisons "to support the development of prison enterprises and reeducation through labor facilities." But some labor camps remained unprofitable due to embezzlement. Still, the state needed the camps for political indoctrination. So they began offering subsidies to financially unsuccessful laogai camps in 2003.

Masanjia was a prime example of a camp that had teetered toward bankruptcy in the late 1990s but was saved by extensive funding from the Chinese government. In October 2002, the Ministry of Justice allocated one million yuan (about $160,000) to the camp, and in 2003, the province of Liaoning spent one *billion* yuan (about $160 million) to upgrade and expand local prisons. Half a billion yuan went to Masanjia alone.

By the time Sun arrived in 2008, Masanjia RTL Camp had transformed into an incredibly productive manufacturer, turning out decorations, cooling filters, oil pumps, welding rod dryers, down clothing for children, and more.

The work itself was often a form of torture. The detainees in the down-clothing division worked in a damp room with poor ventilation as bits of loose feathers drifted in the air. Although they wore masks, their lungs ached from inhaling feather flakes for fifteen to twenty hours a day. There was no air-conditioning in the summer and not much heat in the winter. The guards huddled near the heating pipes as the detainees, with frostbitten hands, stuffed feathers into tiny coats and pants. Their lunch breaks were shortened to meet the daily quota of one hundred to two hundred down coats and three hundred down pants. Masanjia earned hundreds of dollars a day from this division alone.

In order to meet production deadlines, inmates in some divisions went to sleep at midnight and woke at three in the morning to begin work. The obsession over meeting quotas drove some inmates insane. In 2008, a detainee in the diode division, a young man named Xiaobao, stopped drinking water from the bathroom faucet so that he would not have to take restroom breaks. Growing obsessed with diode production, he devised a strategy to maximize efficiency. His left hand would grab a handful of curvy diodes from a tray and spread them across the table. As his right hand rubbed the misshapen diodes into straight ones, his left hand reached for more. He repeated this motion tens of thousands of times a day.

One day, driven to self-harm, Xiaobao swallowed a diode. It was almost three inches long, with metal wires on both ends.

Perhaps due to an increase in production quotas, Sun never did morning exercises after that first day. The camp soon required each detainee in his division to produce a minimum of 160 paper mushrooms a day. To meet the otherwise-impossible daily goal, some inmates stole mushrooms from other people's piles. They were allowed to go to bed by midnight while the rest of the prisoners stayed behind to produce more mushrooms.

The guards ignored the pus that seeped from Sun's blistered fingers, and frequently forced him to work until two in the morning.

"When will we finish?" a detainee asked.

"When will you finish?" a guard said with sarcasm. "Is that a question you can ask? Shut your mouth."

Since the job never seemed to end, time became irrelevant in the camp. Sun regularly slept just two to four hours, only to dream of the repetitive creasing motions of folding paper mushrooms. At dawn, a guard would shout it was time to start the workday. Sun became withdrawn and apathetic. Hating the job, he did it slowly.

As he lined up for dinner one night, he glanced out the window and saw a group of sickly inmates dressed in rags. Their dirt-caked hands held mesh bags filled with bones and skulls. He stared in horror. *Are they carrying human remains?* he wondered.

A detainee who had been in Masanjia longer explained that those people were from Unit Eight, which was assigned to a "ghost job." Sun stared at his mix of rotting vegetables, casually piled together like compost. He did not want to know what a ghost job was.

He had already heard about grisly torture in Unit Eight: a si fang had told him the story of a hunger-striking Falun Gong detainee named Zhao Fei.

"Even if you refuse to eat, you still have to go to the cafeteria," a guard had said to Zhao. Then he'd dragged him by the feet down three flights of stairs. Zhao died from the sustained injuries. His head had slammed against too many steps.

So whatever the ghost job was, Sun didn't want anything to do with it. But he knew that decorative-mushroom production—considered relatively easy work at Masanjia—was for newcomers and that when the next batch of inmates arrived, those currently in the mushroom division would get reassigned.

Sun was now a long way from his former life of contemplating Hegel and thinking about the universe. His existence had been reduced to that of a mechanism: a cowering, shaved head among a sea of cowering, shaved heads, folding and flipping paper. As fragments of personality, agency, and memory broke loose and faded, Sun became a shadow of his former self. Disassociating as he worked, he replayed in his mind a cruel daydream, imagining the moment when the next batch of new inmates would arrive. He dreaded being reassigned to a potentially worse production team, but he had learned that new inmates were the only ones without individual beds at Masanjia, he tried to fixate on that fact. No matter how tired he was, it was hard to fall asleep with so many men sharing a bed. They wore the same uniform every day. They never did laundry. The stench was unbearable.

After a month in Masanjia, Sun learned there was an inmate-guard running a black-market phone-call service. He seized the chance to contact his family. His sister Jing was the first to answer.

"I can't believe you're in Masanjia," she said. He heard the pain in her voice.

"I think they are allowing visitors at the moment," he said softly. "And please send money if you can. I can call frequently as long as I pay the si fang."

Sun's mother immediately bought two Masanjia-bound train tickets. The route from Xi'an to Masanjia was complex and required switching trains several times over the course of three days. Lingyu feared she would get lost by herself, so she asked her younger sister to come with her.

There was a nervous tension in their silence as they watched buildings dart by.

"I knew it all along. I knew he was in trouble," Lingyu told her sister. "I even asked a fortune-teller to find out where he was."

"I have heard of this place," she went on. "This is where female prisoners are stripped down and thrown into male cells to be raped. I can't imagine what other things go on there."

"Sun is smart. He will be okay," his aunt replied, not knowing what else to say.

They arrived in Masanjia on the third morning. Far from urban regions, the town had a rare smog-free sky. Lingyu and her sister flagged down a bright-red electric rickshaw to take them to the labor camp. A poster, BATTLE FOR THE OLYMPICS, STABILIZE SOCIETY, was plastered on the back.

It was a bumpy ride, as country roads were not paved. The driver's name was Cao, and he made his living transporting visitors to and from Masanjia. His business was booming. Although the Chinese government had pledged to improve human rights if the world allowed Beijing to host the 2008 Summer Olympics, promising to ease media censorship and permit designated protest sites, Chinese civil liberties only worsened during the months leading up to the games. An estimated one and a half million Beijing residents lost their homes as the city made space for the new stadium, and when displaced locals went to designated protest areas to express their outrage, they were arrested. The spike in the capital city's police presence led to citizens with a history of dissent being arrested en masse. A new wave of prisoners was flooding Masanjia.

Cao was now driving families to the labor camp several times a day.

"The Olympics have enriched the police," he said. "They now smoke the best cigarette brands."

As they pulled up to the main building, Lingyu and her sister were startled to see groves of trees with lush foliage. They walked up to a security guard by the entrance.

"We are here to visit Sun Yi," Lingyu said. "We are his family."

The guard looked up his name. "You can't see him," he said. "New inmates are not eligible for visitations." Sun had been there for almost two months.

"Please. We rode the train for three days," Lingyu said, getting upset. "Can't you let me see my son just for one moment?"

"No. We can't do that."

Not knowing what to do, Sun's mother and aunt left to search for lodging. None seemed to exist. They settled for a bathhouse with a sign that read ACCOMMODATIONS AVAILABLE. Inside, they found beds lined up in a public corridor.

Tired and disheartened, Lingyu lay down right away. She did not bother using the bathhouse.

When Sun was little, he was always the most responsible one, Lingyu recalled. She thought about the time when Sun applied for a military academy because it offered free tuition. Soft-spoken, sickly Sun was volunteering to serve only to reduce his family's burdens. She had been relieved when the military rejected him.

Lingyu had a hard time staying asleep. When dawn broke, she and her sister tried visiting again. She had hoped to encounter a kinder guard, but the camp denied them a second time. Before Lingyu could say a word, her sister grabbed her hand and pulled her toward the visitation room. No one moved to stop them, so they ran in. Squeezing in with other families, Lingyu walked around and talked to each inmate.

"Do you know my son? His name is Sun Yi. Do you know him?"

One young man said he did.

"Oh, thank God. Can you please give this bag to him? I am his mom," she said.

The man later placed the bag in front of Sun as he was folding paper mushrooms.

"Your mother came," he said.

"What?" Sun asked. "What did she look like? What did her accent sound like?" He could not believe she had made it to Masanjia.

He peered into the bag. It held his favorite comfort foods: cookies, pickled vegetables, and a jug of fermented tofu. The snacks pained him, his thoughts racked with guilt.

This must have been a really difficult, long journey for her. How did she even find this place? She must be so worried and scared. I have caused her so much suffering again.

Outside, Lingyu was having a nervous collapse. She begged the guards to let her talk to Sun, even if only over the phone. "I need to hear his voice," she cried. "Please. I need to know he's alive."

The guards, feeling increasingly uncomfortable as the elderly woman sobbed, allowed her to make one call to the guard who oversaw Sun's division. He handed the phone to Sun.

"Hello, Mom," he said.

Lingyu could not stop weeping.

"It's all right. I'm well," Sun said. "Don't worry about me."

"What are you eating in there?" she said. "What else do you need us to send you?"

"I don't need anything. Don't be sad. Please take care of yourself. I will write to you," Sun said. "Please visit May in Beijing on the way home. How is she doing?"

The line went dead. Without thinking, Sun ran to the nearest window.

"Hey!" the inmate-guard yelled. "Get back here!"

He was desperate to catch a glimpse of his mother, even if only the back of her head.

It was unusual for Sun to get riled up. The inmate-guard, perhaps thinking of his own mother, let him look out the window for a few minutes.

But she must have left from a different exit.

Sun watched the other families leave one after another. He kept his eyes on the empty yard.

6: Audits and Subterfuge

‚‚

Portland, Oregon, 2012, four years
after Sun disappeared into Masanjia

It was a brisk and quiet Monday morning in December. Julie pulled into the Goodwill parking lot in Portland's industrial district, where a wholesale distributor of commercial exhaust fans shared the neighborhood with a gluten-free gastropub. She was on autopilot as she entered the office lobby when a flash startled her. A videographer was scrambling toward her as a reporter, pointing a mic at her, fired questions.

Julie was alarmed. *What did I do?* she thought.

She soon realized: Two months after she had spoken with the *Oregonian* about the note she'd found, they'd finally published the article, and it had mentioned where she worked. The story had caught the notice of New Tang Dynasty Television—the first news crew to arrive—and the *Epoch Times*, two US-based Chinese dissident news outlets staffed mostly by Falun Gong followers. Later that day, five more journalists—from CNN, Fox, and various local news outlets—arrived at Julie's office. For a short while, there seemed to be a media fixation on the mysterious letter from Masanjia.

"I got done with one interview, and then someone else would show up. I was like, 'Oh my God, what is going on?'" Julie said. "Thankfully, my boss was okay with it."

The *Oregonian* article included a response from the China director of Human Rights Watch, Sophie Richardson. "I think it is fair to say the conditions described in the letter certainly conform to what we know about conditions in re-education through labor camps," she told the newspaper. "If this thing is the real deal, that's somebody saying please help me, please know about me, please react.'"

In response to the international press coverage of Sun's SOS note, Kmart's parent company at the time, Sears Holdings, released a statement claiming it found "no evidence that production was subcontracted to a labor camp during a recent audit of the factory that produced the Halloween decoration." This was one of approximately three thousand audits that Sears Holdings said it conducted per year; the company said auditors visited its factories every six to twelve months.

Audits are widely regarded as the most effective strategy for ensuring ethical sourcing. And it's true that comprehensive unannounced audits can sometimes unearth serious problems—like child labor or blocked fire exits. But in general, audits rarely uncover the whole picture. For instance, when an eight-story garment factory building collapsed in Bangladesh in 2013 and killed more than one thousand workers, two of the factories in that complex had recently passed audits. However, the retailers that authorized the audits had not required the auditors to make sure that the factories had been built with proper permits.

The issue is, not all audits are created equal. The price of an audit often limits its thoroughness: A standard audit, which costs a couple hundred dollars, usually means a cursory inspection that might check the cleanliness of a factory, the quality of merchandise, and the efficacy of the equipment. It is unlikely to detect something structural, like a building's stability—and incapable of finding something as complex as a secret subcontract to a labor camp.

There is also a more comprehensive audit, called a social compliance audit, which takes a deeper look at a factory's working conditions and environmental practices. This might include interviews with workers and managers, visits to employee dorms, and a review of wage documents and employee time sheets. Auditors might also inspect how a factory handles chemical usage and waste disposal. An audit like this usually costs $1,000 or more. But even social compliance auditors have told me it is almost impossible for them to know if a factory is subcontracting to a labor camp.

"Throughout my nineteen years working in this field, I personally could not prove any factory actually placed orders to prisons," said an auditor in China who asked to remain anonymous. "But I know it is happening."

An even more extensive five-day audit *might* be able to detect secret subcontracting. This type of review, which often costs about $5,000 per factory, includes having auditors cross-analyze wage documents and working hours for every department of the factory before comparing those wages and hours with the production records and production line output. But this method is not effective unless the factory makes products for only one brand. It is hard enough for one company to cross-analyze its own production records—let alone access and track the records of other brands the factory also works with.

Another problem: the cost of these audits adds up. It is common for a major brand to have over one hundred thousand suppliers at the first level. But when one hundred thousand suppliers are subcontracting to factories that are subcontracting to other factories, even the cheapest audits can quickly become expensive. Although larger corporations can afford more comprehensive audits, it is easy to see why they might resist paying more for these—especially given that audits are not 100 percent effective in detecting labor violations.

Another major stumbling block auditors come across in these types of investigations is a lack of documentation. There is usually no contractual agreement that requires a factory to keep production records for an extended period of time, which means factories can quickly discard any incriminating records.

As an auditor in China explained to me: "A brand says, 'We want to know where you produced this.' The factory says, 'I already threw away the production documents from last season.' That ends the investigation."

When Sears Holdings was still the parent company of Kmart, I asked one of its spokespeople about this loophole specifically. The spokesperson declined to divulge how comprehensive its audits were. Instead, he pointed to a company compliance program addressing record retainment. But according to a guidebook found on the company's website, its Global Compliance Program only requires suppliers to maintain time card and payroll records for "at least one year." Julie's Halloween decorations sat in her shed for two years before she opened them. When I asked Sears Holdings if its auditors were able to access records from the relevant years during its investigation into the note Julie found, the spokesperson told me the company had "no further comment."

After years of declining sales, Sears Holdings filed for bankruptcy in October 2018, and in February 2019 a new corporation, named Transform Holdco, became the parent company of Kmart and Sears. To this day, Transform Holdco still requires factories to maintain time card and payroll records for only one year.

It is striking that in the era of big data, when corporations can store our emails, photos, and web searches for eternity in the cloud, data centers, and blockchains, they do not retain their factories' production records.

What does all of this add up to? With these lax standards for production records coupled with the massive amount of *authorized* subcontracting that occurs in Chinese manufacturing, it is virtually impossible for an auditor to tell if a factory is secretly sourcing from labor camps. And this is by design.

From the beginning, audits were created to protect corporations rather than workers. Our modern auditing practices date to the 1990s, when labor activists, journalists, and NGOs uncovered Nike's reliance on child workers and sweatshops. Nike initially denied responsibility. Its reasoning was this: since the company did not own its factories, the well-being of overseas factory workers did not fall under its purview.

But Nike's dismissive attitude toward its workers appalled an important segment of consumers—college students. Organizers at more than forty universities protested the brand throughout the 1990s, calling for their schools to terminate business relationships with the company.

Then in 1997, Nike commissioned an audit of one of its Vietnam factories, hoping to learn more about what went on inside, and the audit leaked. Global Exchange, an international human rights NGO, obtained a report showing that 77 percent of the plant's ninety-two hundred workers suffered from respiratory ailments; that in parts of the factory, employees were exposed to carcinogens at levels that surpassed the local legal limit by 177 percent; and that most of these employees did not wear masks or gloves when they handled carcinogenic chemicals.

Galvanized by this information, consumers around the world stopped buying Nike products. As a result, Nike made significant changes to improve its factory conditions and become more transparent. It began conducting inspections and shared many of the reports with the public. And it was precisely during this Nike boycott that many other large corporations began monitoring their own suppliers in countries like China as well.

After all, Nike was not the only company sourcing from countries that are known to have poor factory conditions. Gap, Reebok, and Timberland began conducting audits in China in the late 1990s too.

These are good efforts. Still, even Nike acknowledged, in its 2012 sustainability report, that "monitoring does not bring about sustainable change. Often, it only reinforces a pattern of hiding problems." This is due to another major pitfall: the records auditors do see are often fake. There is a cottage industry of companies that specialize in fabricating employment and production records for Chinese factories. Such consulting firms produce phony time cards that look identical to authentic ones—slightly smeared with dirt, punched in and punched out at uneven locations. Some firms sell software that can create fictitious production data for three thousand workers in thirty minutes. China Labor Watch, a New York–based NGO that advocates for workers' rights, found a Shanghai consulting firm that was advertising software that could create fake accounting books and "irregular attendance records that match factory testing standards completely."

The staff at such consulting firms know exactly what auditors look for because they usually *were* auditors. "They get trained by auditing firms and then go work for a consulting company," a current Chinese auditor told me.

Considering all these obstacles, the only effective way to prove a factory is illegally subcontracting is for auditors to copy the tactics of activists—by going undercover. When China Labor Watch investigated the labor conditions of Target's supplier Rushan Alice

Garments Company, Ltd., in 2011, it had someone work undercover in the Alice factory for over a month. During this time, that person witnessed employees mixing outsourced products with the factory's own products before packaging the merchandise into Target boxes. All were labeled as Alice factory products.

But investigations like these can come at a cost. In 2017, three of China Labor Watch's undercover workers were arrested. After they were released on bail, they endured travel restrictions and police surveillance for several months.

So what drives all this subterfuge? As the world's largest manufacturer, China has an excess of suppliers. Factories with paper-thin margins compete bitterly to win contracts with transnational brands. But when it takes so much obfuscation to present an acceptable facade for auditors, why do Chinese suppliers risk ruining their relationships with coveted labels such as Apple and American Girl to subcontract to forced laborers at all?

Obviously, not having to pay wages keeps costs low. But when it comes to *why* they need to keep expenses down, the answer is more nuanced than miserly factory owners chasing larger profit margins. China Labor Watch found that many factory owners believe it is impossible to meet global corporations' demands for desired bargain prices *and* better working conditions. "If clients need us to follow their requirements completely but offer such low prices, how can we produce anything?" a factory owner using the alias Glory posted in an online forum for Chinese manufacturers called the Product Examiners Archive.

In other words, the reasons Chinese suppliers subcontract to forced laborers lead straight to global consumers: to us and the way we buy. In our ceaseless search for the cheapest and the most current design, technology, flavor, or appliance, we reward the companies that offer the lowest prices and sell the latest trends. The most profitable retailers in every industry are the ones that meet these demands.

Since the early 2000s, fast-fashion stores have been refreshing inventories at ever-faster rates, with new items arriving just about every week. But that is not good enough anymore. Online retailers like ASOS and Boohoo are now adding up to one hundred new items every day, while Fashion Nova can introduce more than a thousand new styles every week. "If there was a design concept that came to mind Sunday night, on a Monday afternoon I would have a sample," Fashion Nova's CEO, Richard Saghian, told the *New York Times*.

And these ultrafast fashion brands are pressuring traditional retailers to keep up or lose business. "They want new and they want it now," Nivindya Sharma, director of retail strategy and insights at fashion forecaster WSGN, wrote in a 2018 report. "When competing alongside super-speedy ASOS and boohoo, stores just cannot match up, as they are plagued by long lead times . . ."

A representative of a logistics management company called Cerasis elaborated in an article on its website: "The widespread increase in connectivity, particularly through mobile devices, has taught customers to believe in the power of their voice and demand instant gratification. . . . An order of new mobile devices may need to be filled within 24 hours and all appropriate packaging may be manufactured on-site at the shipping facility."

Our spending habits put brands on a perpetual search for ways to shorten the time between design, manufacturing, and distribution. This process is known as supply-chain optimization. And our current pressure on companies to endlessly optimize is fundamentally unsustainable.

But without a realistic deadline extension to accommodate order changes, factories face a dire situation. For many manufacturers, a few missed deadlines could put them out of business. If suppliers cannot meet the deadline for transporting goods by boat, they must send the merchandise by air, at much higher costs. Overseas garment manufacturers often have a profit margin of only 3 to 4 percent. But the penalty for a missed deadline can require the factory to give the brand a 5 percent discount. In other words, the factory ends up *paying* the brand to take the product.

This leaves factories in a desperate position. Businesses will pay auditors to check how their factories are performing, but no one is paying auditors to check if brands are giving their factories a reasonable amount of time to make these products, or if brands are paying too low of a price for workers to earn a fair wage. So when there is no other way to fill high-volume orders or deal with sudden production changes, forced laborers are a cheap and reliable workforce to turn to. They'll be monitored by guards who will punish them if they fail to complete the work. They can labor for fifteen hours straight to help manufacturers meet deadlines. And no one will ever know.

These pressures were more than likely the reasons decorative gravestones produced by forced laborers in Masanjia were allegedly shipped to a Kmart in Oregon. And there wasn't much stopping the gravestones from entering US ports.

ICE and CBP can issue detention orders at US ports only if there is "reasonable" evidence a product was made by forced laborers. If there is, the agencies can detain those products for up to ninety days. But if CBP is unable to find conclusive evidence of forced labor in that time, it revokes the detention order—and that's usually what happens. Finding hard evidence so quickly, such as eyewitness accounts or verifiable documents, is often impossible. Forced laborers cannot come forward to testify if they're still in China, where they risk execution if they reveal "state secrets" to US officials.

ICE has three special agents in Hong Kong and five in mainland China who are responsible for identifying manufacturers that use forced labor. But even ICE has acknowledged these agents are stretched too thin. Between the burden of proof required in the United States and the lack of manpower abroad, the US government has been able to open and sustain only twenty-six active detention orders for "Made in China" merchandise since 1991.

Besides the daunting requirements for halting shipments, there was, until recently, another major legal flaw that prevented border and customs agencies from effectively stopping laogai products from entering US ports.

The US Tariff Act of 1930, which first gave government border agents the power to seize shipments made by forced laborers, included a "consumptive demand clause," which permitted products manufactured by children, prisoners, and forced laborers to be sold in US stores—if domestic production could not meet consumer demand. Lawmakers had included this measure in response to economic struggles during the Great Depression. But in practice, it meant the rest of the act was nearly unenforceable.

Until the loophole was closed in 2016, CBP faced not only the insurmountable task of demonstrating a product was manufactured by forced laborers; the agency also had to do market research on supply and demand.

"It was a defense that importers could raise when we detained merchandise," a CBP official told me. "They could take us to court over this."

This wasn't the only ineffective law. In 2010, California passed the Transparency in Supply Chains Act. It requires companies doing business in the state with annual sales of more than $100 million to "provide consumers with critical information about the efforts that

[they] are undertaking to prevent and root out human trafficking and slavery in their product supply chains."

Unfortunately, it is nonbinding legislation—which means there are no legal ramifications for brands that don't comply. Under the banner of this legislation, both Sears Holdings and, later, Transform Holdco posted on their websites that they would "terminate a supplier if a violation related to slave labor or human trafficking is cited" anywhere in their supply chains. But did either company really do so? More than ten years after Sun hid his SOS letters in the graveyard decorations, I asked Transform Holdco if Kmart was still buying from the supplier accused of subcontracting from Masanjia forced laborers. Despite repeated requests for comment, the spokesperson chose not to answer this particular question.

In early 2013, as the identity and fate of the sender of the Masanjia SOS note that Julie had found remained unknown, Sun's message faded from the news headlines. But as Julie trawled the internet for updates one day, she came across a comment from a stranger that left her with a slow-burning dread.

"How could you publish the entire letter publicly?" she recalled reading. "It names the specific unit they are in."

If the author of the letter was not already dead, Julie feared she may have just killed him.

7: Desire and Denial

The article about the Halloween SOS letter became one of the *Oregonian*'s most-read stories, surpassing half a million views. It drew nearly seven hundred comments from readers on the newspaper's website and sparked conversations about ethical consumption on internet forums. "It shouldn't take a letter tucked into a package to get people to realize that they're putting money into abusive labor practices," one commenter wrote in a discussion of the Masanjia letter on the online forum Reddit.

Still, some commenters appeared unfazed. "Ethical people don't [shop at Walmart or Kmart]," another Reddit user wrote. "I do, because I'm a piece-of-shit hypocrite like damn near everybody else."

At this point in the information age, most consumers are aware to some degree there is profound hidden suffering behind the abundance of cheap products. Stories about sweatshops and child labor have been extensively covered in books, documentaries, and lifestyle magazines, and on late-night talk shows. But it has not stopped most of us from shopping from brands that likely use this type of labor.

When Brazilian government inspectors unearthed, in 2011, that the clothing brand Zara had been sourcing from illegal workshops where conditions were "analogous to slavery," the news drew public outrage in Western developed countries. The issue made headlines in publications from the *Telegraph* to Reuters to the BBC. In response to this investigation, Zara's parent company, Inditex, said it has stepped up monitoring by assigning auditors to each of its Brazilian suppliers. Although it is unclear if these auditors are equipped to catch secret subcontracting to forced labor, this statement was enough to let Zara off the hook in the public eye. For the most part, people continued shopping at Zara.

H&M has faced similar scandals with little consequence. Various journalists at news outlets from Refinery29 to the *New York Times* have publicized H&M's use of underage labor and sweatshops in Myanmar, Bangladesh, and Cambodia. In a statement to the *Guardian*, H&M responded to the child labor criticism by stating that in countries with developing economies and limited educational systems "when 14- to 18-year-olds are working it is . . . not a case of child labour, according to international labour laws." While this is true and the practice is technically legal, is it ethical?

This question doesn't seem to matter. As of March 2020, Amancio Ortega, Zara's cofounder, remains the world's wealthiest retailer, and Stefan Persson, H&M's chairman, remains the richest person in Sweden.

How can so many consumers continue to financially support the very brands that outrage them? It's not due to a lack of empathy for workers. Studies have shown consumers care very much about working conditions, fair wages, and environmental impacts. In fact, Futerra, an international consulting firm specializing in corporate branding, found in a 2018 survey of more than one thousand US and UK consumers that 96 percent of people believe their actions— whether it's recycling, donating, or avoiding brands with unethical or unsustainable production practices—can make a difference. And more than half believe an individual's ethical choices can make not just a small difference in the world, but a significant one.

Yet many of us knowingly shop from brands that are not ethically manufacturing their products. What exactly causes this cognitive dissonance?

According to Ulrich Orth, an associate professor of developmental psychology at the University of Bern in Switzerland who has studied how consumers justify the ethics of their purchases, the human brain has a limited capacity when it comes to processing complex ethical questions.

When making difficult choices, "[the] process of decoupling one side of a decision problem—for example, the moral side, from the economic side—makes it easier," Orth told me. "In other words, it's less demanding on cognitive resources."

In a 2019 study, Orth and a team of researchers examined 655 consumers who knowingly bought counterfeit products. They found that, during the critical minutes leading up to the decision to buy or not to buy, there are two, often opposing, groups of considerations that rival for our attention.

One group revolves around the obvious considerations: price, quality, how much we like the product. The other one delves into more complex questions: Is the price this low because the workers who made it experienced immense hardships? Has this brand been exposed in the past for using forced labor, sweatshops, or child labor?

The researchers found that our brains have space to hold only one category of questions at a time, and an ethical question—for example, Am I actively contributing to another person's harm by buying this product?—requires more brainpower to answer than, let's say, Does this look better in beige or green?

"On one side, we are interested in saving money. On the other hand, most people don't want to impair other people," Orth said.

"Balancing those two major decision criteria against each other—that's really difficult."

So our brains compartmentalize, and ignore ethical concerns to make faster and easier choices. "What [we're] basically doing is aggregating the decision by saying, 'Yes, I know there are some bad decisions involved in getting cheap products. But on the other hand, it gets me a good product at a good price,'" Orth said. "Separating those two lines of thought, that's what makes the decision easy."

This ability to streamline our decisions is not completely bad. After all, it is a product of evolution. "The sophisticated allocation of attention has been honed by a long evolutionary history," wrote Daniel Kahneman, who won a Nobel Prize in economics for applying psychological insights to economic theory, in his book *Thinking, Fast and Slow*. "Orienting and responding quickly to the gravest threats or most promising opportunities improved [our] chance of survival."

And streamlining decisions still plays an important role in protecting us during dangerous situations today. For example, Kahneman describes a hypothetical scenario where you sit at the wheel of a car that is starting to spin out and you instinctively respond before you become fully aware of what is happening.

But this process ceases to serve a good purpose when we are standing in the safe environment of a store.

So when we simplify our decision-making, what determines which line of thinking will win out? The answer is neurological. Researchers from Stanford, MIT, and Carnegie Mellon found that when we see an item we like on sale, our brains light up. The more we desire a product, the more blood flow goes to our brains.

In their 2007 study, researchers gave each participant twenty dollars to spend. They could keep the money if they refrained from buying anything. Then the researchers watched, from a brain scanner,

how the subjects reacted as they viewed the prices of forty different products—all of which were 75 percent off normal retail prices.
In particular, they monitored three parts of the brain: the nucleus
accumbens, which anticipates pleasure; the mesial prefrontal cortex,
which evaluates our gains and losses; and the insula, which anticipates pain.

They essentially found that when people saw something they
wanted, their brain's pleasure center activated. But when people saw
a higher price than they were willing to pay, the part of their brain
that processes pain flared instead.

This is why we are so tempted by cheap products. We feel pleasure
if the price is low. We feel pain if the price is too high. When we are
standing in the familiar space of a store or in front of the gentle glow
of a computer screen, we don't feel the agony of the workers who
made our products as deeply as we feel our desires.

But why are we buying so much? And so often? It might be
because we use products and brands to communicate who we are.

While some parts of our identities, like parent or sibling, are
more permanent, others are constructed and reinforced through
consumption. A funky-colored nail polish might convey youth; a
black blazer, success; thick-rimmed glasses, intelligence. Brands also
help us shape and express our lifestyles. Someone who buys Red Bull
energy drink seems—and feels—like a thrill seeker. Someone who
buys West Elm furniture appears to be a minimalist. Someone who
buys Lululemon athletic wear might be a fit, modern mom.

These affiliations drive many of our purchasing decisions. For
example, a person who identifies as an athlete is more likely to purchase a sports drink like Gatorade than a health drink like GT's
Synergy Organic Kombucha, which doesn't have any kind of marketing association with athletes.

When certain brands become the basis of our identities, we form strong emotional ties to them. And studies have shown that such consumer attachments to brands can suppress critical judgments about unethical corporate behavior. A 2012 study found that after word got out that Ikea's Chinese suppliers were plucking feathers from live geese to make down bedding for the home furnishings company, longtime Ikea fans expressed outrage but did not actually stop shopping there. (After the scandal, Ikea said it had stopped selling live-plucked down bedding.)

Despite these flaws in the human mind's ethical wiring, most consumers have a threshold when it comes to compartmentalizing. Ulrich Orth examined this in a 2019 study published in the *Journal of Business Research*. The study recruited 365 consumers between the ages of sixteen and seventy-five to consider buying counterfeits of Calvin Klein fragrances, Beats by Dre headphones, Nike shoes, and Ray Ban sunglasses.

The researchers found that when participants had to read a text message, which listed reasons it is unethical to buy counterfeit brands, right before the time of purchase, most people chose not to buy the counterfeits. "If you alert people, 'You really should not disassociate or separate those two lines of thoughts,' then they tend to make more ethical decisions," Orth later explained.

In other words, consumers are more likely to make moral choices when they don't have to invest extra brainpower to do so. Price will dominate our minds unless the unethical considerations are written out for us at the appropriate time. Only then can we override the joy of seeing a cheap price tag.

The caveat is that this only worked if consumers looked at the anti-counterfeit text right before they considered the purchase. The effect didn't last long. "Maybe minutes. Not more than half an hour,"

Orth said. "People tend to forget. There's other things on their minds. They move on."

All things considered, it may not come as a surprise that people have been saying, for the last fifteen years, that they would pay higher prices to support environmentally sustainable businesses—but that few have actually done so.

A 2004 article in *MIT Sloan Management Review* observed that "when consumers are forced to make trade-offs between product attributes or helping the environment, the environment almost never wins." Likewise, a 2008 survey from McKinsey Global Surveys, which conducts research for global executives, found that 87 percent of consumers expressed concern about the environmental and social impacts behind what they buy, yet only 33 percent said they are willing to pay higher prices for eco-friendly products. More recently, the July–August 2019 issue of *Harvard Business Review* revealed that 65 percent of consumers say they want to shop from sustainable companies, but only 26 percent actually buy from these brands.

Despite the vast disparity between consumer intention and consumer action over the years, there is currently a burgeoning countermovement to excessive and immoral consumption. One popular advocate for a more controlled approach is Marie Kondo, a Japanese decluttering expert whose method revolves around buying and keeping only things that "spark joy."

Surveys show that millennials and Gen Zers in particular tend to prefer "socially conscious companies," brands that treat the environment and their workers well. Members of these generations, born from 1981 to 1996 and from 1996 to 2010, respectively, like companies with a purpose that extends beyond profit—particularly brands with a connection to social or political causes. For instance, in the mid-2000s, Toms Shoes developed a buy-one, give-one business model, where it donated a pair of shoes or eyewear for each Toms product it sold. (In 2019, it changed its model to donating a third of its annual net profits.) This multimillion-dollar brand's main consumer demographic is millennial women.

And millennials have crucial purchasing power: Making up more than a quarter of the US population, they are currently the largest demographic of consumers. The next generation to come of age, Gen Z, is the largest generation in US history. According to research published in 2015 by the consulting firm Altitude, Gen Z was expected to make 40 percent of all retail purchases by 2020.

There is already a segment of consumers from this generation who are more environmentally and socially conscious than their predecessors. Perhaps one of the most telling signs that some Gen Z members are, in fact, making serious efforts to shop sustainably, is that they consider it trendy to buy used *and* luxury items. Although these are two seemingly contradicting shopping preferences, they both stem from a desire to save the Earth. The idea is that by buying thrift items, consumers are reducing the number of goods that end up in landfills and limiting carbon emissions. And by investing in luxury brands, they are committing to wearing the same item for years down the line.

Nancy Nessel, a consultant who specializes in marketing to Gen Z, told me the teens she speaks with for her research "express serious concern about the environment and factories, which is the main reason they are more particular and strategic about how they purchase clothing."

Gen Zers are still shopping at fast-fashion stores, but less so than millennials. "They are buying fast-fashion items, just to be mildly trendy, but more thrift-fashion items, because it is more environmentally correct and financially practical," Nessel said. "H&M used

to be teen girls' favorite store, but today they prefer buying one recycled sweater from Patagonia over many quickly made sweaters from
H&M or Uniqlo."

Does this mean all young people are turning away from hyper-
consumerism? Not exactly. Many are still shopping a lot—as exem-
plified by the "haul video" phenomenon, where young YouTubers
produce segments showcasing their excessive purchases. But there
is evidence suggesting that a growing number of young people are
putting their money where their mouths are.

There is another notable Gen Z characteristic worth mentioning
here. Millennials and members of Generation Z may still be buying
products to form and maintain identities. But marketers are noting
that Gen Zers have considerably less brand loyalty than those who
came before them, perhaps due to their increased thrifting habits. As
a result, they're much more willing to boycott a brand after learning
about negative sourcing practices.

"Sustainability is becoming an expectation for Gen Zers. If it's not
being addressed, if you're not sustainable, we will find a brand that
is," Gen Zer Jonah Stillman told me. He and his father cofounded
the consulting firm Gen Z Guru, which advises companies on how
to capture the Gen Z market.

This shift in attitudes may have contributed to the September
2019 bankruptcy of Forever 21 (although it remains open under
new ownership), and to H&M's record loss in 2018, when it failed to
sell $4.3 billion worth of its inventory. And brands are responding
accordingly. In the wake of this loss, in the spring of 2019 H&M
began listing the names and addresses of some of the manufacturers
that made each item. It also describes the number of workers these
factories employ under the "Product Sustainability" section of its
website.

Some examples of popular brands that have successfully marketed sustainability to young people are Everlane and Reformation. They both charge much higher prices than fast-fashion companies in exchange for more eco-friendly sourcing practices. Reformation, a Los Angeles–based fashion brand, says it has been carbon-neutral since 2015. It also provides summaries of its factories' audit scores, although it doesn't reveal the comprehensiveness of its audits. Everlane, an online boutique with a handful of brick-and-mortar stores, has found a niche by sticking to simpler and higher-quality designs. For this reason, it doesn't compete with fast-fashion companies to sell the latest trends. Over the years, it has pulled off some innovative eco-friendly designs, like outerwear made from plastic bottles that have been repurposed as synthetic fabrics. Everlane also shares photos of the factories where each product comes from on its website. But it mentions the audit scores of only a select few factories.

And so the million-dollar question is: Are any brands truly sustainable at the moment? Even companies that market themselves around "transparency" and "sustainability" often reveal little information about whether their audits can actually detect unauthorized subcontracting. I have yet to come across any companies that divulge how often they make sudden production changes, or how fast of a turnaround they expect from factories. And without transparency about these sourcing practices, for all we know, even the most well-intentioned companies could be inadvertently sourcing from laogai factories.

8: Ghost Work

Masanjia used to be a graveyard. The guard told us, "There are ghosts beneath us." But we are the ones living in the underworld . . . The worlds of the living and the dead have mixed together. —LIU HUA, *laogai survivor*

Masanjia, China, 2008, four years
before Julie found the letter

There was a window on the second floor of the workshop from which a paved road beyond the fence was visible. Cloaked by the shadows of trees, the empty road was barely discernible, but once Sun saw it he could not unsee it. He would steal glances outside every time he passed the window on the way to the toilet. The road was always desolate, until one morning, when someone rode by in a red electric rickshaw. Sun's heartbeat quickened as he stared at the human figure.

He had been there so long he sometimes forgot he was alive.

Sun was no longer a newcomer at Masanjia. After two months in the mushroom department, he and the other forced laborers were divided up to be sent to other workshops.

Masanjia assigned the fast laborers—and people with money for bribes—to a facility that manufactured jewelry and small decorations. The jobs were said to be less tiring there. As Sun walked toward his new unit, he was unsure if he would get an easier job.

He was slow. He was not wealthy. But perhaps he had the virtue of luck—a faint hope he clung to as he ascended the winding steps with the rest of his new team.

He turned the corner, and a crippling dread hit him: They were entering the fourth floor. They had the ghost job, the one that required them to carry sacks of skeletons.

The environment in the ghost work facility was brutal. The violence greeted them at once. A guard grabbed a prisoner by his hair, twisted his head, and smashed his face into a heater. Forced laborers died weekly in this division. The executive officer who managed the ghost team hung a string of Buddhist prayer beads in his office to clear the haunted air.

Even the inmate-guards were not safe. On Sun's first night on the ghost team, he met a si fang in his thirties who liked talking about his girlfriend. His name was Hu, and he had a set of clean clothes tucked under his bed, reserved for her visits. Hu stopped by to ask Sun's bunkmate, who was once a graduate student, to craft a love letter for him. A few days later—only a month short of his scheduled release—Hu was dead. The rumor was that he had been killed by a guard. Sun later overheard a police officer say to a guard, "Find people who will testify that Hu suffocated to death when he fell asleep with a quilt on his face."

When Sun first touched the gravestones his team was assigned to make, he was surprised by their softness. It was only then that he realized they were decorations. A guard later told him the merchandise would be exported to countries celebrating a Western holiday that took place in the fall. It was a new concept for Sun. Most Chinese people did not celebrate Halloween.

He and the other prisoners coated the foam with liquid latex before dipping it in black dye, which had a dizzying scent. They waited for the color to dry and harden. With a wet sponge, they scrubbed the foam to create irregularities that lent the gravestones a timeworn appearance. Smudging their faces with black paint as they wiped their sweat, they labored like this from four in the morning until eleven at night, their feet always damp from standing in pools of black water. The fastest prisoners produced up to twenty tombstones a day, but Sun, with his worsening health, could make only five or six. The team was sometimes forced to stay up an entire twenty-four hours to meet production demands.

Sun stole moments of rest by closing his eyes while his hands continued the motion of scrubbing. Fragments of memories came to him: When he used to buy May gifts—shirts, scarves, jewelry—she never seemed to care which colors he picked. "As long as it's from you," she would say.

The decrepit gray building where Sun manufactured decorative gravestones used to house women too. By 2008, the female forced laborers were imprisoned in a separate, newer building. But for decades before that, they ate in the same canteens as the men and experienced torture in adjacent rooms. There were still bloodstains on the walls of what had been the women's torture room, where those who would not submit to authority or change their political or religious beliefs were "reeducated." The men in Sun's unit dreaded working at night, when their minds played tricks on them—they saw moving shadows and heard unexplained sounds. Some inmates claimed they could hear women sobbing, the ghosts of those who had killed themselves.

Historically, and presently, the women at Masanjia experienced arguably worse torture and degradation than men. The guards would jam and twist toothbrushes up women's vaginas, pour chili powder into their genitals, and shock their breasts with electric batons. Then they gang-raped their victims, who often vomited blood afterward.

A female Masanjia survivor named Yin Liping described her sexual assault:

> *As I woke from unconsciousness, I noticed three men lying beside me. One was on my left, and two were on my right. A young man close to my right was groping my body all over with his hands. He looked like he was younger than 20 years old. The other man behind him was also busy groping me with his hands. The man on my left kept touching my face and held his leg against my private parts. Then I felt, above my head, there was another man sitting there. He kept touching my face and my head. Two men stood below me facing the gap between my legs. One was videotaping while the other one watched. They kept talking dirty. I didn't know how many others were there. They were tickling my feet and laughing. . . . I couldn't believe what I was experiencing. . . . The next day, I was beaten by a male inmate. That night, I was gang-raped, just as I had been the night before. We don't know how we survived . . . Even now, years later, I tremble when I think about it.*

According to survivors, the women made uniforms for the Liaoning Forest Fire Prevention Department, shirts for a South Korean company, and down coats for an Italian brand. But unlike the men who worked with feathers, the women did not even have protective masks.

The clothing was exported under a commercial name: Xinyu Clothing Company, Ltd. Researchers from the US-China Economic and Security Review Commission later confirmed that the garment company's corporate address was the same as the labor camp's.

In 2013, a Chinese citizen named Du Bin, a Beijing-based photojournalist, poet, and documentary maker, helped bring the conditions at Masanjia women's camp to light, despite great risk of landing in a labor camp himself. Since 2011, he has worked as a freelance photographer for the *New York Times*, covering subjects ranging from forgotten villagers devastated by mass construction projects; the border between China and North Korea; and victims of China's underfunded mental health system. But it was his documentary about Masanjia that would get him in deep trouble.

In the film, titled *Above the Ghosts' Heads*, a middle-aged survivor named Liu Hua described what it was like to manufacture down coats at Masanjia's women's camp: "Our faces were covered with tiny feathers. We looked like newborn chicks. . . . All covered in fur, except our black eyes. It was June, and it was very hot. We were not allowed to shower for a month. We were drenched in sweat . . . Our eyes were so dry, and our faces were so itchy. For ten months, my eyes were red. It felt like my eyes were rotting . . . I've been released for four months now, and my eyes are still dry and infected." Liu, a nanny, had been sentenced to Masanjia for petitioning the central government to address alleged embezzlement by the party secretary of her village.

In the labor camps, women were beaten so often that when they were allowed showers, the water on the floor bled red. They were often whipped for eating outside the canteen, but they did so anyway because they were starving: "By nine thirty in the morning, we would already feel so hungry that our bodies shook," Liu described. "There was not an ounce of energy left in our bodies. So we hid food in our underwear. We ate our snacks during the five minutes we were allowed to be in the bathroom . . . We were so hungry and so afraid of getting beaten . . . I would hide a cold and hard steamed bun in my pocket. I'd eat it while I took a shit. It made me feel sick to do this. But I had to or I would starve."

The women were not always allowed bathroom breaks. One woman recalled sitting for hours, sewing clothing, as menstrual blood seeped across her bottom. The guards were all men, and there were four male repairmen in the workshop that day, fixing broken sewing machines. She was mortified when the detainees were finally permitted to leave the workshop. She walked backward toward the door to preserve her remaining shred of dignity. Risking beatings, the other women in the room huddled to hide her.

It was at great personal risk that Liu Hua told her story to Du Bin. Despite knowing retaliation awaited her, she wanted to get her account to the outside world. "We also made uniform pants for the police," she said in the documentary. "We had to make three hundred forty pants every day. I can't put into words how stressed and tired we were."

After the film was released in Hong Kong in 2013, the Chinese authorities promptly arrested Du Bin and Liu Hua. Du Bin was detained for thirty-seven days, while Liu Hua was sent to Shenyang No. 1 Detention Center and then placed under house arrest. But with international eyes watching, the authorities chose not to send Liu Hua back to Masanjia.

In the course of reporting this book, I interviewed another female forced-labor-camp survivor, named Yu Zhenjie, who told me the conditions were no better at other camps: From 2000 to 2003, she was detained at the Shuanghe Labor Camp in Qiqihar City, where she manufactured pesticides for more than ten hours a day. The camp never gave the laborers masks, and chunks of powdered pesticide would clog Yu's nose as she processed chemicals. She was later force-fed unknown drugs that made her tongue go stiff.

"It felt more painful than when I gave birth to my daughter," she said, adding that the drugs also numbed the lower half of her body.

Now a soft-spoken woman in her sixties, she told me with a timid smile that she remains partially paralyzed, and she is unable to fully control her bowel movements.

After her release, Yu Zhenjie left China for New York, where she now lives alone; her husband divorced her while she was in the camp. Her daughter remains in China.

Ma Chunmei, a forced-labor-camp survivor in her late forties, told me she experienced similar tortures during her four years at the Heizuizi Women's Labor Camp in Changchun, also known by the business name Changchun City Arts and Crafts Factory. The guards shocked her breasts with electric batons, she recalled, and she and the other women in the camp were forced to manufacture decorative birds, butterflies, fish, ladybugs, and frogs, which all had English labels. They also wrapped single toothpicks in cellophane.

Ma Chunmei was released in 2004 and immigrated to the United States in 2009. Nearly a decade later, on a November evening in 2018 not long after Black Friday, she went shopping at a Sears store. She froze in front of a rack displaying bird Christmas ornaments. Shards of memories of sexual violence emerged as she stared at the familiar long tails and glittery feathers.

"These are the exact birds that I made," she wrote to me in a text message. Then she sent pictures of 4.5-inch Donner & Blitzen Incorporated bird ornaments, selling for $3.99 to $12.99 each.

9: A Laogai Love Letter

There was a culture of self-mutilation in Masanjia. Detainees took great pains to cause just enough damage to get hospitalized but not kill themselves. Some swallowed toothpicks. Others swallowed nails. Some ingested blades wrapped in tape. One Masanjia prisoner who went by the nickname Little Sichuan stabbed himself in the stomach with a pair of tapered pliers because he wanted a break from manufacturing diodes. Anything for a trip to the hospital; it was their only possible respite from the backbreaking work.

If the workshops had lye, some detainees drank it. But it was hard to measure the precise amount needed for a ticket to the hospital. Too little had no effect; too much burned holes into the esophagus. Although sentences were usually less than four years, some detainees preferred to chance losing the ability to eat for the rest of their lives than spend another day in the labor camp.

It was nearly impossible for inmates to break out of Masanjia, in large part because their skeletal frames moved slowly. Rumor has it an inmate once ran away at midnight, but although the camp gate was not extremely far, daylight broke before he reached it. Still, there were prisoners who went to great lengths to escape, despite knowing it was unlikely they would make it; the slightest possibility of freedom was worth any punishment that might await them.

On one summer morning, as the rolling shutters lifted to let in a truck retrieving products, a man in his thirties named Meng darted out. He was young. He hadn't lost his strength yet. For months, he had been bribing a worker in the canteen for sausages, sustaining his muscles for an escape attempt. Meng sprinted away and vanished into a field of corn. But the guards still caught him. They beat him with electric batons until his body convulsed, then hung him by his wrists for two weeks—with his toes barely touching the ground. Meng tried to break out four times before giving up.

Many prisoners recalled considering suicide. An inmate named Yu Xiaohang who noticed the sharp, chipped edge of the stone sink. "If I slashed my wrist against the shard, I could cut my veins," he said. As he lowered his face toward the faucet, he would eye that edge and think, *Death will end all my troubles*. He was later glad that he never went through with it.

In some ways, the ghost team was a relief for Sun. At least he was now allowed one basic dignity: the opportunity to shower. In a frenzied state, he and the other prisoners stripped off their clothes as fast as they could and ran into water, even though it was ice-cold. The bathroom doors were left open in the winter, perhaps to discourage bathroom breaks.

They were permitted to bathe for only a few minutes, however, so the frail and aging inmates often did not finish undressing before they had to put their clothes back on. An older man on Sun's unit named Dong Chen gave up trying to clean himself; he stopped washing his face and brushing his teeth. His body was dead tired from dyeing and scrubbing tombstones all day, and he was near the end of his sentence anyway. Dong, a quiet man in his sixties, had been sent to Masanjia for "disturbing social order" after the authorities discovered he had been holding unregistered Bible studies in his home.

The state-approved Christian churches in China are political institutions first and foremost. They refute some of the defining features of Christianity, such as a belief in the resurrection of Jesus Christ. Instead, most are affiliated with the government-run Three-Self Patriotic Movement, which espouses self-governance, self-support, and self-propagation, and rejects foreign funding and foreign missionaries. For this reason, many Chinese Christians prefer to worship in informal house churches like Dong's. This is troubling for the Chinese regime, which sees independent churches as a fountainhead of dissent—and indeed, several prominent Chinese human rights lawyers are Christians.

Sun and Dong were briefly cellmates. When Sun returned to his cell after a long night of work, he would sometimes find Dong already asleep. Inmates were forbidden to lie down before bedtime, but for a few nights, the guards made an exception for the old man, who had been vomiting. "It's all right," one guard said. "He'll be all right after he sleeps."

Dong died from a stroke two weeks before his release date.

Sun would often think of Dong when he assembled one particular decoration, a hooded skeleton embracing a cross.

Little did Sun know, May was in trouble.

It happened not long after he disappeared. The police cars arrived on the last day of Chinese New Year, a weeklong holiday. As she pulled into her apartment complex with her younger brother, she spotted the cops. A raid was imminent.

As waves of firecrackers shot into the sky and exploded, she decided to destroy the incriminating evidence that Sun had left behind. She asked her brother to help as they quietly entered the building. May barged into her apartment and began frantically grabbing all the Falun Gong flyers and books she could find. She almost tripped over her Pomeranian, circling her feet.

Smoke spread through her home as they burned the materials on the stove. The police noticed the smoke from May's window.

There was a knock on the door. Then the officers entered. Dulled by fear, May didn't say anything. The dog barked a few times before retreating into the bedroom.

The police replaced her light bulbs with higher-wattage ones before inspecting the apartment. Drawers, storage bins, shoeboxes, gift bags, purses, and suitcases were emptied and thrown aside. Then they arrested May and her brother, leading them away in handcuffs.

She initially thought it was going to be a quick detainment, since it was the product of a misunderstanding. She figured they would release her once she proved she was not a Falun Gong practitioner. After all, she was willing to criticize the group for its work against the government.

She signed Statement One, repentance for helping a Falun Gong practitioner. She signed Statement Two, a promise of allegiance to the Chinese Communist Party.

She faltered on Statement Three.

It required her to give the government the name and address of someone who secretly practiced Falun Gong.

Sun had never introduced her to his Falun Gong friends. This was intentional, to protect her. He didn't want the government mistaking her for a follower.

So she only knew one other practitioner, an old woman. She couldn't give her up. But there was no one else May could name.

Since her brother had only a tangential connection to Falun

Gong, they released him after one day. But the authorities refused to let May go until she talked. And so after two weeks of beatings and interrogations, she cracked. As they discharged her into the world, an auntie was about to vanish into a camp.

When May returned home, guilt consuming her, the front door was still plastered with auspicious red Chinese New Year couplets. When she opened it, the bedlam inside shocked her: withered plants, smashed pottery, kitchenware scattered across the floor, her clothes lying in disarray, like lifeless bodies. After the terrors she'd experienced in the detention center, she had almost forgotten the violent night of her arrest.

At least the two-week stint in detention didn't get her fired. Her company preferred freelance accountants like her, whom they paid lower wages and gave no benefits. She picked her dog up from an elderly neighbor before she began collecting the loose items on the floor.

She walked by Sun's devastated study but could not bring herself to enter. Instead, she shut the door. Years passed before she would open it again.

Her family had long been pressuring her to leave Sun. Now that her younger brother had been arrested because of her connection to Falun Gong, she had little choice. She began gathering receipts for packages she had mailed to various detention centers over the years: evidence of Sun's absence, for a divorce filing.

Tears welled in her eyes as she glanced at the moon, a luminous crescent blazing alone in the starless city sky. She often watched the moon, because wherever Sun was, perhaps he was looking at the moon too.

One day, two young employees from the supplier subcontracting to Masanjia came to inspect the labor camp. Their visitor IDs dangled from their necks as they strolled through the workshop, snapping pictures of tombstones. The suppliers near the labor camp were country people with heavy accents. But these two, with their expensive clothing and polished voices, were clearly urban elites. Sun suspected they were working for a big exporter.

The young inspectors did not appear to mind the workshop's unbearable stench due to the ban on doing laundry. Some prisoners washed their clothes in secret and wore wet clothing during the day. Their shirts and underwear were quick to dry during scorching summers, but once the weather turned cold, any damp garments grew moldy.

Sun stared at the inspectors before gluing the black plastic roses and small skeletal feet to the tombstones he was working on. He was no longer a part of their world. Standing in front of them, he felt he was already a ghost.

As he stored the products in boxes, he looked at the English words on the packaging. An idea struck him.

These might be going to America or Australia. Could I sneak a letter into the packaging, let a customer know what my life is like? Is it possible to get away with writing letters now that I have my own bed?

Before he could think this plan through, an unexpected reprieve from making tombstones arrived: the guards recruited Sun, who had a knack for drawing, to make posters celebrating the upcoming Beijing Olympics. To foster a sense of nationalism, labor camps sometimes had detainees draw propaganda posters. He traced the five interlaced rings with colorful markers. *How ironic*, he thought. *The Olympic symbol looks like handcuffs.*

He was writing the words "We Welcome the Olympics" when a guard handed him a parcel containing clothing and a torn envelope.

Sun recognized the handwriting on the envelope. He dropped the marker and sat down.

Sun,

Our home was raided after you left. My brother was arrested and his work was affected. My health has not been good, I'm coughing all the time.

I hadn't hoped for wealth or social status when I married you. I only wanted a peaceful life. But there was always something happening with you over the years because you practice Falun Gong.

I live in constant fear, with only a few quiet days at a time.

My health has become very poor. I feel mental and physical fatigue.

My mental condition is very weak. I can't bear it anymore. If it were only me embroiled in your problems, I could deal with that. But my brother is often embroiled now too. My parents are anxious all the time. They have trouble sleeping.

So I think since you can't change your beliefs, we should break up. I thought about postponing the divorce until after you come back from the labor camp. But once you come back, I know it will be very hard to leave you. So I am filing for divorce now. I am letting you know in advance so you can be mentally prepared. I sent you some old clothes. Write to me if it is not enough.

May
June 3, 2008

Sun picked up the marker but was unable to draw more interlaced rings. The impending divorce did not hurt him. He understood her position. But it shattered him to read about the pain he had caused. He tucked the letter into his pocket with his sole belonging, a plastic spoon.

Sun folded and unfolded the fraying paper several times a day to look at her handwriting. No matter how tired he was, he read the letter every night before he slept. When he came across adhesive tape in a workshop one day, he sealed the entire letter with strips of tape to protect it from tearing further. "It's almost as good as a love letter," he said.

10: Dangerous Words

Tender memories commingled with the present: the smile of his mother; the old woman who sold him cookies in Taiyuan; a metal disc he played with as a child. Sun clung to these images, as if forgetting would mean a permanent disintegration of his former self.

He was less than halfway through his two-and-a-half-year sentence. But it would likely be extended much longer, since he was refusing to tout party lines. Desperate for the slightest chance of leaving earlier, or leaving at all, he decided to write the SOS notes in late 2008.

He faced many challenges. The lights were always on in the cells, and each one had seven prisoners and an inmate-guard. But it helped that Sun slept on one of the top bunks. He began formulating a plan. The paper would inevitably rustle. So he would have to write slowly, taking frequent pauses to limit the noise. He could hide finished letters in the hollow steel bars of the bed.

That night, he stared at the onionskin paper and hesitated. There was a chance he would survive long enough to go home. But if they caught him writing SOS messages, he could die.

He had torn pages out of the back of his political reeducation workbook with care. The paper had green lines, similar to the stationery he'd used to practice English two decades earlier in Chongqing, except that the upper right corner was ripped. Sun wished he could remember more English grammar rules as he lay hunched on the grimy mattress.

He picked up the pen.

Sir: If you occasionally buy, he wrote before stopping. He was nervous. The paper was crinkling louder than he'd anticipated. He listened for changes in his cellmates' breathing patterns. They were still asleep.

It was after midnight; the humid air was cooling with each passing hour. The guards made less frequent rounds as the night wore on. Sun's eyelids grew heavy, but he wanted to complete at least one letter his first night.

His eyes snapped open as heavy footsteps echoed in the hallway. He froze, listening to the footsteps pass him and fade. The night sounds dwindled back to snores and chirping crickets. He slipped into a deep sleep.

Throughout the next day, as he went over the risks again and again in his mind, he became more determined to write the letters. To survive, he needed hope.

He managed to finish that first letter the second night. He tried to include as many details as possible, filling all the lines on the sheet. Writing became easier once he had a solid draft. After two weeks, Sun had completed more than twenty slightly varied letters.

Now, how to get them out?

He waited almost a month until the ghost team finished another batch of Halloween decorations. Sun was sometimes alone when he packaged the gravestones—he was a slow worker—so it wouldn't look suspicious if he lingered behind. He retrieved the rolled-up letters from the bars of his bed in preparation. He took all of them, including the earlier drafts with crossed-out words.

Trucks came every few days to pick up shipments. But he was not certain that this was the final production step. The guards might open the packages again to inspect quality before loading them onto the trucks. He could get caught before even a single letter got out.

Sun likely did not know this, but a similar SOS note ploy had been thwarted at the Heizuizi Women's Labor Camp in Changchun just a few years earlier, in 2005. This was Ma Chunmei's camp, where women glued sequins onto foam birds and stuck kitschy wings onto plastic butterflies. Feeling nauseous from breathing toxic fumes all day, a small group of forced laborers plotted to write messages inside the boxes of their products. But a guard noticed the writing during a routine quality inspection. Several detainees were smacked with extended sentences.

On a day when a truck was scheduled to arrive, Sun began inserting his letters into the gravestone packaging. His heart pounded. He waited for commotion, for someone to yell, for the ire of the guards.

But then—nothing. Sun was stunned. A rush of euphoria hit him: he wanted to do it again.

Sun saved two of his letters to give to two other Falun Gong detainees. One was a man named Laopo, a dexterous man assigned to glue the skeletons' hands to their arms. The glue gun had a piercing odor, and Laopo did not have a mask to wear. Still, many forced laborers in the ghost team envied his job; it was less tiring than dyeing and scrubbing tombstones.

Laopo and the other forced laborer immediately agreed to help even though they didn't know English. Using Sun's letters as templates, the two of them forfeited sleep to duplicate SOS notes at night.

A few weeks later, Sun lingered behind again. A quiet fell over the warehouse as the detainees trickled out. Sun was nervous, but less nervous than last time. Growing bolder, he may have stayed a moment too long.

As he was tucking a note into a package, someone walked in on him. "Hey! What are you doing?" a detainee named Wang Guige said. "What are you putting inside?"

Sun stiffened. A tense silence passed as he tried to read the man's face.

Wang, a detainee from Inner Mongolia, had recently been transferred to their team to help package products. Never having worked together, he and Sun had no rapport. And Wang could get a reduced sentence if he reported Sun to a guard.

"Forced labor is illegal," Sun finally said. "I am telling the world how these products are made. People need to know."

Wang's eyes widened. "I'll help you. Do you have any more letters?"

Sun grew more paranoid with each passing hour. As he chewed his rotten cabbage at dinner, he regretted handing Wang a copy. For all he knew, Wang could be planning to show it to a guard. He also feared he should not have given the letter to the other people. There were now more risk factors out of his control.

A few days went by without any guards approaching Sun. Just when he thought he was in the clear, an unforeseen incident knocked the plan off-kilter.

A prisoner broke out, triggering a lockdown. Although he was later caught and brought back to Masanjia, the guards did an exhaustive inspection of each cell. As they searched for hidden tools that could help detainees escape, one lifted a Falun Gong practitioner's mattress. There was a piece of paper underneath.

The guard could not read English. But the Chinese words interspersed throughout were red flags. Torture (酷刑折磨). Illegal reeducation through labor (非法勞教). The guard handed the note to his supervisor.

It took a few days for the entire letter to get translated. But once it was, Masanjia RTL Camp was placed on red alert. The guards handcuffed all the male detainees to each other and led them outside.

Standing under the early afternoon sun, they looked at one another with horror in their eyes. The guards surrounded the man whose mattress they had found the letter under. For hours, they struck him with high-voltage batons, his guttural screams ringing through the empty rice field.

"You're a simple man from the countryside. You couldn't possibly have the English skills to write this by yourself," a guard yelled. "Tell me. Who wrote the English for you?"

Sun stood in terror, waiting to hear his name.

11: Historical Complicity

In the early 1990s, when the prominent pro-democracy organizer Chen Pokong was forced to toil in the quarry at Guangdong No. 1 Reeducation Through Labor Camp, detainees worked under scorching sun to haul large rocks onto boats that tossed on a turbulent river. The rocks often slipped from their grips, smashing their hands and feet, as smoke crept from the cargo ships that came to retrieve the prisoners' bounty.

The prisoners were always thirsty. The only place to drink was from the brown river swelling with flecks of garbage and industrial waste. "It tasted awful," Chen told me. "We called it 'horse urine.' But you had no choice but to drink it."

They were beaten for stopping for water, pausing to breathe, having a resentful facial expression. Seven or eight guards and inmate-guards at a time would club one forced laborer. Many prisoners lost consciousness, collapsing into the reeking river. The inmate-guards poured cold water on the pus-stained bodies that lay bleeding in the mud until the laborers woke, got up, and resumed work.

There were nine or ten units, Chen recalled, with each unit containing three hundred people. The camp collaborated with the public security bureau. Whenever it fell short on forced labor, the police filled beds by making arbitrary arrests of rural migrant workers.

"I did not have a trial," Chen said. "The public security bureau sentenced me by giving me a piece of paper."

After working eight hours a day in the quarry, prisoners had to manufacture artificial flowers for six more hours at night. Chen folded adhesive labels around garish lilies, tulips, and poppies. He glued fake stems to polyester and silk flowers. The mustiness of the silk mingled with the strong glue, covering the iron scent of blood.

The trademarks were labeled in English, the prices marked in US dollars. And this was not the first time Chen had noticed this.

Chen was first arrested in 1989 for helping to organize the pro-democracy protest at Tianamen Square. Prior to his informal sentencing to a labor camp, he was forced to manufacture small souvenirs in pretrial detention centers. "Even in the detention centers, I saw the trademarks and prices were in English as well," he said. "At that time, I was thinking, 'Why are the prices in US dollars?' I did not immediately think it was for exports. When I saw it again in the reeducation through labor camp, I was certain it was being exported. I even confirmed with camp officials, who showed off and said they had connections with a Hong Kong company. When I asked more questions about where the products were going to be sold, they stopped talking."

Chen knew that if he wanted to tell the outside world, he had to act fast. It was 1994 and he was halfway through his sentence, but he was living on borrowed time. One man had already died in the quarry.

Relying on a feeble streetlight that shone through his cell window, Chen started writing a secret letter. He did not have strength to work on it every night; it took him weeks to finish.

I understand that once my letter is published, I might be perse-cuted even more harshly, he concluded his first message. *I might even be killed. But I have no choice!*

Then he folded it up and inserted three labels:

"SILKY TOUCH," BEN FRANKLIN STORES INC., CAROL STREAM, ILLINOIS

"LADY BUG COLLECTION," UNIVERSAL SUN RAY OF SPRINGFIELD, MISSOURI

UNIVERSAL SUN RAY

At the wharf, when no one was looking, Chen slipped his letter and 50 yuan to a deckhand on a boat. The man gave a small nod without changing his expression.

After the boat pulled away, Chen let out a deep breath.

He had addressed the letter to a friend in Guangzhou. It passed through several hands before landing in the California home of Harry Wu. Holding the letter in his hands, Wu was emotional. A survivor of forced labor himself, Wu had once attempted to sneak out a similar message from a Beijing camp. He was caught and placed in solitary confinement, and the guards tortured him by force-feeding him for eleven days. But now, as the cofounder of the Laogai Research Foundation, Wu knew what to do. He took the letter to Washington, DC.

"He sent a compelling appeal for help, relating the terrible tale of ill treatment and slave labor in a world where political prisoners labor fourteen hours a day," Congresswoman Nancy Pelosi said of Chen's letter at a congressional hearing in October 1994.

The hearing did not ultimately lead to any meaningful policy changes that would prevent laogai products from entering US markets. But since Chen was able to sneak labels out from the camp, it was a rare case in which the United States had concrete evidence to detain specific products. On December 21, 1994, Customs and Border Protection issued a detention order for artificial flowers from Kwong Ngai Industrial Company, based in Hong Kong, named as the culpable supplier sourcing from Guangzhou No. 1 RTL Camp. The detention order remains active today. (Unless an importer submits evidence that it has addressed the forced-labor concern, a detention order can remain active indefinitely.)

Detention orders are a good start, but they're not enough. Kwong Ngai Industrial Company may not be allowed to export artificial flowers to the United States, but it can still export other forced-labor products. "Theoretically, you can have an importer that imports a variety of merchandise—peeled garlic and onions maybe," a CBP official told me, regarding Chinese companies that import goods into the United States. "Their peeled garlic shipments we can detain . . . but we don't have any [detention orders] on onions at the moment. So they could, in theory, [still] import onions."

And there is another loophole. Since other suppliers from that region can still export artificial flowers to the United States, Kwong Ngai could too if it changed its name.

Over the years, US-China trade expert Jeffrey Fiedler has been calling for industry-wide bans instead. "It's a bit meaningless [otherwise]," he told me. "You name a company, and they change the company name to avoid the detention order. It's so easy to get around."

I was unable to find a website for Kwong Ngai Industrial Company in recent years. But there is a Ngai Kwong Industrial Company—also based in Hong Kong—that now exports household appliances.

CBP could ban artificial flowers from Kwong Ngai because the labels that Chen had snuck out of the camp, with their CAROL STREAM, ILLINOIS and SPRINGFIELD, MISSOURI text, were unequivocal evidence that China was exporting forced-labor merchandise to the United States. And this was not the first time the US government had seen hard proof like this.

In the summer of 1991, Harry Wu, a naturalized US citizen, went undercover with CBS journalist Ed Bradley. Posing as a Chinese American businessman, Wu visited more than twenty laogai facilities with a hidden camera.

Returning to camps where he had attempted suicide, where his weight as a grown man had dropped to seventy-two pounds, was an unraveling experience. Despite the disturbing memories he had to face and the fear of being discovered at any moment, Wu filmed his conversations with laogai officials for the *60 Minutes* program.

In one clip, Wu discussed business matters with managers from the Shanghai Laodong Machinery Factory, which was sourcing products from a prison that manufactured hand tools.

"Our products are never exported directly," said Lu Weimen, a manager at the factory. "We always go through the import-export company system."

"As far as I know, the US has a trade law that prevents importation of products made by prison labor," Wu replied. "This will give us trouble, because customs will find out."

"Not if we don't export directly," a second manager assured him.

Wu also visited a labor camp in a desert in the province of Qinghai, where detainees in blue uniforms processed sheep hides into leather, and he caught a glimpse of a man working inside. "I noticed a prisoner who seemed to be hiding behind a vat of chemicals used to cure the lambskins," he recalled in his memoir, *Troublemaker*. "Ultimately he emerged and, to my astonishment, began to strip off his uniform. When he was stark naked, he climbed into the vat and began to stir the chemicals with his body. The chemicals were intended to cure the lambskins, and I shuddered to think what they were doing to his skin."

The camp's commercial name was Qinghai Hide and Garment Works. On the wall hung a framed exporting license and an award that proclaimed: ADVANCED COLLECTIVE FOR SUPPRESSING REBEL-LION AND CEASING CHAOS. MINISTRY OF JUSTICE. OCTOBER 1989. It was one of thirty-one camps that had detained pro-democracy activists after the Tiananmen Square massacre.

The camp's sales representative told Wu the facility exported to Japan and Australia, and gave Wu the name and address of a Hong Kong import-export firm that handled their foreign transactions.

60 Minutes producers wanted an undercover journalist to schedule an in-person meeting with the Hong Kong trading company. But they feared their correspondents might be recognized. So Ned Hall, an audio engineer for the show, ended up posing as the president of a US company looking to import leather from a labor camp. He used a hidden camera to film his conversation with the trading company.

"Have you had experience with this type of labor in the past?" Hall asked. "Have you found them to be dependable?"

"We send our people to keep on checking the quality," a woman from the trading company said in English. "Once we report to them the quality is not up to standard, the prisoners will have punishment, beatings . . ."

The *60 Minutes* segment caused quite a stir when it aired later that year. The US Congress invited Wu to testify at its first-ever hearing on laogai products. And when the United States demanded answers of China, China's Ministry of Justice revealed that the value of products from laogai farms and factories ranged anywhere between $300 million and $1 billion.

In response, President George H. W. Bush signed a memorandum of understanding with China in 1992 that was supposed to enable US officials to inspect Chinese forced-labor facilities suspected of exporting. But the agreement was willfully weak. Bush allowed China to sanitize the agreement's language by describing the issue as "prison labor" instead of "forced labor."

In doing so, China was able to make a direct comparison between its gulags and the US prison system. And there are some similarities. According to Unicor, a.k.a. Federal Prison Industries, a government-owned corporation that sells goods made in prisons in the United States, US prisoners manufacture products ranging from air purification equipment to textiles to office supplies—some for wages as low as twenty-three cents an hour. In some states, inmates work for no pay at all. But as problematic as the US prison system is, it does not violate international labor laws. This is because the International Labour Organization, the UN agency that defines labor standards, says involuntary work "as a consequence of a conviction in a court of law" is not forced labor.

This explains why China was eager to whitewash laogai labor as merely prison labor. If the agreement with the United States did not specifically address laogais, then the US government couldn't hold China accountable for forced labor being used in laogais.

In truth, though, there is no functional difference between a prison and a forced-labor camp in China, because while people have trials before they disappear into prisons, most of these trials are meaningless. According to a statement in 2018 by Zhou Qiang, the head of China's Supreme People's Court, criminal courts in China convict in 99.9 percent of all cases.

Regardless of the legality of labor in China's prisons, its laogais are definitively in violation of international law. Although US officials are well aware of the crucial legal difference between prisons and forced-labor camps, the 1992 agreement has never been updated to address this discrepancy, even though it has long been known to be an issue. Back in 1997, Jesse Helms, then-chairman of the Senate

Foreign Relations Committee, said during a hearing: "This distinction has created a major problem in enforcement of the agreement between China and the US on prison labor, with China refusing access to 'reeducation through labor' facilities on the grounds that they are not prisons."

President Bush also allowed China to delegitimize the 1992 memorandum of understanding by agreeing to use the term "visit" instead of "inspect." "In international law, the word 'inspect' has a rigorous connotation," Fielder told me. "You go in when you want to and they have to let you in . . . In that context, and in practice, we have to *request* a 'visit.' The time period between request and visit was, in many cases, years."

After the Laogai Research Foundation pressured US officials to step up enforcement, President Bill Clinton slightly revised the agreement by signing a statement of cooperation with China in 1994. It clarified that US diplomats should be permitted to visit suspected facilities "within 60 days of the receipt of a written request."

Despite the sixty-day rule, US requests to visit labor camps remained pending for years. Frustrated US officials have described scenarios where China's Ministry of Justice rudely rebuffed a US diplomat in charge of investigating forced labor.

Meanwhile, China has never faced consequences for not holding up its end of the agreement. After receiving documentation from the Laogai Research Foundation that suggested that Fuyang General Machinery Factory was sourcing from forced labor, US officials requested to visit the factory in 1995. China waited ten years before approving the visit. Needless to say, US investigators could not find evidence of forced labor after a decade.

This lack of progress demoralized Harry Wu. He realized most of what the world knew about Soviet gulags and Nazi concentration camps surfaced only after the collapse of the regimes, when researchers and journalists finally had access to records. The Chinese Communist Party was not showing any signs of disintegration. So Wu took it upon himself to continue documenting the laogai system by returning to China in 1995. He knew he could be executed if the authorities caught him. But a longing for the world to know—to *care*—drove him. "People remember Anne Frank. We Chinese are human beings, too. Who will remember us?" he wrote in his memoir.

He was caught as soon as he entered China, and the CCP charged him with espionage.

China ended up letting Wu go after sixty-six days, due to pressure from US human rights activists who campaigned for his release. But the Chinese government could have easily chosen not to. This is the price of documenting the laogai system, a risk that every researcher considers when they go to China to do this work.

There is one exception, though: activists and diplomats may not have the authority to visit labor camps without China's permission, but US businesspeople can. Unlike diplomats, they do not need to make formal requests to the Chinese government before seeing factories. After all, most businesspeople aren't visiting factories on behalf of the US government, so they are not subject to the 1992 agreement.

And it was exactly this loophole that Peter Levy, a bespectacled man with side-parted brown hair, used in 1996.

Levy, a descendant of Holocaust survivors, had taken it upon himself to prove and publicize the fact that China was exporting laogai products. Some human rights considerations motivated him, but he was also a businessman—and his company was tanking as a direct result of China's labor camps.

Levy was the owner of Labelon/Noesting, a modest manufacturer of office products in Mount Vernon, New York, that employed twenty people. They distributed office products, including those ubiquitous binder clips, to companies across the United States. But with the office-supplies industry consolidating, small manufacturers like Levy's faced increasing pressure to lower prices. "We are all looking for a competitive advantage," Levy later said, during congressional testimony in May of 1997. So it hurt when one of his competitors, the New Jersey–based Officemate, began selling binder clips for impossibly low prices.

When someone in the industry told Levy that Officemate was undercutting him by sourcing from a Chinese detention center, he grew angry. This illegal competitive advantage was allowing Officemate and Allied International Manufacturing Stationery Company, a supplier that Officemate owned, to dominate one-third of the US market for binder clips. The Allied International facility in Nanjing, China, was the largest spring-clip factory in the world.

Levy contacted the US State Department and Customs and Border Protection for advice. But the agencies could not help.

"The State Department . . . told me that the Customs Service was not allowed to make unscheduled inspections of the camps. It was my opinion that the US government was not in any position to effectively investigate this matter," Levy said, "and it was at that time that I made the decision to research this matter on my own."

And so Levy went to Nanjing to follow the trucks that left Officemate's supplier, Allied International. During a traffic jam there, Levy got out of his rental car. He stood out among the sea of Chinese faces. It was risky to draw attention to himself like this. But there was no other way to gather evidence.

Carrying a video camera, he approached the Allied International pickup truck in front of him and peered into the crates: The binder clips inside were unassembled. Some crates held metal clip handles. Others contained only black plastic backbones.

When traffic picked up, he got back into his rental car and followed the truck to Nanjing Detention Center's women's division. He couldn't see this, but behind the barbed wire, there were more than sixty women, each assembling thirty-six hundred clips a day for no payment. Their fingers bled from working so much.

Levy waited outside the detention center—a bucolic area with trees and wild grass. Several hours passed before the truck came out. He filmed the vehicle leaving, making sure to capture the words ALLIED NANJING on the door of the vehicle as it passed.

When the truck stopped on the street, he jumped out to look inside the crates again. This time, the binder clips' silver winglike handles were attached.

Levy took two trips to China to prove that his competitor was consistently sourcing from forced laborers. Even though Chinese officials never cooperated with the US government's investigation, Levy's video footage and eyewitness testimony served as hard evidence. In 2001, Allied International pleaded guilty to federal charges in US District Court in Trenton. The company admitted it began using forced labor in 1995, when it "came under pressure from its primary customer in the United States to increase production volume."

Customs agents seized twenty-four million Officemate binder clips across the United States, forcing the Allied International factory in Nanjing to close. Yet, more than twenty years after Levy proved the link between Chinese labor camps and US companies, as far as I can tell, Officemate remains the only US corporation to have ever been prosecuted for sourcing from Chinese forced labor.

There was one business owner who came close to getting a competitor charged in 2005, but he was ultimately unsuccessful. Gary Marck, a US ceramics importer, knew something was wrong when his competitor Photo USA, based in Sunnyvale, California, lowered the prices of its already-inexpensive coffee mugs by sixteen cents. Photo USA was reportedly sourcing from Shandong Zibo Maolong Ceramic Factory. Marck, who partially owned a ceramics factory in the same area of China, knew it was impossible to make a profit charging such a low price unless Photo USA was not paying workers.

Determined to investigate, Marck visited the Maolong facility himself. He saw that the factory, which advertised an ability to meet high-volume orders, had only one kiln, and he knew it was impossible to produce the number of mugs Maolong said it was making with only one kiln. What's more, the factory was located just outside a known labor camp called Luzhong Prison. The Laogai Research Foundation had independently confirmed that Luzhong Prison was producing over seventy million ceramic products a year. By some estimates, the prison factory produced over 50 percent of US ceramic imports.

"A number of US importers are importing mugs made at Luzhong and exported by Maolong. Most of these importers are aware of the Luzhong-Maolong relationship but choose to ignore the fact that prison labor is used to make their mugs because of the price advantage they receive," Marck said at a US-China Economic and Security Review Commission hearing in 2008.

Marck filed a lawsuit against Photo USA in federal court, accusing the company of distributing Chinese prison products. He gave eyewitness testimony. He provided photographic evidence that Maolong, with its single kiln, could not produce the volume of products it marketed. He proved it was located close to Luzhong Prison.

But to protect itself from pending investigations, ceramic production at Luzhong Prison had stopped after the lawsuit was filed. And the court ruled that Marck did not have enough hard evidence to prove there was a relationship between the Prison and the Maolong factory.

In 2009, Beijing finally allowed the United States to inspect Luzhong Prison. But after the time lapse, US officials could not find evidence that the prison was exporting ceramic mugs.

According to a 2017 US-China Economic and Security Review Commission report, China has not allowed US officials to visit any suspected forced-labor facilities since 2009. When I asked if the United States has made any new requests since 2017, a Department of Homeland Security official acknowledged in an email that it has "made several requests." But, he admitted, "To date, those requests are pending."

Time after time, there has not been enough hard evidence to convince prosecutors and customs agencies that US companies are sourcing from forced labor. That is why, despite a string of legislative hearings and diplomatic agreements since the 1990s, Western consumers are still finding Chinese forced laborers' SOS messages today.

In December 2019, a six-year-old girl in London found a prisoner's SOS message inside a box of Christmas cards purchased from Tesco, a British grocery chain. The note was scribbled in capital letters:

WE ARE FOREIGN PRISONERS IN SHANGHAI QINGPU
PRISON CHINA. FORCED TO WORK AGAINST OUR WILL.
PLEASE HELP US . . .

It's starkly clear, looking at all these cases, that the US government is demanding an impossible burden of proof to ban products from China. Surely, the policy makers who worked on these laws are aware of the loopholes. Why are they so reluctant to close them?

Some argue it is because corporate America would not want them to.

In 1989, after the massacre of student protestors at Tiananmen Square, the United States said China's most favored nation (MFN) trading status would be contingent on improvement in human rights. This status, renewed every year, gave China favorable trade conditions such as low tariffs and high quotas. But it wasn't until the late 1990s that Chinese forced-labor imports became a talking point, alongside other human rights offenses, during annual congressional debates over the renewal of China's MFN status.

Although the rationale for linking the status to human rights was strong, big businesses wanted the United States to renew China's most favored nation status regardless of China's poor human rights record. They wanted US companies to continue sourcing cheaply from China.

And while the agreements that President Bush and President Clinton signed in the early 1990s did not help the United States inspect China's prison factories, they did help Clinton justify his decision to reverse his previous position and renew China's MFN status, despite the country's lack of human rights progress.

As the *National Journal*, the publication of a company that sells strategic policy research, pointed out in an article in 1998: "Suspicions linger that Clinton's conciliatory approach is a payback to the corporate interests that do business in China and that so generously supported the President's 1996 reelection campaign."

In 2001, the issue of forced-labor exports was raised once again in Washington. Despite growing evidence that Chinese factories were still selling forced-labor merchandise abroad, China was permitted to join the World Trade Organization (WTO), a club of trading nations that enjoy lower trade barriers with one other. The justification was that steady trade and economic development would help China transition to a democracy. But that never happened.

What did happen: China's new status helped it obtain long-term economic growth. As its manufacturing sector rose, more and more US corporations turned to China to buy dirt-cheap products. According to a 2017 study by the Economic Policy Institute, China's accession to the WTO caused the United States to lose 3.4 million jobs. And as manufacturing migrated to China, it created more opportunities for Chinese factories to outsource work to labor camps.

These events were the opposite of what Chen Pokong had imagined would unfold after he wrote his SOS letter from the Guangdong labor camp in 1994.

The congressional publicity helped Chen leave the gulag five months before his sentence finished, in 1995. And he was initially optimistic when he immigrated to New York City about two years later, after receiving a visiting scholar invitation from Columbia University. After all, it had been less than ten years since the pro-democracy protests at Tiananmen Square. He was anticipating more mass movements.

I first arrived in the US in my thirties," Chen told me. "I thought for sure that China would transition to a democracy before I turned fifty."

In his fifties now, he is no longer hopeful. He looked tired as we talked about the state of human rights in China today.

Chen is now a political commentator and author of several books on China. Although he works full-time as the principal of an English as a second language school in New York, his official YouTube channel, Chen Pokong Zong Lun Tianxia (陈破空纵论天下) has an impressive number of subscribers: more than 234,000 as of March 2020. It's a no-frills one-man daily political commentary show, where he films and uploads unedited videos himself.

I met with Chen during an eventful time in 2019, as pro-democracy demonstrations in Hong Kong were starting to make headlines for demanding democratic reforms, like the freedom to elect Hong Kong politicians without Beijing's approval. (Although Hong Kong is technically a part of China, it is a former British colony that is supposed to have autonomy until at least 2047 under the One Country, Two Systems policy.)

As Chen watched the young activists in Hong Kong, it hit him how much time had passed since he was the starry-eyed leader of democracy movements in China himself. When asked whether he still believes he will see democracy in his homeland in his lifetime, he looked solemn. "After so many disappointments," he said, "I don't think about that question anymore."

12: Transplanted

Ma Chunmei thought it was strange. They wouldn't give her medical care after she lost consciousness during electric baton beatings. Or that time when her fingernail had detached from her thumb after a particularly violent encounter with the guards. Yet out of the blue, without any apparent need for medical attention, she was escorted out of Heizuizi Women's Labor Camp to get a physical at Jilin Province Hospital.

There, the doctors ran thorough tests on her eyes, head, chest, and abdomen. They also collected urine and blood samples. They never told her the purpose or results of the exams.

Years later, Ma came to a disquieting realization as she learned about an underground trade. She fears they were collecting her medical data for the organ transplant industry. "I think I was very close to dying then," she told me. "I was lucky because I probably wasn't a good match for anyone."

There is mounting evidence that laogai camps not only supply free labor for China's enormous manufacturing sector, but also organs for the nation's transplant industry—which is estimated to be worth a billion dollars. While this may sound like the plot of a horror film, the United States and the European Union have held hearings on the matter. In 2016, both the US House of Representatives and the European Parliament passed resolutions condemning the practice of harvesting the organs of executed prisoners of conscience—people imprisoned for their political or religious beliefs.

According to the European Parliament, there have been "persistent credible reports on systematic, state-sanctioned organ harvesting from non-consenting prisoners of conscience in the People's Republic of China, primarily from practitioners of Falun Gong . . . but also from Uighurs, Tibetans and Christians."

This issue first came to light in 2006, when human rights lawyer David Matas and former Canadian parliament member David Kilgour released a report examining why between 2000 and 2005, there were 41,500 organ donations in China from unknown sources. The recipients of these organs likely included both Chinese nationals and foreigners traveling to China to receive transplants.

By 2008, the issue had risen to the United Nations, whose Committee Against Torture formally requested "a full explanation of the source of organ transplants" in China.

An investigative journalist named Ethan Gutmann also examined this issue in his 2014 book, *The Slaughter: Mass Killings, Organ Harvesting, and China's Secret Solution to Its Dissident Problem.* Gutmann interviewed over one hundred witnesses, including doctors who had been pressured to kill prisoners on operating tables and former detainees who underwent blood tests for seemingly no reason.

According to Gutmann's research, forced organ harvesting of prisoners of conscience began in the northwestern region of Xinjiang as early as the 1990s; there, members of the Muslim Uyghur ethnic group may have been the first such prisoners killed for their organs. By 2001, Gutmann found, the practice of selling organs of executed prisoners of conscience had spread beyond Xinjiang; at this point, the Chinese government was also targeting Falun Gong followers, underground Christians, and Tibetans.

By 2016, Gutmann and the authors of the 2006 report estimated that China was transplanting somewhere between sixty thousand to one hundred thousand organs a year, sourced primarily from those same four groups.

Although all healthy prisoners are at risk, there is evidence that suggests Falun Gong practitioners and other religious minorities are especially targeted for organ harvesting because they tend to not smoke or drink alcohol. Over the years, many Falun Gong survivors have recounted inexplicable blood and urine tests, x-rays, and ultrasounds that medical professionals say are consistent with organ evaluation tests. Perhaps it is no coincidence that China's organ transplant industry started experiencing rapid growth in 2000, shortly after the crackdown on Falun Gong began. According to an article in the *Journal of Political Risk*, there were only ninety-one hospitals performing organ transplants in China that year; just six years later, there were one thousand. Yet the article points out China had no functioning voluntary organ donation system during this period.

Falun Gong–affiliated investigators have reported that between 2006 and 2018, they called various hospitals and transplant doctors across China, posing as prospective patients who needed new organs. They specifically requested organs from Falun Gong practitioners. Over the decades, they say, many doctors confirmed to these callers that they had been transplanting organs taken from Falun Gong prisoners, and they suggested that they could fulfill the requests.

Although the calls were recorded, some have questioned their credibility, given that Falun Gong researchers may have a bias. But regardless of whether most of these transplant organs were taken from executed Falun Gong followers or not, China's then–vice minister of health Huang Jiefu admitted in 2005, before the Falun Gong investigations began, that more than 95 percent of the nation's transplant organs came from executed prisoners.

In some sense, it doesn't matter which inmates the organs are coming from. The fact that China is selling the organs of executed prisoners is highly problematic in itself. The World Medical Association, a global network of physicians that represents over one hundred national medical associations, has long been urging China to stop selling prisoners' organs.

Even if China's vice minister of health had not admitted they were extracting organs from prisoners, the short wait times for finding organ matches in China says just as much. As early as 2006, the China International Transplantation Assistance Center's website boasted that any patients who needed a kidney transplant would have to wait only "one week to find a suitable donor, the maximum time being one month . . . If something wrong with the donor's organ happens, the patient will have the option to be offered another organ donor and have the operation again in one week." (The website was taken down that same year, after this was publicized.) For comparison, the average wait time for a kidney in the United States is 3.6 years.

In 2006, Kirk Allison, then-director of the Program in Human Rights and Health at the University of Minnesota, pointed out that the reported speed of the operations in China's transplant tourism industry was impossible unless China was executing prisoners on demand. As Allison explained at a congressional hearing in September of that year: "The short time frame of on-demand system transplantation requires a large pool of donors pretyped for blood group and human leukocyte antigen (HLA) matching to prevent rejection. It is consistent with execution timing. Given a twelve- to twenty-four-hour window for kidney tissue and a twelve-hour window for liver matching for transplants, tourists cannot be assured on a random death basis." In other words, it is statistically impossible for natural deaths to produce so many fresh organs in such a short time.

Questions continued to mount over the transparency of China's organ transplant industry until, in 2019, the China Tribunal in London, an independent panel investigating the allegations of forced organ harvesting from Chinese prisoners of conscience, gathered all the existing evidence to evaluate. The tribunal consisted of reputable human rights lawyers, doctors, and other relevant experts, and was chaired by Sir Geoffrey Nice, who had been the lead prosecutor in the war crimes trial of the former president of Serbia at The Hague.

The group spent a year reviewing academic papers, China's medical records, and reports from human rights groups, such as Amnesty International, Freedom House, and the UN Committee Against Torture. They also examined recorded telephone calls with Chinese transplant surgeons and undercover video footage filmed inside Chinese hospitals.

In the end, the tribunal said there was "proof beyond reasonable doubt" that China has been harvesting a large number of organs from prisoners of conscience, although it was impossible to verify exact numbers. The panel reached this verdict based on major inconsistencies in China's voluntary transplant data, including the fact that, until recently, China had no voluntary donor system at all. (What is more, even China's current donor system is not credible. In late 2019, the *BMC Medical Ethics* journal published a study that strongly suggested systemic falsification of data in China's voluntary donor registry.)

The tribunal concluded: "Falun Gong practitioners have been one—and probably the main—source of organ supply" in China, and it is likely in the years to come, evidence will emerge of continued mass organ harvesting from indigenous Turkic people in Xinjiang.

13: Wrong Answers

In the weeks after guards found the SOS note under the mattress, Masanjia saw the first snowstorm of the year. Sun and the other Falun Gong detainees shivered as they squatted outside. The camp's barricade, once a simple thirteen-foot concrete wall, was now reinforced with barbed wire and an electric fence.

Hours passed as they waited in the snow while the administrative staff filled out paperwork documenting their transfer to a special disciplinary division.

The man blamed for the note had endured intermittent electrocution for an entire afternoon, but he never named Sun or the others. And the camp didn't investigate the message further because, not long after the incident, two detainees attempted to run away. The SOS letter was a more serious breach than the attempted escapes, but Masanjia RTL Camp reported only the latter to government officials. "The authorities can't learn about this," Sun overheard a guard say. "The products have been packed and shipped already. Imagine the workload of tracking down and opening every shipment we've made since who knows how long ago. If the manufacturer finds out, we might not get paid."

Camp officials may not have known who spearheaded the SOS

initiative, but they knew this much: the Falun Gong forced laborers in Masanjia were not reforming.

And so Masanjia formed Team Three—for the sole purpose of brainwashing these detainees. The term "brainwash" is a direct translation of the Chinese phrase *xinao*, which is also known as *sixiang gaizao* ("thought reform"). Chairman Mao first carried out these coercive persuasion techniques in the 1950s.

The focus of the detainees' imprisonment would shift from hard labor to reeducation, and the transformation rate of their political attitudes would determine the guards' salaries, bonuses, and promotions. A satisfactory "transformation" would consist of a disavowal of faith, a pledge of allegiance to the Chinese Communist Party, and a disclosure of the names and addresses of other Falun Gong followers. "All of you will recant eventually," a guard told them. "If you are smart, you won't go through unnecessary suffering."

When the paperwork was done, the freezing detainees eagerly followed the guards inside. They were taken to a room on the fourth floor, where a whiteboard read: ADVOCATING SCIENCE. OPPOSING THE CULT. REINVENTING ONESELF. HAVING A REBIRTH. They were told to fill out a multiple-choice survey on their current views. The guards promised they could give candid answers without repercussions.

What is Falun Gong?
a) A cult.
b) A righteous faith.

Will you practice Falun Gong after you are released?
a) No.
b) Yes.

How would you describe the government's policy toward Falun Gong?

a) Wise.

b) Oppressive.

Those who gave the wrong answers were pushed out into the hall. The guards grabbed the first detainee, a burly man about six feet tall, and dragged him away. There was silence—then a scream echoed down the corridor. It was an unfamiliar sound: the screams were bare, not coupled with baton buzzes or the thuds of fists hitting flesh.

About ten minutes passed. "I'll quit. I'll quit Falun Gong," the man yelled.

The other prisoners murmured among themselves, surprised. Grisly scenarios ran through Sun's mind. *What did they do to him? The man's legs were limp as the guards brought him back. He's not bleeding. They must have hurt his legs with a baton. But I didn't hear it.*

One by one, each Falun Gong detainee they dragged down the hall denounced his faith. When the guards finally led Sun into the torture room, the emptiness of the space startled him. There was nothing inside but a metal bunk bed.

The bed was a tool for a technique that Masanjia had learned from other camps. It had two advantages: it was easy to transport, and since it did not leave permanent scars, it was unlikely to invite legal troubles. The guards had been instructed to limit their use of electric batons for the latter reason. And this torture could inflict more pain with less risk.

A stocky guard with a childlike face bound Sun's ankles with rope to the posts at the foot of the bed. He put cotton mittens on Sun's hands before leaning him forward at a ninety-degree angle, over the metal footboard of the bottom bunk, and cuffing his wrists to the bottom of the top bunk. He tied a bedsheet around Sun's waist. Then he yanked the sheet down, jerking Sun's belly downward and forcing his back into an impossible angle.

Sun gasped for air but was unable to breathe. His wrists and back muscles were tearing. A paroxysm of pain burst in his chest. It felt as if his arms were separating from his shoulders. But the mental torture was harder to bear. He didn't know how long the guards would leave him in that position, or whether they would yank the sheet again.

Perspiration dripped from his face. Edging in and out of consciousness, he let his head hang low. He woke on the floor to two si fang massaging and wriggling his limbs. Seeing that Sun was regaining consciousness, they lifted him only to retie him to the bed.

The guards carried on like this for a while, releasing Sun whenever he lost consciousness, yanking him whenever he was cognizant enough to feel pain. "You can kill two of them," Sun heard one guard say to another. "You won't be held accountable. Just don't kill them all."

After a week or two, the guards realized the bunk-bed torture was not having the desired effect on Sun. He was the only one who still had not renounced his faith.

"Let's change it up," a guard said.

It was past midnight when Sun was sent to a storage space reserved for torturing the most defiant prisoners. The room held three bunk-bed frames, some flattened cardboard boxes, and two ping-pong tables, where the guards sometimes played to pass time. But that night, the guards were in a dark mood.

They were rough with Sun as they cuffed his wrists to the sides of the upper bed frame. With the balls of his feet barely touching the ground, Sun hung from the railing as if he were nailed to a cross.

This was called the Big Hang. Previous detainees had tried to kill themselves by slamming their heads against the metal rail; a quilt now covered that part of the bed.

Sun was hung like this for twenty-four hours a day in the windowless room. His feet became so swollen that his socks and shoes no longer fit. In the grip of pain, he searched for relief in the amber of his memories. He tried to find lighter moments from his early years with May. But it was the unhappy ones who came to him.

Chinese New Year: Sun and May were visiting her parents. Only after confirming Sun was not followed did his father-in-law let them in the house. The celebratory gathering turned into an intervention as May's family surrounded Sun, criticizing him. "We put May into your care, but you did not carry out your responsibility as a husband," her father said. "You did not take good care of her. You should get a divorce if you're not willing to change."

"I really have not cared for her well, all these years," Sun said. "But you should know what I have been doing. I haven't been gambling or having affairs. I haven't done anything wrong to her. I am doing something for the greater good. Many people have been persecuted and killed. I can't just ignore this and live an easy life."

Unable to find common ground with his son-in-law, May's father shook his head.

While Sun was suspended in the air, he strained to stand on tiptoe. Whenever he dozed off, he slumped forward and the handcuffs sliced into his wrists. After nearly a week of sleep deprivation, he began hallucinating. The aberrations struck at sudden and uneven intervals. The room twisted and churned into a ballroom. Objects in front of him blurred and dissolved as the tiles on the floor transformed into TV screens.

As time went by, it became harder for Sun to differentiate reality from the dream state. His moods shifted violently. Between bursts of hysterical laughter, he sobbed whenever a memory of his mother or his childhood entered his brain. He knew he was losing his sanity.

He sometimes wavered. *What other tortures do they have in store for me? Should I just sign the papers?*

But then he thought:

Am I already dead?

No, at least I'm not dead yet.

It will be a long time before I die.

Since I'm not dead yet, I can hold on a little longer.

It was the seventh day of this new torture, Sun was told, when they unshackled him to let him sleep on a gurney.

When he woke up, he was hung again.

Those who stood watch avoided looking at him. When their gazes met Sun's by accident, their eyes revealed a soft pity. Years later, a si fang with deep creases on his face would look back on this time and say about Sun: "Even though he looks like a frail academic, he has a lot of backbone. I really admire him. He wasn't a harm to society. He just had his own thoughts, his own beliefs."

The former inmate-guard paused to blink back tears. "I don't want to remember these things," he said. He placed one hand stiffly on his knee. "We weren't friends. But anyone with a conscience can't bear to see this."

Sun knew it was morning when the hallway erupted with the sound of the other detainees marching and shouting political slogans, like "I firmly adhere to the Chinese Communist Party!" He strained to hear their voices and footsteps for as long as he could, before the halls fell silent.

Every now and then, he heard the commotion of a detainee being dragged into his room: screams, electricity zapping human flesh. Sometimes, as many as four detainees at once were hung in the storage space. Most stayed only a few days before signing a pledge to reform their thoughts. Afterward, they returned to the workshops.

A month passed; Sun still had not signed the pledge. His resolve came from a remarkable stubbornness, and a deep-seated belief that there was meaning to his suffering. He was standing up to injustice. He was accumulating good karma. He believed this experience would amount to something worthwhile in the next life.

He couldn't remember the last time he spoke; the guards and si fang were prohibited from talking to him. There was one inmate-guard, though, who took pity on him by reading the daily gazette out loud. He read the entire paper, including missing-persons notices and obituaries. It was the smallest reprieve from loneliness.

And Sun had more pressing problems than alienation. His body was disintegrating. Blood and pus seeped from the pores of his legs. His calves swelled into tree trunks, thicker than his thighs.

It is unclear how many months Sun was hung, released to sleep for roughly four hours each night. Dr. Xu, the barefoot doctor from the countryside, occasionally came by to check Sun's vital signs. A nervous man, the doctor kept his eyes on the ground.

"His blood pressure is really high. He has heart problems too. Take it easy on him," the doctor said to the guards once, but to no avail. And when Sun still hadn't disavowed his faith after several months, he was subjected to the next torture.

At the end of 2009, Sun's sister Jing received a call from a stranger.

"Sun is in trouble," said a man recently released from Masanjia. Sun had given Jing's number to him a while ago, knowing that this man's sentence would end before his own. Sun had asked him to give his family an update.

"But he called us when he was making decorations," Jing told the man. "He said he was fine."

The man knew better. He had heard horror stories from prisoners who were occasionally sent to the storage room with Sun.

"Things are getting worse for him," he said. "You have to save him. He is about to be tortured to death."

14: Legal Channels

A heavy snowfall hit during Jing's visit to Masanjia. The wind stung her face as she waited for someone to let her in.

"He's not performing well. He cannot see visitors," a guard told her when he finally came out.

"He has been here for two years, and we have never been allowed to see him," Jing cried. "I don't know if my brother is dead or alive. I must see him this time. Prove to me he's even alive."

After some time, a tall guard stepped outside. He showed her a picture of Sun from his cell phone. "See? He's alive."

Her eyes watered as she examined her brother's sunken face. The photo showed only his upper body and one of his arms, which was raised in an awkward way. There was something unsettling about the picture.

Jing contacted Jiang Tianyong, a Christian lawyer based in Beijing. She was uncertain if he'd take Sun's case. Jiang, then in his late thirties, had a lot to lose. He had a wife, and a small round-faced daughter with messy bangs.

But Sun's story may have reminded Jiang of his own battles with the Chinese government. On one May afternoon in 2007, Jiang was praying and singing hymns in a private room in Beijing when several dozen police officers barged into the unregistered church. "Stop your illegal activities and remain where you are!" an officer yelled. "We are with the Beijing Municipal Bureau of Religious Affairs. Your gathering is not authorized by the state."

The police wrote down the identities of each church member. They interrogated Jiang and many others until past one in the morning. Jiang was released, but for the past two years, he'd had no place to express his faith. His isolation and frustration, he might have imagined, was similar to what the Falun Gong meditators must feel.

Jiang had decided to become a lawyer in 2005, giving up his safe job as a schoolteacher to focus on human rights. It was a career that had been unfathomable to him during his childhood. In the early 1980s, there were only a few hundred lawyers in the entire country. Then in the mid-1990s, Beijing implemented reforms that made it easier for foreign NGOs to register and operate in China, which in turn helped improve human rights and government accountability.

By the late 2000s, there were over six hundred law schools there, accepting more than three hundred thousand students a year. Law was the fastest-growing major in Chinese higher education, and that became a concern for the Chinese Communist Party. Attorneys who took on human rights cases were frequently disbarred, placed under house arrest, or tortured. But there were many like Jiang who still chose to fight for a freer country.

It was always risky to take on human rights cases in China. But Sun's case would not be Jiang's most dangerous one. He had already defended nearly twenty Falun Gong followers and represented members of several persecuted groups: petitioners, HIV/AIDS activists, and, perhaps most controversially, Tibetan dissidents in 2008, when a series of protests erupted.

The protests occurred on the forty-ninth anniversary of the 1959 Tibetan uprising, a failed rebellion against Chinese rule that resulted in the Dalai Lama fleeing Tibet. On this anniversary, the Chinese authorities locked Tibetan monks and nuns in their monasteries, and they forced the monks and nuns to attend patriotism classes that included cursing the Dalai Lama and spitting on his portrait. This plan backfired. Somewhere between eighty and two hundred nuns in the Burongna and Ya-tseg Convents broke out into the streets to resist their political indoctrination.

Jiang was one of eighteen lawyers who risked their law licenses to represent the Tibetan dissidents afterward. He defended Phurbu Tsering Rinpoche, the Tibetan abbot who oversaw the monasteries in the regions where the protests occurred. In the end, the abbot was sentenced to eight and a half years in prison, and Jiang was put under house arrest. But Jiang's efforts likely reduced the abbot's sentence. Some Tibetans with state-appointed lawyers were sentenced to life. Several were executed.

When Sun's sister came to Jiang with her request, the secret police was pressuring his landlord to stop renewing his apartment lease. But he looked up at Jing from behind his rectangular rimless glasses and agreed to help with one more controversial case.

Jing told him she had traveled to Masanjia several times to investigate Sun's condition, independently from her mother and aunt. "Even condemned criminals have the right to meet their family members. How can the labor camp deprive them of these rights?" she said. "I was not allowed to see him in August 2008 because it was the Olympics. I wasn't allowed to see him in November 2008 either. They did not give a reason. I just went again a few weeks ago, where I was told I could not see him because of his 'poor performance.' What does that even mean? I am afraid he is being tortured."

Jiang knew if they applied enough pressure from the outside, it would be possible to scare the guards into improving Sun's conditions. Torture was illegal in China. It was also illegal to force detainees to work an excessive number of hours. These laws were rarely enforced, but since the labor camp was technically operating illegally, Masanjia's guards and supervisors could get in trouble if Jiang made enough noise to the central government. As a cosmetic measure to address citizen grievances, the Chinese Communist Party often diverted the blame for systemic problems to small bureaucrats or other individuals. Scapegoating a guard or a local official sent an effective message: The problem lay with one rotting apple, not a rotting barrel.

At the time of his sister's last attempt, Sun was forbidden from seeing visitors because a steel gag was clawed into his face and he was being force-fed—because he still hadn't renounced Falun Gong. Whenever a nurse twisted the gag handle, it snapped his mouth open, jiggling his now-loose teeth.

"Don't keep the gag on too long or it will fracture his jaws," Sun heard Dr. Xu say. "Have him take a rest every two to three hours."

But the inmate-guards sometimes kept the gag on for more than twenty-four hours at a time. And when the nurses removed the feeding tube from Sun's stomach after a month, the tube was black. During this time, Sun would remember his Halloween letters and lose hope; he assumed his message never reached anyone outside of China.

The authorities at Masanjia suspected Sun was going to die soon, so a deputy commander at the camp named Yu Jiang began making preparations to divert the blame for his death. To show that Masanjia had been attentive to its reeducation students' medical needs, Yu told Dr. Xu to take Sun to the local hospital.

When Sun tried to get up from the force-feeding gurney, he collapsed. After enduring various tortures for almost a year, his atrophied legs could no longer support his weight. Dr. Xu and two guards held him as they made their way out of the camp. They passed a mirror, where Sun stopped to look at his hazy reflection. With a uniform draped over his skeletal frame, he looked like a Holocaust victim—pale, gaunt, and bald. Sun, detached, was unable to fully register the image.

In the car, his hands remained chained. His dull eyes observed the asphalt street as they drove off. This was the road of his countless escape fantasies. The surrounding fields, blanketed in snow, reminded him of how remote the camp was. *Oh. This is a really long road,* he thought. But he was too weak to attempt an escape now anyhow.

At the hospital, Sun received strange looks from some of the other patients. But most avoided eye contact; they saw him as a criminal.

"His organs are close to failing," the local doctor said, after a checkup.

"He is not allowed to eat," Dr. Xu said. "What else can I do?"

"His organs will fail if he is force-fed any longer," the local doctor said.

After the cursory hospital visit, they returned to the camp and shackled Sun to a bed. They gave him food on some days but not on others. Too weak to move his limbs, he lay in his stiff red uniform stained with dried gastric juice. The pus that had oozed from his legs during the Big Hang remained crystallized on his pants.

As he lay sprawled on what he thought would be his deathbed, he examined his life and the cost of his search for meaning. He knew he could still be released if he signed statements denouncing Falun Gong, promising to never meditate again.

Only I can make this decision for myself, he told himself. *Humans are made of skin, bones, and organs. But that's only on the surface. The difference between a man and someone who has achieved spiritual enlightenment is not a surface difference, but a difference in their thoughts.* With this realization, he believed he had entered an altered state of consciousness. He homed in on this transcendental feeling. He was a caged animal, but, in his mind, he felt free.

Sun now focused on the future: He was going to get out alive. And he was going to add extra layers of encryption to the technology he used. He was not going to be reeducated.

Jing returned to Masanjia with Jiang Tianyong in March 2010.

"You cannot visit Sun because of his poor performance," a guard said, the same thing Jing had been told when she came several months before.

This time, however, Jiang took a *Rules and Regulations on Reeducation Through Labor* booklet from his bag. "You see here?" he told the guards. "It says, 'It is a violation of the law to prohibit visitation.'"

The guards did not care. But they did not realize Jiang was prepared to fight. Although the lawyer and Sun's sister risked landing in a labor camp themselves, they spent weeks visiting central government departments like the Legal Affairs Office, and a powerful political advisory body called the Chinese People's Political Consultative Conference to petition for Sun's right to see visitors. As Jiang had anticipated, it made a difference. Masanjia invited Jing to come see Sun.

She was tense as she stood alone in the waiting room, anticipating the reunion with her brother; their mother could not come because their stepfather had had a stroke. To calm her nerves, Jing walked to the door to see if she could look down the corridor and spot Sun.

In the distance, a slow figure staggered toward her. It looked like an old man, struggling to lift his legs. When he got to the threshold of the waiting room, he was unable to step over it. He grimaced as the guard bent down to help him raise his leg.

Jing was stunned when the crippled man was carried in.

My God, she thought. *It's him.*

Without his glasses, Sun did not immediately notice her.

"Brother!" she called.

A wave of emotion swept over his face: he recognized her voice.

Sun sat down behind the glass partition and looked at her with dazed eyes. In the silence that followed, she noticed the specks of white hair on his shaved head.

It was the first time in two years that Sun was seeing someone from his old life. He could not think of what to say. And he had not spoken in so long he had trouble formulating words. "Jing, you are here," he said.

Her face, wet from a stream of tears, softened. They were not allowed to use the intercom to talk. Instead they sat hunched, trying to catch each other's words through a slot at the bottom of the glass.

She leaned toward the slot to talk about their hometown, how the local government was building a new highway. Sun listened with a blank face.

"How is Mom?" he asked.

"I didn't hear you," she said. "Can you say that again?"

As Sun started to speak, the guards grabbed him, dragging him away. He summoned his remaining strength to yell: "Find a lawyer."

Jing didn't get a chance to tell him she already had. She stood up, pressing her face and hands against the glass. Her vision was blurred by tears. But she could see he was falling over as they pulled him down the hall.

The fact that Masanjia allowed her to see Sun gave her a glimmer of hope. She and Jiang worked on bringing Sun's case to the appeals court. Gradually, Masanjia began feeding Sun three meals a day again. And they eventually permitted regular visits.

The guards would release Sun from his chains a few days before the scheduled visits so he could practice walking. But practice didn't help. Sun now had bone spurs, which caused knifelike pains when he bent his knees. The ligaments in his arms were also damaged.

Jing's next visit with her brother was brief, but they were allowed to speak to each other through the intercom.

"How did they torture you?" she asked. "Tell me the specifics."

Sun hesitated, looking at the guards nearby.

"Don't be afraid," Jing said. Her voice was rising. "We found a lawyer for you. Tell us who has been torturing you!"

Likely fearing he could be scapegoated, a guard hurried after Jing as she was leaving. "What is Sun's impression of me?" he said to her. "Did he say anything about me?"

She and Jiang continued appealing to the central government, which made the authorities at Masanjia uneasy. The guards must have begun giving Sun and his sister more privacy during their visits, as Sun was able to help document the illegal tortures by discreetly giving her the names and identification numbers of the guards who dealt with him. Although she and Jiang never heard back from the central government, they kept Masanjia updated on their efforts.

The authorities at Masanjia informally extended Sun's two-and-a-half-year sentence by twenty days because he never disavowed his faith, but fearing impending legal troubles, they chose not to detain him any longer than that.

Sun's last night in the labor camp was no different from the others. He slept on his side, with one wrist handcuffed to a bunk-bed ladder. No one had informed him he was going home. He found out only when the guards handed him a white T-shirt and a pair of gray sweatpants the next day.

He was also given two sheets of stamped documents that showed he had completed his reeducation through labor. The labor camp had deducted the little money Sun had earned to cover his medical expenses.

The guards patted him down to make sure he wasn't sneaking out any damning materials, like a secret diary documenting his torture.

When he was told he could leave, Sun lingered.

"Where's my wife's letter?" he asked. It had been confiscated during a cell search two years ago.

"It's gone," the guard said.

On that Wednesday in September 2010, Sun finally stood outside without shackles. His vision cleared as he put on his glasses. It was a radiant day, but he could not feel the sun's warmth.

He slowly walked by the building where he had been tortured for a year. Still desensitized, he felt only numbness as his soft, bruised legs carried him slowly past the gate. *I went through hell and came back,* he thought. *I have to record my experience somehow.*

15: We Made It

Hesitant to contact his ex-wife, Sun spent his first night in Beijing at a friend's home. He waited until the next evening to call her.

"Where are you now?" May asked. Her voice held the emotions of years of unsaid words.

"I'm close to home," he said. "Are you home?"

"Yes," she said.

They were both quiet for a moment.

"Then I'll be home soon," he said.

May opened the door. She had more wrinkles, but still the same elegant eyebrows and porcelain skin. She noticed his hair was white but said nothing. They were strangers again.

Sun stepped inside. He took in the familiar furnishings: the Swiss cheese plant, the empty fish tank, the bamboo wave screen illuminated by an early evening light. A faint fragrance wafted in from the clothes that were drying on the balcony. It was the same fabric softener as before.

The old Pomeranian, Cong Cong, wobbled out, looking up at Sun.

"Our dog is still alive," he said, moved.

The dog did not jump to greet him.

"He probably doesn't remember you anymore," May said.

A pause.

"Did anyone follow you?" she asked. She looked worried.

"Cong Cong has no teeth now," Sun said, caressing the dog's jaw. "Why doesn't he bark anymore?"

"He's too old," she said. "He only barks when he's in pain."

"Did you check to see if you were followed?" May asked again.

"I wasn't followed," Sun said.

He opened the door to his study and turned on the light. Dense cobwebs veiled the room, which had not been touched since the raid two and a half years ago. He watched a spider scramble across the lampshade.

His chair was flipped over on the floor, next to jumbled papers, books, and power cables. The white window screen was gray from dust. Sun knew about the raid, but seeing the residue of violence from that evening unmoored him. "She suffered a lot because of me all these years," Sun later said. "I don't know how I could ever"—he paused to search for the words—"make it up to her."

Sun tidied his office a bit before going to bed. There was a new incense plate next to the TV in their bedroom. Unaccustomed to space, he stretched his arms out slowly. He observed the outlines of family pictures on the wall. He had trouble falling asleep in the dark; the lights were always on in the labor camp. Darkness was the shade of freedom.

By the next morning, May had gotten over the initial shock of his return.

"Are you sure no one was following you?"

"I don't think I was followed."

"Then you can live at home?" she said, her expression softening. She handed him a set of house keys. "What did you feel when you read my letter?"

Sun was quiet.

"Never mind," she said. "I don't want to know."

"I don't want to know," she said again.

Although Sun and May had divorced to keep May and her family safe, they remained married in their hearts. Unable to lift his left arm, Sun struggled with daily tasks such as showering and walking down the stairs. With May's support, however, he began reacclimating to a normal life little by little. He was relieved to hear that his friends who were arrested with him, Lu Daqing and Tian Guide, made it out alive. They had gone on to live quiet lives. Sun, too, was taking it easy as his injured knees and ligaments recovered.

But there were some strange habits he could not shake. He found himself storing razors in a plastic ramen bag. Everyone stored their belongings in ramen bags in the camp. Regular plastic bags were a rare commodity, and when they were available, they were usually repurposed as belts. "After leaving labor camps, all of us had many strange behaviors. Like mental problems," Sun said. "It is difficult to live like a normal person again."

May noticed the eccentricities but did not ask questions about life in Masanjia. She knew it was too painful to discuss. For years, she also refrained from telling him about her two weeks in the detention center. She ended the conversation curtly whenever Sun asked. "Maybe we should actually be divorced," she said.

To hide his injuries from his mother, Sun waited a while before visiting her. When he went, although he had healed a little, she could tell his legs were hurt.

"I didn't know what to do, Sun Yi," she said, crying. "Your aunt took me to a fortune-teller, who said your life was not endangered. But you were tortured and suffering. The fortune-teller said you would be fine after you turn fifty years old. You will have whatever you want then. But please be alert," she whispered. "We are being watched. The Office of Retired Cadres asked me to sign a statement of guarantee that I would not practice Falun Gong. A comrade of your stepfather's is monitoring me."

Harsh metallic bangs interrupted their conversation. His stepfather, now paralyzed from his recent stroke, had recognized Sun's voice from the other room. He was banging against the bed rail to convey a message: Sun was not welcome in their home.

For six months, May and Sun almost never left the apartment together. When they did, May led the way while Sun lingered behind at a safe distance. She knew from experience the police were likely still monitoring them.

Since as early as 2004, China has built the most extensive surveillance and internet censorship system in the world, with currently an estimated one hundred thousand human censors inspecting the web for politically sensitive content and manually deleting posts on various Chinese social media platforms. They are employed not only by state propaganda departments, but also by Chinese companies that have privatized censorship. And then there are the commenters, who are paid to guide online discussions in a pro-government direction. A 2017 Harvard study estimated that 448 million paid comments appear on Chinese social media every year.

Although it can be difficult to navigate the maze of propaganda on the Chinese internet, activists have had some online success rallying people against labor camps.

The most notable case took place in Chongqing—the city where Sun and May met many years ago. Even though reeducation through labor was prevalent across China, the city of Chongqing was infamous for its excessive use of the system. "Anyone [in Chongqing] could end up in a labor camp by saying something insignificant online," human rights lawyer Pu Zhiqiang told the *South China Morning Post* in 2012. Between 2007 and 2012, the city's then–party secretary, Bo Xilai, had initiated a series of political campaigns that led to mass incarcerations of activists and other Chinese citizens who had merely posted online comments expressing discontent with the local government.

In August 2011, one young civil servant in Chongqing, a twenty-five-year-old man named Ren Jianyu, was informally sentenced—without trial—to two years in a labor camp for "spreading negative comments and information online." With the help of social media, Pu Zhiqiang and several other bold human-rights defenders quickly rallied a sizable number of people to discuss the case nationally. Ren's two-year sentence was ultimately reduced by nine months.

A year later, reeducation through labor remained a hot topic in Chinese public discourse. After an eleven-year-old girl in the province of Hunan was kidnapped, raped, and forced into prostitution, the child's mother, Tang Hui, spent six years petitioning the government for her daughter's perpetrators to receive heavier sentences. For this annoyance, in August 2012 the local police informally sentenced the girl's mother to eighteen months in a labor camp for "disturbing social order."

Her story went viral too. Even the state-run *Global Times* reported on it, acknowledging that there were more than 1.6 million posts in solidarity with the mother on Sina Weibo, a Twitter-like social media platform. With more than three hundred million Sina Weibo users at the time, a number almost equivalent to the entire US population, the Chinese government was forced to start paying attention to people's grievances toward reeducation through labor.

In the same month, human rights lawyer Wang Cheng launched an online signature campaign demanding the abolition of RTL.

According to the *Global Times*, the petition received more than one hundred thousand signatures. It was a remarkable figure, given the risks associated with signing.

Fearing a revolution, the authoritarian government began to consider policy adjustments. Two months later, in October, China announced that reform was on the table. Official news outlets began openly criticizing the RTL system. The government's mouthpiece, the Xinhua news agency, even published an article affirming that "[many] cases have shown that the labor reeducation system has been misused to persecute innocent people and illegally punish protestors. The system has infringed on human rights and the rule of law . . ."

And it was on a December evening that same year when Sun learned some stunning news. Celebratory music had been blasting from a festival outside, so Sun had gone into his study, shutting the window to mute the noise and turning on his computer.

Using Freegate to circumvent the Great Firewall, Sun was surfing the uncensored web when a headline caught his attention: CHINESE SOS LETTER DISCOVERED IN OREGON, USA.

He did not think of his own letters at first. He had almost forgotten about them. But he was still curious. He clicked on the article and zoomed in on an image of the letter. It looked familiar.

He felt a tingle of excitement and fear.

He couldn't remember what he had written exactly, but this was *his* handwriting. And there was that familiar ripped corner of the page that all his letters had. Then he read the words:

Unit 8, Department 2, Masanjia

He sat for a moment, not knowing what to make of this.

In the labor camp, he had waited in agony for someone to find one of his letters. He never expected his message to resurface four years after he wrote it. "I achieved my purpose. All I wanted was for people to know," he later said. "But I was afraid to believe it."

"May, quick, come here," he said.

The Pomeranian was snuggled by May's feet as she lay on the convertible couch, watching a dating show. Sun called for her again before she got up.

"I wrote this letter!" He pointed to the monitor. "This made the news outside the country."

"What?"

Although she could not read English, she remembered writing the Chinese characters for "Masanjia Labor Camp, Unit 8, Department 2" when she mailed his clothing. She turned toward him. "You barely survived last time. All these years, our lives were complete and utter chaos," she said. "We are finally having a normal life now—"

"But this is bringing international attention for those who are still there," he said.

She was quiet. "Maybe you should go into hiding again."

They were both scared, not knowing what the implications were for this publicized SOS note. It helped that the state-controlled media was beginning to criticize RTL camps. But even if the SOS note had not resurfaced, it was still a risky time for Sun.

Just a month before, another important political event—the Eighteenth Party Congress—had occurred, causing a few people in Sun's circle to disappear as the Chinese Communist Party tried to create a facade of public support for the government. And six months earlier, the police had arrested Sun's lawyer, Jiang Tianyong, for trying to visit another human rights lawyer. They beat Jiang with such force that, after several blows to the side of his head, he lost hearing in his left ear. Then they forced Jiang to return to his hometown in the province of Hebei, three hours away from the capital. The police told him he could not return to Beijing until after the Congress.

Sun also learned from Falun Gong news websites that dozens of Falun Gong followers, including two of his friends, had been arrested in Beijing before the Eighteenth Party Congress. He read that one had received a fourteen-year prison sentence, an even harsher punishment than usual.

Despite such dangers, Masanjia survivors were elated to learn that the letter had been found by an American. Laopo, the dexterous detainee who had helped Sun copy SOS letters, cried when he read the article.

Laopo had completed his sentence at Masanjia in 2009. He left with an injured waist. His mind, dazed from torture, was still unwell. But after realizing one of the SOS notes had arrived in the United States, he was ecstatic. He wanted to shout the news. Tears covered his face as he thought to himself, *We made it. We finally made it.*

Laopo had copied and hidden two letters in his shipments. Not knowing English, he had only a general idea of what the letter said. He read a Chinese translation of the full letter for the first time on Dajiyuan, a Chinese dissident news site run by Falun Gong practitioners outside China. "I feel so proud that I participated in this," he said.

He began typing in the comments section. In the grip of unbridled emotions, he pressed the wrong key and submitted the comment before finishing his thoughts:

This is true. I'm one of the witnesses . . . We risked having our terms extended and torture to write these letters in order to have the truth known to the world . . . If we did not work well enough, we would face corporal punishment, electric shocks,

and even have our terms increased . . . We had written many
SOS letters that we slipped into the packages because we knew
those products were going to be exported abroad. It was the only
way to make it known to people around the world . . . It hurts
so much to recall all these memories. I don't know how many
times I've wiped my tears as I write this post . . .

16: Fight and Flight

Although Sun's SOS note would not stop any specific forced-labor products from entering US stores, it proved to be a domino in a series of high-profile embarrassments for Chinese authorities, ultimately leading to the abolition (if just in name) of reeducation through labor camps. Although international articles about Masanjia were blocked in China by the Great Firewall, some Chinese citizens accessed the news via virtual private networks (VPNs), a common method of circumventing censorship through encrypted connections. Information about RTL camps began to spread.

A bold domestic journalist named Yuan Ling decided to investigate this story for his state-controlled publication in China. While most state-controlled media are government mouthpieces and nothing more, a handful are run by more audacious editors. This is largely due to the journalists' guanxi. These connections to powerful people aren't enough to let them pursue every controversial story they want to cover. But it allows them to publish a few, as long as they do not directly criticize the central government.

After interviewing a dozen female Masanjia survivors and a number of former camp officials, Yuan Ling published an exposé on the camp in *Lens* in April 2013, four months after the initial *Oregonian* coverage on the letter from Masanjia.

The article, "Leaving Masanjia," detailed the grueling working conditions and torture inside the camp. According to the piece, Masanjia housed more than five thousand forced laborers at its peak, and its annual revenue was nearly 100 million yuan ($16 million). After the article appeared, *Lens* magazine ceased publication for several months, which the reporters and editors had likely anticipated. This is the cost of investigative journalism in China.

And so, following a steady sequence of criticisms of the RTL system—from online petitions to viral social media posts to Yuan Ling's article—China began to relent. Less than two months after a CNN story about Masanjia labor camp came out, in December 2013, the Chinese government announced that it was abolishing reeducation through labor.

For a moment, activists like Sun were stunned. Reform seemed possible. A more just China was, suddenly, conceivable.

Human rights defenders hoped that, without RTL camps, more people would enter the formal criminal justice system, which would mean a chance to see lawyers and judges before receiving a sentence. Without further reform, though, this would not mean much, because of the 99.9 percent conviction rate in China's courts. Still, perhaps fewer people receiving extralegal sentences would signify that more reforms were possible down the line.

The party had just selected Xi Jinping to become the new president in March 2013, and the rest of the world knew very little about him. Western academics hoped he would be more open to democratic reform than his predecessors.

But this was not the case. After the initial burst of hope, Sun and other human rights activists soon realized the camps were not really closing. Not long after the abolition, government websites and state-run media posted directives to rename RTL camps "compulsory isolation drug detox centers."

Given that Chinese drug rehab centers had been functioning as de facto labor camps for years, this was a logical step. Although the majority of detainees in these detox centers were drug abusers, dissidents with no history of drug addiction had also been disappearing into these facilities. According to the Joint UN Programme on HIV/AIDS, as many as half a million people across China were held in drug detox centers at any given time before the abolition of reeducation through labor. And on the inside, the only major difference between RTL camps and detox centers was that the detox centers placed less emphasis on brainwashing.

As RTL camps across China quietly changed their names, dissidents continued disappearing into these new "detox centers."

"They haven't changed their methods. It's only more secretive now," Sun later said. "There are people I know who are still in the camps doing slave labor. Life in a dark endless prison . . . I worked and lived with them. I don't know when they can be freed like me."

So he did what he had always done: carry on with activism.

Not long after the Western media published Sun's SOS note, one of his friends connected Sun to journalists from CNN and the *New York Times*. The international press had been looking for him.

Sun would wait by a subway entrance carrying a frayed bag. The bag's strap was mended with transparent tape, not unlike how he had taped May's letter in Masanjia. His humble demeanor masked his fear. Standing in the crowd, he appeared unremarkable, and maybe a little irrelevant. He often wore faded shirts and a wide-shouldered, loose-fitting suit from the 1980s. Some of the journalists searching for him had trouble spotting him.

The CNN crew brought him to a secret location to film his first television interview. Sun sat in a stiff posture as he faced the cameras. Having focused all his mental energy on getting to the meeting place safely, he had not put any thought into his appearance. The friend who had connected him to the foreign journalists glanced at his tattered shirt, limp collar, and uncombed hair.

"You should have worn a newer shirt," he whispered. "This is a major media company."

"I always wear this," Sun said. "There is nothing wrong with this shirt."

Needing time to heal his physical and mental injuries after Masanjia, Sun did not have a steady income. He was lucky that May could hold down a job. He tried his best to avoid spending money, even on necessities. When his wallet broke, he began clipping his cash together with a paper clip.

Promising to blur his face, the TV crew began recording. "I saw the packaging and figured the products were bound for some English-speaking countries," Sun said through a translator. "I had this idea of telling the outside world what was happening there—it was a revelation even to someone like me who had spent my entire life in China."

Sun gave an interview to the *New York Times* under the pseudonym Zhang. The *Times* corroborated his story with other Masanjia survivors before publishing the article in June 2013.

Having the chance to communicate to the outside world via the foreign journalists gave Sun another idea. He wrote a letter to Julie Keith to thank her for publicizing his SOS message. In his eyes, there were not many people in the world who had a sense of justice. He was grateful that his SOS note had landed in the hands of someone who cared.

He included his email address, in case she wanted to contact him. But he did not dare write down his phone number or sign his real name. He gave the handwritten letter to a journalist to pass on to Julie.

Julie was shocked to receive a second letter. She had learned, from the *New York Times* article, that the anonymous letter writer was a man. But that was all she knew. In some ways, the second letter was more astounding than the first. It raised more questions: How did he leave the camp? What is he doing now? Where is he? She began drafting an email to him right away. But she wasn't sure what she could ask. She knew their emails could be monitored by the Chinese government.

The *New York Times* article opened one door, but it closed another. According to emails and documents I obtained through a Freedom of Information Act request, US Immigration and Customs Enforcement closed the Masanjia case file after reading the *Times* piece. "The mystery surrounding a letter found in a box of old Halloween decorations seems to have been solved . . . On Wednesday, the New York Times reported they have now found the man behind the letter and his chilling story appears to be true," an ICE agent wrote in a summary of the case. "OKAY...........NOW Case Closed."

It is unclear why the story's verification would lead to ICE closing the case. But ICE did not respond to my queries about the Masanjia investigation, despite repeated requests for comment.

At the end of 2015, Sun began collaborating with a Chinese Canadian filmmaker named Leon Lee to chronicle China's forced-labor system. Sun filmed ordinary moments from his own life, as well as interviews with former inmate-guards, victims, and activists. (Much of the footage he shot would end up in Lee's 2018 documentary, *Letter from Masanjia*.)

Sun knew that working on a foreign documentary to expose a "state secret" was a crime that qualified for execution. But when Lee asked him why he was willing to put himself in such danger, Sun responded, "As China's technology becomes more sophisticated, it becomes easier to monitor dissidents. So the persecution of dissidents is intensifying. This makes China one big modern, technologically savvy labor camp."

Freedom had come to mean far more to Sun than just the freedom to meditate.

When Falun Gong activism began in the late 1990s, practitioners were originally only advocating for the legalization of the group itself. Ironically, if the Chinese government had simply unbanned Falun Gong during the early days of persecution, it might have successfully silenced the group from any further critiques of the party.

But as the persecution carried on, the fight for Falun Gong became entwined with the fight for Chinese democracy. Before landing in labor camps himself, Sun had not known China had a forced-labor problem. In Masanjia, he saw all kinds of people—petitioners, Christians, petty criminals—unjustly trapped in the brutal laogai system. In some ways, he did leave the camp a reeducated man. It just wasn't the reeducation the government had intended.

Even if the Chinese Communist Party were to legalize the group today, it would be hard for many meditators like Sun to untangle their Falun Gong identity from their pro-democracy work. "I risk my life for this because it's my responsibility to society," Sun said. "No matter what the risk is, no matter what we lose, it's worth it. We are being responsible for the future."

Besides, the Falun Gong network has become a valuable tool for exiled pro-democracy activists. Chen Pokong, who sent an SOS letter from a labor camp in the 1990s, is not a practitioner himself, but he told me he uses his Falun Gong contacts in China to covertly spread his latest writings and videos there.

"Apart from the Chinese Communist Party, Falun Gong is the most organized group in China. A lot of the Chinese democracy groups are divided by their own internal politics. But Falun Gong is very united under one cause," said Chen. "Their media is the most influential one that gets to China. In terms of organization and reach, no other group can replace Falun Gong."

Sun was embarking on his new resistance project—the documentary—just as it was becoming increasingly perilous to do so. Much to the world's disappointment, President Xi Jinping was showing even more authoritarian tendencies than previous Chinese leaders.

The facade of civil liberties was crumbling under Xi's rule. Since the 1980s, domestic and foreign NGOs had helped expand environmental, educational, legal, and gender-related policies in China. While previous Chinese leaders at least recognized that NGOs from abroad were necessary for the country's economic and social progress, the Xi administration severely restricted these groups, often referring to them as "hostile foreign forces."

On July 1, 2015, China passed a controversial and vague law expanding the definition of "national security" to anything that would safeguard the political regime and "other major national interests." A few days later, on July 9, a nationwide crackdown on civil rights and activists began. Police arrested over three hundred lawyers and activists within a span of a few months. This became known as the 709 Crackdown.

At one law firm alone, the Beijing-based Fengrui, thirty-eight lawyers and staff disappeared. The police did not allow their families to see them; their trials took place behind closed doors. Zhou Shifeng, the law firm's founder, received a seven-year sentence for subversion. His crime? His firm had represented activist artist Ai Weiwei and Falun Gong followers, and had fought a powerful company that produced tainted baby formula. Later, several of the disappeared lawyers made confessions on state television, saying that "hostile foreign forces" had used them to harm the Chinese government.

As a part of the larger crackdown on journalism spearheaded by President Xi, *Southern Weekly* (*Nanfang Zhoumo*), a domestic newspaper previously known for its willingness to stray from party lines, had come under heavy-handed censorship in 2013, with the Chinese Communist Party's Department of Publicity directly stepping in to alter texts before the paper hit the press. Up until then, journalists there could get away with publishing first and dealing with consequences later. When they realized they could no longer push boundaries, many *Southern Weekly* editors and reporters quit. Conservative writers who refused to question the party replaced them.

A few years later, *Yanhuang Chunqiu*, a monthly journal known for publishing politically sensitive topics, ceased publication after the government fired most of its editorial staff.

Besides these government crackdowns, a new kind of modern horror was festering in the northwest. China was developing an unprecedented high-tech predictive policing program—one that would use artificial intelligence and big data to teach computers how to select "suspicious people" for the police to arrest. At a brazen press conference in March 2016, the China Electronics Technology Group Corporation, a major state-owned military contractor, announced that it had received funding to build a big-data collection program that could predict terrorism before it happens.

Mostly, "suspicious people" meant Turkic Muslims. Although Sun was not yet aware of it as he quietly documented China's forced-labor problem, the Xinjiang region was beginning to transform into an open-air prison for the Turkic people who lived there, and his work gained more urgency. The authorities in Xinjiang had begun routinely administering "health checks," to collect blood, fingerprints, voice recordings, and facial scans of Turkic people.

The biological information from these ongoing checks is entered into a database called the Integrated Joint Operations Platform. This platform is used at ubiquitous checkpoints to establish predictive policing in the region. The computer program generates lists of people for the police to interrogate and send to reeducation camps, using software to sift through checkpoint data for "suspicious" patterns. These patterns include infrequent use of Mandarin in conversations, nonattendance of nationalistic flag-raising ceremonies, and other "abnormal" behavior, such as missing phone bill payments or using too much electricity. And perhaps most ominously of all, the checkpoints in Xinjiang employ AI-backed facial recognition cameras to distinguish race.

Not coincidentally, Xinjiang is essential to a trillion-dollar economic development strategy called the Belt and Road Initiative (BRI). Bordering eight countries, the region was once a strategic intersection on the Silk Road, connecting China to central and west Asia, the Middle East, and Europe. The BRI finances new highways, ports, and other infrastructure in developing countries, which will link China's markets with more than seventy nations via a modern Silk Road. The project is too big to fail. And if the Turkic people in the important BRI juncture of Xinjiang, who already live like second-class citizens, were to start an uprising, it could significantly hamper trade in the region.

China is deeply afraid this will occur. Right after the Belt and Road Initiative began, the Chinese government unleashed a salvo of draconian policies. Schools, parks, hospitals, and gas stations were topped with barbed wire. New passbook systems barred Muslims from traveling, even within Xinjiang. Uyghur intellectuals, even moderate ones who supported the Chinese government, were "disappeared" or imprisoned.

"What's really driving the incarceration is that a part of the Belt and Road Initiative means that Xinjiang has to be opened up," Anna Hayes, a senior lecturer in politics and international relations at Australia's James Cook University, told me. "It's going to expose all of those Muslim minorities to external influences that Beijing has been really carefully trying to keep them away from for so long. Rather than wait for something to happen farther down the track, they've decided, 'We'll identify the people who are influential.' That's why they are locking up university lecturers. They are the ones who shape and mold education. They are also incarcerating elderly people, because they have familial influence. And I think the younger people, that's really about the labor."

As Muslims in Xinjiang were rounded up for labor camps, Sun continued to live the lonely postprison life of a Chinese activist. He'd had to move out of his apartment in Beijing to protect May. They still saw each other on occasion, although never in public spaces.

As Sun lost touch with most of his family members for the same reason, his mother passed away from an illness. Her sudden death was a blow to him. The years she'd spent agonizing over his safety, he suspected, had contributed to her poor health. He blamed himself for her death.

"I've never seen him cry like that," a friend of his later told me.

And so Sun buried himself in his work. He prepared for another raid by building hidden storage spots in his room: a power outlet that was not really a power outlet, and a secret drawer at the bottom of his desk that required a hand tool to crack open. Inside, he hid the laptops he used to send encrypted video files to Leon Lee for the documentary.

With his knack for technology, he taught other Falun Gong practitioners how to use encryption software. "If you can't break through the network blockade, outside information cannot come in," Sun said. "The government has us living in a state where we are deaf and blind. Communication is key if we are going to fight against an autocratic, totalitarian state. This is how we can fundamentally resist the Chinese Communist Party." As part of this objective, he also taught the elderly and people with limited education how to use computers and access the uncensored internet.

When Sun left for these missions, he wore an oversized coat and a surgical mask that hid his face. It helped him blend in, since people often wear masks in China due to air pollution. Switching buses multiple times, he never traveled directly to his destination. His eyes were always searching for surveillance cameras. He usually did not enter buildings from the main entrance, and he would change his clothes before leaving.

For a while, it seemed like the encryption and safety measures were working. So for one special occasion, May made an exception to her rule and went out with Sun. To celebrate what would have been their twentieth wedding anniversary in the summer of 2016, they went on a date at the Beijing Botanical Garden. For one day, they forgot their worries, as if they were adolescents in love. Sun surprised May with half a dozen giant balloons—pink Hello Kitties, yellow monkeys, red hearts—and she laughed as she struggled to hold them.

He watched her fondly. "Last time we came here . . . it was snowing."

"That was in 1997 or 1998," she said.

She closed her eyes as she sat down to rest. Sun reached over to massage her temples.

"Although we've been married twenty years, we've only spent a few years together," she said, looking melancholy. Perhaps she was thinking of how their lives had changed since that afternoon when he'd showed up at her door unannounced and asked her to marry him. "I never thought, because of your beliefs, we'd have to live separately."

They went to a movie theater that night. Laughing as they waited in the concession line to buy fries, they looked like a normal couple. But they both knew Sun's safety was a ticking time bomb.

May and Sun were never certain if they were being overly cautious or not cautious enough. They couldn't live like this anymore: always together, but not together. Shortly after their anniversary, they decided to risk it all by remarrying. They planned to seek asylum as a couple. They wanted to start over.

In a pink velvet *qipao* dress, May led Sun down a brick alleyway. They crossed the street and entered a photography studio, where they were going to get pictures taken for a marriage-certificate application. "We want to live a normal life together, so we have to leave China. This is the only way we can be together," she said as Sun recorded her. Almost everywhere he went, he was filming, collecting footage for the documentary.

The studio was a shoestring operation. Walking past columns of boxes, the photographer directed them to a sliver of space in front of a royal-blue wall.

"The man's shoulder goes behind the lady's," the photographer said.

A few shots were snapped. Without fuss, the session ended.

They left to fill out paperwork at the marriage registration office. And like that, they were remarried. For one year, May and Sun lived something akin to a normal life. They were still afraid, and Sun did not stop his political activities. But the dream of leaving China, together, made this tenuous state feel temporary.

They took a trip to Sun's hometown in Xi'an, where they stopped to take a photo of themselves in front of the ancient Xi'an City Wall. In the picture, Sun looks like he's unsure he's using the selfie stick correctly. But May's eyes contain a subtle look of hope.

They applied for tourist visas to the United States in October 2016. But when the Chinese consular section of the US embassy saw that Sun had no children, no real estate, no job, and a history of persecution, it rejected his application. The Chinese government considered him high-risk for leaving and never returning.

They tried getting tourist visas for Canada next, but it wasn't any easier. And as Sun was looking into a Canadian work visa, May brought him some sad news. The doctor had diagnosed her father with lymphoma. She cried while squeezing Sun's hand. "I can't leave my parents behind."

A month later, in November, Sun made the mistake of showing up at a Falun Gong practitioner's trial at the Tongzhou courthouse in Beijing. Police officers ran into the courtroom, arresting Sun and the other attendees.

As he was cuffed, the police confiscated his cell phones. This meant the authorities now had his encrypted correspondence with Leon Lee.

In custody, Sun became gravely ill. The police department allowed May to bail him out three days later to receive medical care.

"He could die at any time. His blood pressure is over 230. If it goes higher, his blood vessels could burst," the doctor told May. "We've done everything we can."

But that wasn't Sun's biggest concern. He knew it was only a matter of time before the police would break the encryption on his cell phones, and when they did, it was likely he would be killed.

He realized he must leave China.

"Here's a copy of his parole papers," a police officer told May. "If he wants to leave Beijing, he has to contact the police department and get permission."

May held her husband as they left the hospital together. His frail body leaned on her for support as she tucked in his shirt.

On the way to their apartment, they stopped at a convenience store to buy a razor for Sun. As he was scanning the shelves, he broke the news to May: he was planning to board a flight to Indonesia the following morning. He had thought about this before. Indonesia did not require Chinese citizens to have a visa to enter, so when facing imminent danger, it was the best option. "They have my cell phones," he said. "I have no choice."

Paralyzed by fear, she told him not to speak above a whisper.

They stood in the subway station, looking at the arriving train but not really seeing it, dread in both their eyes.

He gathered his remaining belongings from the apartment in a hurry. He had no luggage, so May gave him her pink suitcase to take.

It was too dangerous for them to spend one last night together.

She told him to have a safe trip, as if this was not the last time they would see each other. But they both knew that, whether he made it past customs or not, this was their final farewell. They shared a quick kiss. It was too painful to linger any longer.

Then he was gone.

17: Blending In

As the morning smog descended upon Beijing, Sun blended in with the crowd of masked pedestrians pushing their way to work. He was sore, having slept on the bare floor of a friend's apartment the night before. He eyed the closed-circuit cameras on the streetlights as he got into his friend's car.

On the way to the airport, Sun looked out the window. They were on the highway now. Emotions and thoughts rocketed forward— once in motion, unable to be rescinded. "My wife doesn't dare to come and send me off. I don't dare tell the news to my sisters, my relatives, my friends. This is quite a feeling," he said. "I am fifty years old this year. I have lived in China for so many years. I never imagined leaving China this way."

He had with him May's pink luggage, which held a sparse collection of his belongings: underwear, socks, the new razor, several pictures of his mother. At the thought of his mother the night before, he had broken down. "Her death has a lot to do with me," he said. "Each one of my incidents was a big blow for her. She could not sleep well for years. I am taking her pictures with me. It will make me miss her more, but I must take them."

The plane ticket was purchased only moments before he left for the airport, leaving a small window of time for the government to detect his plans to leave the country. It felt more imminent with each passing minute. The police had arrested him over the weekend, but now that it was Monday, more public security personnel would be back at work. He feared they would crack his cell-phone encryption very soon.

There were several police cars when they pulled into the airport parking lot. But no officers appeared to be inside.

"Let's park here," his friend said, with a hint of unease.

The car engine shut off.

"Okay," Sun said. "Let's go."

As they scrambled toward the terminal, an airport police kiosk came into view by the entrance. Sun hadn't known it was there, and there was no way to avoid it. To calm himself, he focused his eyes on an airplane in the distant sky. *I will be far away from the police soon, just like the people on that plane,* he told himself.

They stood still for a moment as they entered the airport. His friend filmed him as Sun said his last farewell.

"What is there to say?" Sun looked down with a nervous smile. "I feel I will succeed today."

At the China Southern Airlines desk, a young woman checked him in. As she gazed at the computer monitor, Sun thought of a Falun Gong practitioner in Beijing named Wang Zhiwen whose passport had been canceled a few months earlier, shortly after he booked a flight to the United States.

As the young woman verified his information, Sun searched for changes in her tired eyes; if her expression were to betray a sudden alertness, it would be a signal that he needed to run.

He breathed a little easier as she handed him his passport and boarding pass. She did not appear to have seen any red flags in his file.

The wait in the security line, however, was agonizing. He opened his bag to check his belongings for incriminating evidence. He zipped it up. He reopened it to check again. He was suddenly aware that by folding and refolding his clothing at the airport, he was drawing attention to himself. He observed the other people in line; they were all on their phones.

As he tried to calm himself, his mind wandered to his two hometowns: Xi'an and Taiyuan. On his last trip back to Taiyuan, on the train, an elderly lady had recognized him. He didn't remember her, but the encounter had moved him. Taiyuan was where his roots were. He longed to go home one last time. But he had almost no contact with his family. And it would do more harm than good if he called his sisters' tapped phones.

"So that's it. It is time to leave," he had said into the camera earlier that morning. "It is a pity I cannot say goodbye. I can only think that when I get to the free world, I will tell them I have left. It can only be like this."

He stepped forward in the security line and removed the faux-leather shoes from his feet. He took out his new wallet, which his friend had given him as a gift the night before. Sun had initially declined the present. He was used to holding his cash together with a paper clip. "But this is very strange, carrying a wad of cash in a paper clip," his friend had said. "It will draw unnecessary attention to you at the airport. For your safety, please take this wallet."

Sun had looked at the wallet. "I used to have a kind of life where I had a wallet, where I ironed my pants and wore a tie," he had said to his friend. "It was a dignified life. I never would have guessed that after so many years of persecution, I would be like this."

His luggage passed the security screening. As his insides pounded, he located his gate and boarded a flight to Xiamen, a port city on China's southeastern coast. Hours passed once he got to Xiamen as he waited for the connecting flight to Indonesia. He was convinced he wasn't going to make it: the question was not if they would rearrest him, but when.

Yet against all odds, Sun slipped past the final checkpoint undetected. He found his seat on the plane and sat down. He was numb. He could not focus on the pilot's announcements. *I have finally escaped an invisible prison,* he thought.

For the first time in seventeen years, Sun was free.

18: Jakarta

The slums of Jakarta had a pervasive stench: a mix of burning trash and diesel fumes. Skeletal cats prowled in a narrow back street that led to a cluster of apartments. Inside one of the three-story structures, where mosquitos whined and tenants shared communal toilets, Sun settled into his new home.

For one hundred dollars a month, he lived in a bare studio about the size of a walk-in closet. It was on the second floor. That was better than the third. In this humid city, the odor worsened higher up.

Sun owned two pieces of furniture: a TV tray and a vinyl mattress with no sheets. On the tray sat his laptop, which he used to watch TED talks to practice English. "It's not what I imagined," Sun told Leon Lee. "I didn't know much about Indonesia. I imagined a society that was better than China, with better human rights . . . The government needs to do better. There's lots of people in poverty."

A friend of a friend had picked Sun up from the airport when he first landed in Jakarta. Sun had stayed with him for twelve days, where he met other Chinese asylum seekers. They helped him begin the complicated process of registering with the UN High Commissioner for Refugees.

But until his request for sanctuary could be processed, he lived in limbo. Refugees, largely perceived as illegal immigrants in Indonesia, are unable to legally work. At the time, Sun was one of about 13,800 refugees—from nations such as China, Afghanistan, and Myanmar—waiting for resettlement.

The Indonesian government forbids permanent refugee resettlement in its country. Indonesia is supposed to be a stopping point for asylum seekers like Sun, as they wait for the UN to find them a permanent home somewhere else. But with tens of millions of people displaced around the world, all waiting for permanent resettlement, there were not many slots opening up anywhere when Sun arrived.

His new friends warned him many asylum seekers remained in Jakarta for three to five years before resettling. He soon learned he wouldn't even have an asylum interview until March 2019.

It was then that Sun realized: Leaving China wasn't the most difficult part. It was more challenging to figure out how to live on the limited cash savings he had brought with him. Unable to earn an income for years at a time, some refugees in Indonesia have died by suicide.

On top of the stress of adjusting to life in a new country, Sun struggled with survivors' guilt. In August 2016, his lawyer, Jiang Tianyong, had met with Philip Alston, the UN special rapporteur on extreme poverty and human rights. Three months later, Jiang disappeared. He would remain in a secret detention center for more than nine months before he was sentenced to two years in prison for "inciting subversion of the state."

Sun did not know this, but Jiang's health was declining rapidly. "Jiang Tianyong was force-fed unknown medication, and his memory is deteriorating. He doesn't even remember how old his kid is," Jiang's wife, Jin Bianling, told Amnesty International in 2018.

Forcing political dissidents to receive involuntary and unnecessary psychiatric treatment is psychiatric torture, a method China had borrowed from the Soviet Union. (Jiang was ultimately released in February 2019, after completing his sentence. His safety remains tenuous, as police officers still closely monitor his home. It is unclear if he will ever be able to reunite with his wife and daughter, who have escaped to the United States.)

Although the state of human rights in China remains grim, a notable legislative change in the United States brought a glimmer of progress in 2016. Around the time when Sun arrived in Indonesia, the US government finally closed the "consumptive demand clause" loophole, a longstanding policy that had allowed products manufactured by children, prisoners, and forced laborers to enter US markets if domestic production could not meet consumer demand.

In the 1990s, then-representative Bernie Sanders and Senator Tom Harkin addressed the controversial clause by introducing modifications to the US Tariff Act of 1930, but their efforts were unsuccessful. It wasn't until 2015, when Senators Sherrod Brown and Ron Wyden introduced an amendment to the Trade Facilitation and Trade Enforcement Act that the loophole was finally struck down. In the contentious political atmosphere of the times, this was one of the few pieces of legislation that received bipartisan support, and the Senate passed the bill with a 75–20 vote on February 11, 2016. President Barack Obama signed it into law thirteen days later. For the first time in eighty-six years, consumer demand could no longer be used as an excuse to allow products made by forced laborers to be sold in the United States.

This legislation was a step in the right direction, as it put more pressure on companies to be aware of the conditions in their factories.

But it remains difficult to gather enough evidence to actually stop these products from entering the country.

Back in Jakarta, the sweltering weather and confusing bus system persuaded Sun to stay indoors most days. He passed the hours studying English and Indonesian. At his age, he found that foreign languages did not come as easily as before. He started with Indonesian numbers, so he could know the prices of groceries, and then moved on to the names of landmarks, so he could follow the map on the bus. He also learned the word "stop," because he kept getting on the wrong bus.

It wasn't until four months after Sun arrived in Indonesia that his life started to improve. A Chinese dissident news website called Apollo Network (a.k.a. A Bo Luo Wang) hired him, under the table, to do online tech support. With his basic necessities met, he had space in his mind for more reflection.

However, after the initial chaos of transition had passed, loneliness settled like sediment. He was free to meditate. But was it a Pyrrhic victory?

"The more time I spend in a free society, the more I become desensitized to the value of freedom," Sun said. "In some respects, it is easier for an animal to value this primal instinct for freedom. Take wolves, for example. Wolves would rather forage by themselves in the lonely wilderness, risking starvation and death than be well-fed in a cage. But humans are not the same."

Of course, Sun still believed that freedom, the foundation of democracy, was valuable. But he had become a prisoner of solitude, and it dominated his thoughts. Sun and May had limited contact; she feared the police would accuse her of helping him escape. His communication with his sisters was also superficial. "My family is very concerned my life is too hard abroad," he said. "I am scared to tell them too much, so that they will worry. I try to only say good things."

He shed the pseudonym he had used in his first interviews about the Masanjia letter, revealing his identity to the international press. Fearing retribution, May's communication with him waned even further. They went back to exchanging occasional emojis.

"We just celebrated our twentieth wedding anniversary. Then suddenly, I had to leave China permanently," Sun told Leon Lee. "I don't know what the future will hold for us . . . She, alone, is living fine in China . . . She is worried if she joins me neither of us will have a [good] job. Her parents are old and sick. She doesn't want to seek asylum, because then she can never go back and see her parents."

He emailed Julie Keith again to let her know he was safe. He casually mentioned that she was welcome to visit him in Indonesia anytime. And he signed this message with his real name.

Julie was, at first, baffled by the email. It was from a different address than the one Sun had previously used. And the sender's name was in Chinese. It was not immediately clear it was him. She wondered if the message was spam.

But when she read the email, she felt, at last, a wave of relief. He had often taken months to respond to her messages, leaving her to wonder: Had the authorities identified him because the *Oregonian* had published his Masanjia unit number? Had the Chinese government killed him?

And she still knew so little about him. The language barrier, and the fear of surveillance, had limited the depth of their conversations. But now, four years after she found his SOS letter, she had a chance to hear his full story.

She wanted to go to Indonesia.

Hello Sun Yi,

It is wonderful to hear that you are well and now free from danger.

Yes, I would very much like to meet you in person. I believe it would be a wonderful ending to our story!

I am able to travel to Indonesia . . . [My husband and I] would be available during the months of March, April, and May.

Warmest regards,
Julie

She longed to meet the mysterious human being whose pain had plagued her. "I was just curious to hear his story . . . his whole life story, how he ended up in Masanjia," she later told me. "What happened to him after he was released? I just wanted to hear him tell me." She also felt partly responsible for Sun's current situation; it saddened her that he'd had to leave his family.

Her husband, Chris, was worried. "What if the Chinese government is trying to set you up?" he asked her. He feared China wanted to punish Julie for publicizing the conditions in Masanjia.

She didn't believe that. Instead, she reframed the trip as a two-week vacation in a tropical country. They could go to Bali after meeting Sun.

And so they embarked on the thirty-four-hour trip from Portland to Jakarta in March 2017.

The warm southern sunshine was a pleasant change from Oregon's cooler temperatures at that time of year. Julie couldn't believe she was finally going to meet the author of the note. She waited anxiously in Jakarta's congested traffic.

Their car finally arrived at their destination: some decrepit buildings in the northern part of the city. A small and wiry Chinese man stood outside waiting for them. Julie was taken aback by his genial demeanor. He did not look withdrawn, on edge, or hardened—what she had imagined a gulag survivor would be like.

"Hello," she said, laughing.

"You come here so long distance," Sun said slowly in English. Emotions swept over his face as they hugged. "It feels like you are my blood sister . . . I never imagined I would meet the person who received my letter. I wasn't even sure if someone would receive my letter. I didn't have a lot of hope."

His voice was warm and soft, and that saddened her. His gentle bearing added a layer of vulnerability that was not there before in her mind. It made it more painful to know he had been in a forced-labor camp.

Over the next few days, Sun and Julie exchanged stories and pictures from their lives.

"My wife and I," he said.

"She's very beautiful," Julie said.

"We managed to remarry last year," he said, his voice full of melancholy.

He showed Julie photos from his childhood—his old village, baby pictures—before stopping on one of him with an inmate-guard, whom he'd met up with recently, for the first time since their release. Sun explained to Julie what si fang were, and how he had convinced two of them to participate in the documentary. They were the only two who had shown him kindness in Masanjia.

Julie examined the photo. The inmate-guard, wearing a purple Ralph Lauren polo, was in his late twenties and heavyset. He looked solemn as he posed with his arm around Sun. Sun looked like he was trying to smile but was unable.

Inevitably, the conversation turned to torture.

"Do some people try to kill themselves to be free of the pain?"

"You can't," Sun said. "They will keep you from self-injury. Two men guard you . . . They watch you day and night."

Julie knew from his first letter, and from the subsequent articles, that Sun had been tortured. But sitting there, in front of him, the details of the horrors he'd experienced gained a new immediacy.

Many consumers might read about poor labor conditions over-seas, only to compartmentalize once they return to the store. But after physically receiving an SOS letter from a gulag and meeting the person who wrote the cry for help, something fundamental changed in Julie. She could never forget that Sun's life was the true cost of those cheap, disposable decorations.

It wasn't just discount stores she was avoiding now. She could no longer see any MADE IN CHINA label without immediately think-ing of Sun. Although Julie still purchased Chinese products when they were the only option available, she stopped buying things just because they were cheap.

It troubled her, the fact that she had not needed those Halloween decorations. And what ever happened to Sun's other letters? Were they in boxes that were mere impulse purchases too? Still sitting in a basement or shed unopened?

"I had some people tell me the people in Masanjia would be pun-ished because I published the letter," Julie said to Sun. "They told me that I should not have done that. I was always concerned that I had put you in danger."

"I thank you forever," Sun said.

Sun died abruptly from a lung infection and acute kidney failure not long after meeting Julie, on October 1, 2017. May and Sun's sister Jing flew to Indonesia to say a sorrowful goodbye. Some of his friends believe he died under suspicious circumstances. They say there was a Chinese woman who had befriended him, claiming to be a Falun Gong practitioner, not long before his death, and she has not been seen by the Falun Gong refugee community in Jakarta since. His friends suspect she may have had something to do with his death. But since his body was cremated without an autopsy, there is no hard evidence of this.

Sun's remains rest with his mother's and father's in Xi'an, his beloved hometown.

19: The State of Camps Today

So where does Sun's death leave us? I wish I could say a freer China, or that his sacrifices changed something fundamental in the laogai system. But the truth is: in the years following his death, not only has forced labor in China increased, but it has gained more disturbing implications.

According to the Chinese government's official statistics, there were some 160,000 detainees in reeducation through labor camps when the system was abolished in 2013. This could lead us to believe that those prisoners were soon freed. But RTL camps were never the only kind of gulags in China. And in reality, China shuffled RTL detainees into the many other types of informal, unregulated detention sites.

Exiled human rights lawyer Teng Biao saw this right away. "If we are talking about extralegal detention, there are 'black jails,' targeting petitioners. There are 'legal education centers,' targeting mostly the Falun Gong practitioners," he told me. "In all of these kinds of black jails, the detainees are forced to work."

According to incomplete statistics from human rights defenders, the number of detainees in so-called legal education centers, also known as brainwashing centers, increased by sixfold as China shut down reeducation through labor camps.

In some ways, legal education centers are worse than RTL camps, because the government does not formally recognize the existence of these black-site facilities at all. In 2013, human rights lawyers estimated that thousands had already been tortured to death in these centers. If Sun had been locked in a legal education center instead of Masanjia, his lawyer would not have been able to go through any legal channels to help him. Black jails are considered a state secret, and their guards have physically attacked and temporarily detained foreign journalists for documenting these informal prisons. Although horrific torture and murder often took place in RTL camps, there was at least some minimal oversight. In legal education centers, anyone who cannot be brainwashed can be murdered with impunity.

Some RTL detainees were also reshuffled into "custody and education centers," where sex workers and their clients were detained without trial. These centers could force them to do manufacturing work for up to two years. In December 2019, China announced that it had abolished custody and education centers as well—although it remains unclear if sex workers will simply be forced to labor in other types of extralegal detention centers going forward.

And then there are compulsory isolation drug rehab centers. Many of these are located in former RTL facilities. According to Human Rights Watch, these centers are staffed with more police officers than doctors and social workers, and are run by the police instead of substance-abuse professionals. A combination of high-tech surveillance and ordinary street sweeps land drug users and sellers in detox centers.

Some are indeed addicts, but after they disappear into these rehab centers, they receive little to no help with recovery.

"There is absolutely no support for quitting drugs inside detoxification centers; factory work is all there is," a drug user who had been detained in one such facility told Human Rights Watch. Another detainee reported that heroin addicts experiencing withdrawal symptoms received nothing but a pail of cold water in the face. Then, it was back to work.

And, of course, there are also the detainees with no history of drug abuse who have disappeared into these centers since the closure of RTL camps.

Masanjia Women's Reeducation Through Labor Camp remains open today by disguising itself as a drug detox center. In 2014, survivors said the "new" Masanjia employed the same guards as before and continues to detain political prisoners who are not drug addicts. Other production facilities at Masanjia were transferred to the formal prison system, where prisoners convicted in a court of law—albeit, a biased court—must labor.

According to more recent survivors and the families of detainees who gather on internet forums to share information, the Masanjia prisons and drug detox center continue to manufacture products.

In early 2019, I visited the old Shanghai No. 4 Reeducation Through Labor Camp and saw that the building was still encircled by barbed wire and surveillance cameras. SHANGHAI QING DONG COMPULSORY ISOLATION DRUG DETOX CENTER was now emblazoned next to the gate in Chinese characters, along with China's national emblem, a red circle with yellow stars.

At the gate, I encountered two detox center employees on their way to work. I posed as a buyer, inquiring about purchasing merchandise from their facility. At first, both employees referred to the facility as a prison during our conversations.

"Wait—is this a drug detox center or a prison?" I asked.

"Drug detox center," an employee said after a pause.

It was an incredibly productive facility. I watched freight trucks come and go every two hours or so. Although I couldn't see the cargo inside, I followed the drug detox center's trucks to a number of manufacturers: one that made pet products such as rubber dog toys and leather collars, one that made cutting machinery, one that manufactured electronics, one that made bike brakes, and one that produced school supplies. According to customs records, most of these companies export their goods.

The pet products manufacturer was called Shanghai Yixiao Pet Products, which exports dog chews, cotton rope, rubber toys, and plastic bags for pet waste, all under the brand name Ruffin' It, to retailers such as Kmart, Walmart, Amazon, and Target.

The school supplies company was called Skool Tools. Import records show that a New York–based wholesaler called Kikkerland Design Inc. received many Skool Tools products. A number of large US retailers sell Kikkerland school supplies, including (at the time of writing) Amazon, Nordstrom, and Walmart.

A Kikkerland marketing director told me that since the company buys its products from trade shows in Hong Kong and Guangzhou, they "don't have any information about the factories." Meanwhile, Amazon says it "aspires" to audit its manufacturers before ordering products. But its representatives did not respond when I wrote to ask if it has ever audited the manufacturers of Ruffin' It and Kikkerland.

Perhaps the most notable exporter that I followed a drug detox center's truck to was an electronics manufacturer called Primax. When I Googled that factory's address, I found Apple's official 2018 supplier list.

Although I couldn't see if the truck was transporting Apple products, I thought it was troubling that Apple's factory had a relationship with a reopened labor camp. I emailed an Apple media spokesperson to alert the company of my findings. Someone from the communications department responded, saying Apple would not comment on this specific factory but that Apple "strictly prohibits" any "involuntary labor" in its supply chain.

To reassure me of Apple's humane treatment of workers, the spokesperson also referred me to reports on how Apple has, since 2007, trained 17.3 million supplier employees on workplace rights, such as "local labor law requirements" and "permissible working hours and overtime policies." In 2018, Apple mandated that its suppliers reimburse $616,000 to workers who had been forced to pay their employers or third-party job recruiters for the opportunity to work.

These are good steps. But I gave the Apple spokesperson an eyewitness account that one of its factories has a relationship with a prison. Will it be doing anything to address this? Apple did not respond to that question.

The Chinese government claims it has ended state-sanctioned forced-labor practices. But the expansion of the Belt and Road Initiative, combined with the onslaught of artificial intelligence, has worsened conditions in the long-existing Muslim labor camps. In the past few years, the Xinjiang camps that detain Turkic minorities have turned into something akin to concentration camps. As of this writing, a quarter of the twelve million Turkics in the region are estimated to be detained. Although these facilities are known as reeducation camps, they have a different aim than Masanjia and other extralegal detention centers. What China wanted from the former camps was free labor and the silencing of dissent. But the Xinjiang camps have a new goal: to erase an entire racial identity.

Once inside reeducation camps, the Turkic detainees attend daily indoctrination classes on official state ideology. They must prove they can reject Islam, forget their native tongue, and learn fluent Mandarin. There are reports of camps sterilizing Turkic women, while Turkic children are stolen from their parents and given to "orphanages" that raise them as Chinese. In 2020, the Jamestown Foundation released a report analyzing Chinese government documents such as "family planning" records. It found that between 2015 and 2018, forced sterilizations and abortions decreased the birth rate in two of the largest Uyghur prefectures by 84 percent. But this drop was not steep enough for China. The local government of one Uyghur region set a family planning goal of lowering the birth rate to nearly zero in 2020. Through forced sterilization and policies that strongly encourage interracial Han Chinese and Turkic marriages, the Chinese Communist Party is proceeding to wipe out an entire ethnicity.

The Chinese government initially denied the existence of these Muslim reeducation camps. But in 2018, researchers used satellite imagery and China's domestic security budgets to prove that these facilities not only existed but that they were expanding rapidly— drawing condemnation from the UN.

So the CCP began giving conflicting narratives to try to explain the camps. They sometimes said they were a counterterrorism initiative, detaining "suspicious" people to prevent potential incidents. Other times, they called the facilities "vocational schools," intended to lift people out of poverty.

Vocational training is, of course, a euphemism for forced labor. Through a network of Uyghurs living in exile, the DC-based Uyghur Human Rights Project identified 435 Uyghur intellectuals—doctors, poets, journalists, professors—detained in these facilities as of April 2019. Did they need vocational training in manufacturing? And according to Nathan Sales, the US State Department's coordinator for counterterrorism, the camps in Xinjiang aren't an anti-terrorism measure either. "The scope of this campaign is so vast and so untargeted that it simply has nothing to do with terrorism," Sales told Radio Free Asia in July 2019. "Instead, what's going on is the Chinese Communist Party is waging war on religion. It is trying to stamp out the ethnic, linguistic, cultural and religious identities of the people that it's been targeting."

The camps are supposed to ensure long-term stability for the regime. The Chinese Communist Party's "ultimate goal in Xinjiang— as elsewhere in China—is to exercise complete ideological supremacy, and that also entails trying to transform the very identity of the country's minorities," Adrian Zenz, a leading researcher on China's ethnic policies, wrote in a July 2019 *New York Times* op-ed: "The C.C.P. lives in perennial fear that, short of having a complete grip on Chinese society, its long-term survival is in danger."

The regime is worried because the Turkic minorities of Xinjiang have a long and bitter history with China. The region was once an independent territory known as East Turkestan, until the Manchu Empire invaded in 1759. After many skirmishes, the Chinese annexed East Turkestan in 1884. They renamed it Xinjiang, which means "new frontier."

After several Uyghur uprisings and two short-lived periods of independence in the 1930s and '40s, the Chinese Communist Party took over and established the Xinjiang Uyghur Autonomous Region (XUAR), supposedly recognizing the Uyghur majority in the region. But since their land was teeming with minerals, oil, and natural gas, the Turkic minorities didn't have anything close to autonomy.

The party enforced the hashar program, forcing Turkic people to do hard labor on farms and public works projects for no payment. It also went on to implement various forced assimilation policies over the decades, including the mass relocation of Han Chinese people to Xinjiang to dilute the Turkic population. In 1949, the Han Chinese population in the region was just under 7 percent. By 2008, it had surged to 40 percent. As the Chinese demographic grew in Xinjiang, the better-paying jobs were often earmarked for the Chinese.

The Chinese government also highly discouraged Uyghur children from speaking their native tongue. According to Amnesty International, the Uyghur language began disappearing from schools in the 1990s, when the party started restricting professors in Xinjiang from conducting classes in Uyghur. By 2006, Chinese was well on its way to becoming the primary language taught in Xinjiang preschools. In some cases, children and teachers received fines for speaking Uyghur on school grounds.

According to Radio Free Asia, the Chinese government was, by 2011, launching "ethnic harmony" campaigns, which required children as young as seven to attend political education sessions. Religion was also suppressed, even though the vast majority of Uyghurs lived relatively secular lives.

The Chinese government's heavy-handed cultural extermination policies have led to sporadic, mostly small-scale protests over the years. In a handful of cases, Uyghurs have reacted with violence. In 2014, eight Uyghurs carried out a knife attack at a train station in the city of Kunming that left thirty-one people dead. This type of violent outburst, no matter how rare, reinforced the CCP's fear of a Uyghur and Kazakh revolt and gave the party justification to detain Turkic people in the name of counterterrorism. But the police are now flagging even harmless life habits—like a tendency to store a large amount of food at home or a decision to quit drinking and smoking—as indicators of religious extremism and possible reasons for arrest.

It doesn't matter that prominent Uyghur leaders have always discouraged violence. Rebiya Kadeer, an exiled activist, business mogul, and former president of the World Uyghur Congress, has always vocally denounced such extreme acts. Other influential Uyghur intellectuals, such as the economist and professor Ilham Tohti, have done so as well. But even Tohti, who believed in fostering dialogue with the Chinese Communist Party, was charged with separatism and sentenced to life in prison in 2014.

So what happens to these Turkic people after they disappear into these extrajudicial reeducation camps? Mihrigul Tursun is a rare survivor who managed to leave China to shed light on the CCP's disturbing ethnic-cleansing methods.

The guards took Tursun, a young mother of triplets, to what looked like an execution chamber, she testified at a US congressional hearing in December 2018. It was a sparse room: one light, one electric chair.

There was a click. The guards locked her arms and legs in place and pressed a button. Her shackles tightened. She felt the weight of the helmet on her head and, without warning, the electric shocks began. The electricity convulsing through her veins caused foam to seep from her mouth. The shocks stopped before starting again, stopped, then started again. She screamed as the cruel, slow moments passed.

"Kill me," she begged. She could not endure the electrocution any longer.

"You being a Uyghur is a crime," a voice said to her as she lost consciousness.

But the guards did not jolt her with voltages high enough to kill her. Like the bunk-bed torture Sun had endured, the mock execution was designed to "reeducate."

"Long live Xi Jinping," Tursun sang the next morning.

After their "release" from political reeducation camps, most Uyghur detainees have to work in factories for little or no payment, making cheap products for export. After spending ten months in various camps, Tursun was one of the few Muslims not sent to a factory right away. This was because her kids, who had been born in Egypt, were not Chinese nationals, and one of the three had already died in the hands of Chinese authorities. Tursun was told she would be allowed to take her two surviving children to Egypt to stay with relatives there but that she would have to return to China. If she did not come back, she was told, her mother, father, and siblings in Xinjiang would be sent to camps.

Facing an impossible choice, twenty-nine-year-old Tursun took her kids and went, instead, from Cairo to the United States.

"I never thought I would come out of the cell 210 alive. I still cannot believe it," she said, through an interpreter.

"The Chinese government made it clear that the cost of my speaking out would be the lives of my parents and siblings. I feel unbelievably guilty for that, and it is a form of ongoing mental torture I suffer every day," she said. "But I believe I also have a moral obligation to tell the truth to the world so that someone can take an action to stop this atrocity."

Tursun knew most of the women in her cell: her former doctor, neighbors, and the daughters of old teachers. At night, they listened with fear. They could hear men screaming nearby and the rattling of chains, which made terrible grating noises when the guards dragged bodies away. "The thought that these men could be our fathers or brothers was unbearable," she said.

She witnessed nine deaths in her cell in three months.

There was a twenty-three-year-old woman named Patemhan, detained for attending an Islamic wedding without alcohol. Each day, Patemhan agonized over her two small children, who had been left in the backyard when the police took her away. They were probably the last thoughts on her mind before she collapsed and died in the cell. Several masked guards came, dragging her body away by the feet.

Also in the cell was a sixty-two-year-old woman named Gulnisa. She was so sick she had trouble eating. The guards humiliated her for not memorizing political slogans well enough. One night, she cried herself to sleep and did not wake up the next morning.

Gulnisa's and Patemhan's fates in the reeducation camp were not so different from the fate of Dong Chen, the underground Christian who perished while on Masanjia's ghost team. And just as China never truly closed the RTL camps, the CCP's July 2019 claims of releasing the majority of Muslim detainees are improbable. Turkic exiles still cannot get in touch with their missing loved ones. New camps—with their nearly identical block shapes, watchtowers, and razor-wire fences—continue to pop up on satellite images.

And perhaps most significantly, starting at the end of 2019 at least one Chinese official has leaked a series of internal documents to news organizations such as the International Consortium of Investigative Journalists and the *New York Times*. The documents—which include directives, reports, and President Xi's internal speeches—confirmed that the Muslim reeducation camps are not voluntary vocational training centers, but concentration camps. The documents also revealed the party's plans to extend the crackdown on Islam beyond Xinjiang to other parts of China. China did not deny the authenticity of these documents. What's more, there is evidence the region's recent spike in factories is the result of a strategic plan to use these populations for forced labor. The *New York Times* found that, in 2018, the Xinjiang government offered economic incentives to textile and garment companies to open factories in the region, especially if the factories were built near camps.

In March 2020, the Australian Strategic Policy Institute, a think tank based in Canberra, found that between 2017 and 2019, more than eighty thousand Uyghurs were forcibly transferred out of Xinjiang to work in militarized factories in other parts of China. According to the institute's report, which cites government documents and Chinese media, some had been sent directly from reeducation camps.

The institute found at least eighty-three global brands—including Nike, Apple, and BMW—sourcing from factories where Uyghur workers are held against their will. Of course, Nike's, Apple's, and BMW's official company policies forbid forced labor. When I asked BMW if it will be investigating the factory that the institute found was using Muslim forced laborers, a spokesperson told me the company had no comment.

So where is this all going?

As China continues to expand the camps, there is a real concern about escalation. After all, the Chinese government will eventually need to confront the limitations of its indoctrination strategy. No matter how extensive China's reeducation programs become, there will likely be a significant number of Uyghurs and Kazakhs who simply cannot, or will not, assimilate to an extent that would satisfy the government. For instance, learning a second language is more challenging for some than others. It will not be possible for all Uyghurs and Kazakhs to become fluent in Mandarin. And there will always be some Muslims who will refuse to eat pork or drink alcohol. What, then, will happen to those people?

Although there are currently no reports of mass executions in the reeducation camps, some have expressed concern that they share disturbing similarities with the earliest phases of Nazi concentration camps. Ostensibly comparing the facilities to Nazi camps and to Soviet gulags, in March 2019 the then-head of the US State Department's human rights and democracy bureau, Michael Kozak, said he had not "seen things like this since the 1930s."

After all, the Nazis did not start off building death camps. The initial plan was to drive Jews and other "undesirable" minorities out of the German Reich. Adolf Hitler did not implement the so-called Final Solution, which called for mass executions, until several years after the first Nazi concentration camps formed.

"It was eight or nine years before [the concentration camps] were connected to a program of mass killing," Rian Thum, a historian of Chinese Islam told NBC in a conversation about what the Chinese regime might do once it realizes it cannot completely change the Turkic people's racial and cultural identity. "Goals can change, and the function of these things can change, especially when you're looking at such a massive system that has no appeal system, no regulation, no oversight."

And indeed, there is not much preventing China from turning its reeducation camps into death camps. After all, the government has been collecting the Turkic population's biometric data. This would be useful for ensuring accurate organ matching if the CCP were to execute detainees en masse and sell their organs. And international response to the camps has been slow and weak. This is partially because more than seventy countries have accepted development funds from China as a part of the Belt and Road Initiative. Although Pakistan initially criticized Beijing over the Muslim camps, Prime Minister Imran Khan later backtracked, saying he didn't know much about the Uyghurs.

The United States is not a part of BRI, which may be one reason it has delivered a firmer response to the camps. In October 2019, the

US Department of Commerce blacklisted Xinjiang's entire public security bureau as well as eight Chinese tech companies that developed AI surveillance technologies that help target Turkic people. These entities are prohibited from buying any US products without the US government's permission.

A month later, the Congressional-Executive Commission on China formally asked Customs and Border Protection to consider banning all products manufactured in Xinjiang. In an open letter, representatives of the commission wrote: "Manufacturing using forced labor is not only widespread but integral to the Chinese government's campaign of repression in the XUAR. . . . The risk of forced labor is so great that it is difficult, if not impossible, for companies to conduct appropriate due diligence of their supply chains in the region." And in March 2020, a bipartisan group of US lawmakers proposed the Uyghur Forced Labor Prevention Act, which, if passed, will ban all products manufactured in Xinjiang from entering the United States.

But for now, CBP is still offering a Band-Aid solution by banning one supplier at a time—and only after an enormous burden of proof has been met.

In September 2019, the agency finally issued a detention order for Hetian Taida Apparel Co., almost a year after the Associated Press revealed that the Chinese factory shared an address with a reeducation camp in Xinjiang. It was the first detention order CBP had issued for a Chinese supplier in more than a year. And seven months would pass before the agency issued a second detention order for a supplier in Xinjiang, this one for Hetian Haolin Hair Accessories Co. Ltd.

Clearly, banning one supplier at a time is not enough.

With that said, in spring 2020 the US Congress did pass the Uyghur Human Rights Policy Act, which does not ban products from Xinjiang but *does* aim to sanction the Chinese officials who are most responsible for the re-education camps. Republican Senator Marco Rubio and Senator Bob Menendez, the most senior Democrat on the Senate Foreign Relations Committee, introduced the bill, and more than fifty senators cosponsored this bipartisan legislation. This is an incredibly meaningful step toward holding the Chinese government accountable. But as of June 2020, it remains to be seen how this legislation will be enforced.

And still, after all of this—the congressional hearings, exposés in national and international papers, and sacrifices of dissidents to make the horrors of forced labor known to the public—the world at large remains oblivious of China's gulags.

Executives of some Western corporations claim ignorance of the situation. When asked about the ethics of having a car production plant in Xinjiang, Herbert Diess, the CEO of Volkswagen, told the BBC in April 2019 he was "not aware" of any Muslim detention camps. And in October 2019, Japanese companies Muji and Uniqlo went so far as to advertise their Xinjiang cotton as a selling point. And why wouldn't they? There aren't exactly mass demonstrations around the globe calling for companies to stop sourcing from the region.

The international community did little about Nazi Germany's concentration camps until six million Jews had died. It is unclear which direction the arc of history will bend this time, but it is evident we need systemic changes to address the full scope of the problem.

It remains unclear whether the immense sacrifices of people like Sun will fundamentally alter anything.

Sun and May could have had a child. They could have grown old together, as they had hoped to do that day by the river in Chongqing. But in order to resist and expose Masanjia and the laogai system, Sun traded some of life's most meaningful experiences away.

Mihrigul Tursun lives with the knowledge that she has more than likely killed her parents by testifying about reeducation camps in Xinjiang. It is an unspeakable guilt that she carries with her every day.

Countless others have given up their health or their lives to China's forced-labor system.

We have been shown the underbelly of excessive consumption. The ball is in our court. But nothing will change unless we help change it.

What We Can Do

ʮʮʮ

If there is one sign of hope when it comes to the harrowing events unfolding in China, it lies in the fact that Beijing responds to financial pushback. It was foreign trade (the Belt and Road Initiative) that sparked the reeducation camps. It is foreign trade that can end them.

When Turkey, another BRI country, criticized the Chinese government over the rumored death of an acclaimed Uyghur singer named Abdurehim Heyit, Beijing responded with a video showing that he was still alive. With international eyes on Heyit, China can no longer kill him.

"That kind of pushback matters. That's why consumer boycotts matter," politics and international relations lecturer Anna Hayes told me. "If a significant multinational corporation like Volkswagen says, 'We're going to pull out [of Xinjiang] because of reeducation camps,' that's the kind of thing that is going to change Beijing's mind. Beijing has opened up Xinjiang. They want European investment there. They want Middle Eastern investment there . . . So if companies started to pull out on the basis of concerns over labor, that would work."

As conscientious consumers, we can take things into our own hands. After all, we *are* foreign trade: our purchasing choices are the source of demand, and our boycotts serve as accountability. We need to ask our favorite brands: If you are still sourcing from Xinjiang, are you willing to pull out?

One way to get in touch with corporations is to call the company's main number and ask for the person who handles "corporate social responsibility." Most companies these days have a corporate social responsibility department or an ethics team. The phone number and email for these departments are sometimes listed on the company's website.

But a more effective way to get the attention of large corporations may be through social media platforms like Twitter. Brands tend to respond to social media campaigns fast, as the spread of negative information can quickly gain momentum and soil their reputation. Whether tweeting these questions at companies with a catchy hashtag or signing and sharing online petitions asking that companies address these questions, consumers can help create crucial changes that will discourage factories from outsourcing to labor camps.

Raphaël Glucksmann, a European Parliament member who is a part of the Progressive Alliance of Socialists and Democrats, has been particularly successful in launching social media campaigns that hold corporations accountable for using forced labor. In the summer of 2020, he began pressuring the eighty-two major corporations the Australian Strategic Policy Institute found to be sourcing from Uyghur detainees to cut ties with those forced labor factories.

Although most of Glucksmann's social media accounts are in French, those of us who don't speak French can still take part in his campaigns by following the English version of his Instagram account. As of this book's publication, the handle is @raphaelglucksmann_english.

To ensure that corporations are doing the most they can to deter their factories from outsourcing to laogai facilities in China, you can also contact corporations and ask questions like these:

Can you disclose how fast you expect production turnarounds to be?

How long does it take for your auditors to audit each factory? Is it a cursory one-day audit?

How much do you spend per audit?

Can you release all of your audit reports to the public?

Were any of the issues you found in your audit fueled by your own sourcing practices (e.g., last-minute production changes without waiving late penalty fees, or unreasonably fast production expectations)?

Can you disclose what changes you made to prevent these issues from occurring again?

To ensure that your factories have no secret relationships with laogai camps, will you rewrite your contracts with your suppliers to allow auditors to covertly follow the trucks leaving your factories? (This is the best way to let your suppliers know you are serious about forbidding illegal subcontracting.)

It may be too expensive to do such thorough audits for all of your factories, but will you spot-test a few suppliers by following their trucks?

Will you begin retaining a permanent electronic version of all your suppliers' production and payroll records?

Can you disclose the prices you ask from manufacturers?

Can you disclose your factory workers' wages?

These are important questions for companies to answer because these are the precise factors that push manufacturers to secretly sub-contract to terrible places. Only by removing the main incentives for factories to outsource to laogai camps, and by increasing the factories' chances of getting caught if they continue to do so, can we significantly reduce the number of forced-labor products landing in our stores.

For companies that can prove they have made significant efforts to address all the questions above, I would suggest a new LAOGAI-FREE label to help consumers find these brands. This could be similar to the FAIRTRADE label, where independent third-party inspectors verify that companies are paying their workers and farmers living wages and ensuring decent working standards. Only products from companies that the inspectors can vouch for receive the label. For the LAOGAI-FREE label, an independent third-party certifier would affirm that a corporation has implemented critical changes in its sourcing practices that would reduce the likelihood of their factories secretly subcontracting to labor camps.

Until there is such a label, perhaps we can reduce unnecessary consumption. After all, Chinese manufacturers often have no choice but to secretly source from de facto gulags because they cannot meet the global consumer demand for budget prices *and* the newest trends. To practice more thoughtful consumption, we should consider a few points before we buy something. The following list is inspired by a sustainable shopping post on Man Repeller, an independent fashion and lifestyle website:

1. Do I already own something that serves the same purpose?

2. Is this item so much better that I would feel compelled to donate three things in its place?

3. If it were more expensive, would I still try to figure out a way to afford it? Or am I feeling an urge to buy this only because it's extremely cheap?

4. If the product I'm considering is an updated version of one that I already own, is my current one working just fine?

5. Am I sure I will wear or use this product a lot? Or will this likely end up sitting in storage after one use?

Of course, there is no panacea. The Chinese Communist Party will continue to use the labor of imprisoned dissidents and religious minorities as long as it has power. As individuals, we cannot force the Chinese government to embrace democracy. But we can use our spending power to limit how much an authoritarian government will profit from the abuse of prisoners of conscience and ethnic minorities.

Even if we cannot achieve the complete abolition of forced labor in China with our phones, tweets, and wallets, our actions can make a difference. If labor camps start losing international contracts, perhaps detainees will never have to work any more twenty-hour days to meet production deadlines. Without high-volume orders from foreign companies, perhaps there will be fewer arbitrary arrests to help prison factories meet production quotas. It all starts with small changes from each of us.

Author's Note

ᒣᒣ

This is a work of nonfiction. There are no invented or composite characters. Over the course of a year, I interviewed Sun Yi through Skype video calls. We also had many email exchanges, where I asked him to recount the details of his experience at Masanjia. The details he gave match the accounts of other Masanjia survivors, and those of former detainees of other reeducation through labor camps across China. Similar accounts are reflected in reports by human rights organizations such as Amnesty International, Human Rights Watch, and the Laogai Research Foundation.

I asked Sun about small sensory details in particular: sights, sounds, colors, and textures, as well as emotions and thoughts. I wanted to take readers beyond Beijing's brightly lit Chanel and Gucci storefronts, and inside this hidden system contributing to China's colossal economy.

To my great regret, I didn't get a chance to meet Sun in person before his sudden death. If it weren't for documentary maker Leon Lee, who generously shared his transcripts and documentary footage with me, I wouldn't have been able to finish telling Sun's story. The scenes in this book describing Sun's experiences since leaving Masanjia come from the resulting documentary, *Letter from*

Masanjia. Many of the scenes toward the end of this book come from footage that didn't make it into the documentary.

One of Sun's close friends shared video footage and recounted to me the details of his final days in China. Another friend of his shared some footage from Jakarta.

But May, fearing for her safety, declined to be interviewed for this book. Parts of May's story were recalled by Sun, and by their neighbor. Other details and dialogue came from footage filmed for *Letter from Masanjia*.

In addition, May is a pseudonym. Even though it may seem futile to use a pseudonym after Sun revealed his real name to the world, she asked Sun to not draw attention to her. I felt for her fear, and wanted to offer her at least a semblance of anonymity.

Before Sun died, he connected me to a writer and researcher in China who has been compiling stories from more than thirty Masanjia survivors and a few guards. To protect her safety, I will call her Yun Zhao. The stories of other Masanjia survivors, including the inmate-guards and those who died in the camp, came from Yun Zhao. The names of almost all of the survivors who are still living in China have been changed. The only exception is Liu Hua, who has been using her real name to give interviews to the foreign press.

In the United States, I interviewed a group of Falun Gong labor camp survivors who regularly travel to DC to hold events and meet with legislators. For years, they have been campaigning for US senators and representatives to put pressure on China to end the persecution. Although there is little that Congress can do, these refugees have never given up on trying to build momentum and awareness for their cause. They survived various RTL camps across China, and their descriptions of torture and working conditions in those camps match the accounts from Masanjia.

To document the camps and their connections to Western corporations, I traveled to Shanghai, which is simultaneously a metropolitan city and a region with a lot of forced-labor facilities. Because the city is a popular travel destination, someone like me, with a foreign passport, could spend time there without raising red flags from the police.

During this monthlong reporting trip, I visited several different kinds of Chinese prisons and extralegal detention centers that engaged in manufacturing work. I followed the freight trucks that left these camps to various exporting factories. I also posed as a businessperson, striking up conversations with guards about the products they made inside. Since it is not illegal for Chinese companies to source from these facilities, the guards openly called these factories "prisons." And they welcomed me, with enthusiasm, to buy from their camps.

Acknowledgments

I am deeply grateful to Jeffrey Fiedler and Peter Mueller, and all the former Laogai Research Foundation researchers who generously shared their intimate knowledge of the laogai industry. Thank you, especially, for teaching me how to pose as a buyer when calling and visiting camps.

Many thanks to Chris Hedges for pushing me to stop procrastinating with the book proposal, and for the helpful tips on how to escape surveillance while reporting in an authoritarian country. I would not have been able to follow freight trucks in China safely without invaluable advice from experienced journalists such as Chris, Clément Bürge, Yuan Yang, Kiki, and Katie.

I also owe a special gratitude to the auditors and industry consultants who took the time and risks to explain their byzantine world to me. They all have added so much more depth to this book. I am also grateful to the CBP and ICE officials, as well as congressional staffers, who gave me terrific policy background. This book would not have been possible without the admirable researchers from the Congressional-Executive Commission on China and the International Labor Rights Forum who shared their rich insights and connections.

I am deeply indebted to my brilliant and meticulous editors Betsy Gleick and Abby Muller, who have contributed so much intellect and value to this book. I am embarrassed to say how many drafts we went through. I will always be grateful for their vision, patience, and wisdom. My deepest appreciation to my tenacious fact-checker, Ellen Shapiro—who worked right up until her surgery to double- and triple-check so many obscure facts—and to my very impressive copyeditor, Elizabeth Johnson. I will always be thankful for my agent and most impassioned advocate, Laney Katz Becker, who put so much time into shaping the book proposal. Her expertise has steered me through the chaos of the publishing world. I don't know where I would be without her.

My deepest appreciation to the Nieman Foundation and Columbia University School of Journalism, for recognizing this manuscript while it was still a work in progress. I would also particularly like to thank my writing and journalism professors from the New School, especially Heather Chaplin and Alex Halberstadt, who made me feel, for the first time in my life, that I had something.

I owe a very important debt to Caylan Ford, Leon Lee, and Yun Zhao, who have contributed so much to this book's foundation. None of this would have been possible without the three of them. And a special thanks to Dr. Nieh, who initially introduced me to renowned human rights activists such as Chen Guangcheng. My eternal gratitude to the sacrifices of Chen Guangcheng and other fearless human rights activists, including Chen Pokong and Teng Biao. I owe everything to the survivors who were willing to be interviewed for this book. Especially Sun; I wish you were here to see this. I hope I did your story justice.

My friends at Wiscoy, who are the most socially conscious people I know, all have been an inspiration. My dearest thanks to Julie

Johnson and Bob and Emily Copeland for being early readers with such helpful critiques. A special thanks to Joyce Ford and Jim Riddle for providing the most beautiful space to work and think.

To the old and new friends who have kept me sane during the reporting and writing process: Trinh, Lian, Kat Eng, Anna Mae; Gloria Alatorre, Carmen Carter, Shirley Dai, Angela Zhao, Angela Wang, Camille Gray, Pokuaa, Shakia Jackson, Zaina Sesay, Myah Lipscomb, Jenna Jones, Ursula, Rose, Eric, Niyati, and Dave, Alina, and Mel. I am also deeply grateful to the Gray family for all the support during the early years.

To my sweet husband, Z, who supported me every step of the way, and my parents, Lianping, Lynn, and Mike—thanks for putting up with me as I went bonkers when the printer broke before the deadline. Thanks also to my brothers, Josh and Ethan; my sisters, Kara and Lauren; my family, si yi and si yi fu, Hong and Jessica, Lucas and Logan. And last but not least, thank you to my family in China, who knew nothing about this book; I'm so sorry if this will make your lives difficult.

Notes

րդ

Prologue

1   **totally ghoul**   Details of the Halloween decorations are drawn from a photograph of the product published in "Halloween Decorations Carry Haunting Message of Forced Labor," *Oregonian*, December 23, 2012, https://www.oregonlive.com /happy-valley/2012/12/halloween_decorations_carry_ha.html.

3   **crossed-out words and broken English**   Ibid.

4   **across the Pacific Ocean**   "Behind Cry for Help from China Labor Camp," *New York Times*, June 11, 2013, https://www.nytimes.com/2013/06/12/world /asia/man-details-risks-in-exposing-chinas-forced-labor.html.

4   **established in 1956**   "Masanjia Re-Education through Labor Camp," Wikipedia, https://en.wikipedia.org/wiki/Masanjia_re-education_through_labor_camp.

5   **"I found this in box of Halloween decorations"**   Author interview with Julie Keith.

5   **stores like . . . Walmart**   "Arizona Woman Discovers Note from 'Chinese Prisoner' in Purse," Fox News, May 1, 2017, https://www.foxnews.com/us/arizona -woman-discovers-note-from-chinese-prisoner-in-purse-bought-at-walmart.

5   **Saks Fifth Avenue**   "An S.O.S. in a Saks Bag," *New Yorker*, June 3, 2014, https://www.newyorker.com/business/currency/an-s-o-s-in-a-saks-bag.

5   **News outlets such as the *New York Times***   "Behind Cry for Help," *New York Times; New Yorker*   "S.O.S. in a Saks Bag," *New Yorker*.

5   **BBC**   "Primark Investigates Claim of 'Cry for Help' Note in Trousers," BBC, June 25, 2014, https://www.bbc.com/news/uk-northern-ireland-28018137.

5   **seven different Chinese SOS letters**   "S.O.S. in a Saks Bag," *New Yorker*; "Primark . . . Note in Trousers," BBC; "Arizona Woman Discovers Note," Fox News; "Chinese Plea for Freedom Found in Cupcake Box in New York," *Epoch Times*, April 24, 2017, https://www.theepochtimes.com/chinese-plea-for-freedom -found-in-cupcake-box-in-new-york_2245039.html; "Another 'Cry for Help' Has Been Found in a Pair of Primark Socks," *Metro*, December 21, 2015, https://metro.co.uk/2015/12/21/another-cry-for-help-has-been-found-in-a -pair-of-primark-socks-5578156/; "Behind Cry for Help," *New York Times*; "Tesco Halts Production at Chinese Factory over Alleged 'Forced' Labour," BBC, December 22, 2019, https://www.bbc.com/news/uk-50883161.

5   **first well-documented case**   "Bloodstained Flowers," Laogai Research Foundation, National Endowment for Democracy Library, Washington, DC.

5   **US congressional hearing** "Chinese Forced Labor," *Congressional Record* 140, no. 143 (October 5, 1994), https://www.govinfo.gov/content/pkg/CREC-1994-10 -05/html/CREC-1994-10-05-pt1-PgH81.htm.

9   **"Where did you buy this product?"** Conversation with ICE agents, recalled by Julie Keith.

9   **ICE made a formal request** *Prison Labor Exports from China and Implications for U.S. Policy*, US-China Economic and Security Review Commission, July 9, 2014, https://www.uscc.gov/sites/default/files/Research/Staff%20Report_Prison% 20Labor%20Exports%20from%20China_Final%20Report%20070914.pdf.

9   **China refused to cooperate** Ibid.

9   **one of twelve pending investigations** Ibid.

10 **not allowed US officials to visit** An ICE official told the author on background.

10 **"One piece of evidence"** A CBP official told the author on background.

Chapter One

11 **diodes . . . and disposable underwear** "Witness: Working Conditions in Masanjia Forced Labour Camp," Falun Dafa Information Center, December 4, 2013, https://en.faluninfo.eu/2013/04/12/witness-working-conditions-in-masanjia -forced-labour-camp.

13 **between 1958 and 1962** "Mao's Great Leap to Famine," opinion piece, *New York Times*, December 15, 2010, https://www.nytimes.com/2010/12/16/opinion/16iht -eddikotter16.html.

13 **As many as forty-five million people died** "Milder Accounts of Hardships under Mao Arise as His Birthday Nears," *New York Times*, October 16, 2013, https://www.nytimes.com/2013/10/17/world/asia/advancing-a-milder-version -of-maos-calamities.html.

13 **rapid industrialization** Wei Li and Dennis Tao Yang, "The Great Leap Forward: Anatomy of a Central Planning Disaster," *Journal of Political Economy* 113, no. 4 (August 2005), 840–77, https://www.jstor.org/stable/10.1086/430804.

13 **political violence, disorganization** Daniel Houser, Barbara Sands, and Erte Xiao, "Three Parts Natural, Seven Parts Man-Made: Bayesian Analysis of China's Great Leap Forward Demographic Disaster," *Journal of Economic Behavior & Organization* 69, no. 2 (February 2009): 148–159, https://doi.org/10.1016/j.jebo .2007.09.008.

13 **migrated from the province of Henan** "China: Henan: Leveraging Rural Revitalization and Building a Strong Modern Agricultural Province," *MarketWatch*, July 26, 2018, https://www.marketwatch.com/press-release /china-henan-leveraging-rural-revitalization-and-building-a-strong-modern -agricultural-province-2018-07-26.

13 **more industries bolstering** "Taiyuan Industrial Heritage Transformation," OMA, https://oma.eu/projects/taiyuan-industrial-heritage-transformaton.

14 **transcended ten thousand feet** "To Be Left Alone, China's Buddists Open a Door," *New York Times*, October 16, 1984, https://www.nytimes.com/1984/10/16 /world/to-be-left-alone-china-s-buddists-open-a-door.html.

15   **In AD 629, a scholarly monk**   "The Travel Records of Chinese Pilgrims Faxian, Xuanzang, and Yijing," *Education about Asia* 11, no. 3 (Winter 2006), http://afe.easia.columbia.edu/special/travel_records.pdf.

15   **seventeen-year-round-trip**   "Xuanzang: The Monk Who Brought Buddhism East," Asia Society, https://asiasociety.org/xuanzang-monk-who-brought -buddhism-east.

15   **thirteen hundred manuscripts**   "Three Journeys to the West from China," iLook China, December 30, 2014, https://ilookchina.com/tag/buddhist-monk-xuanzang/.

15   **founded in 1992 by Li Hongzhi**   "China's War against Itself," opinion piece, *New York Times*, February 15, 2001, https://www.nytimes.com/2001/02/15/opinion /china-s-war-against-itself.html.

15   **former government clerk**   "China Sentences Sect Follower," *Washington Post*, May 9, 2001, http://www.washingtonpost.com/wp-srv/aponline/20010509 /aponline144443_000.htm.

15   **four-thousand-year-old history**   "What's New 2017," Qigong Institute, https://www.qigonginstitute.org/category/83/what-s-new-2017.

16   **mind and body are connected**   Li Hongzhi, *Zhuan Falun*, 2014, trans. by US and UK practitioners, 44–45, https://falundafa.org/eng/eng/pdf/ZFL2014.pdf.

16   **elevate a person's plane of consciousness**   Ibid., 2.

16   **resolve personal issues and even illnesses**   Ibid., 3; 207.

16   **blocked energy channels and karma**   Ibid., 3; 207.

16   **political upheaval began in 1966**   "China's Cultural Revolution, Explained," *New York Times*, May 14, 2016, https://www.nytimes.com/2016/05/15/world/asia /china-cultural-revolution-explainer.html.

16   **college and high school students**   "Chinese Red Guards Apologize, Reopening a Dark Chapter," NPR, February 4, 2014, https://www.npr.org/sections/parallels /2014/01/23/265228870/chinese-red-guards-apologize-reopening-a-dark-chapter; "Heritage Conservation in China: Why 'Daughter of Dunhuang' Devoted Her Life to Keeping Buddhist Caves and Relics Alive," *South China Morning Post*, Nov 17, 2019, https://www.scmp.com/lifestyle/arts-culture/article/3037939 /heritage-conservation-china-why-daughter-dunhuang-devoted.

16   **"four olds"**   "The Cultural Revolution: All You Need to Know about China's Political Convulsion," *Guardian*, May 10, 2016, https://www.theguardian.com /world/2016/may/11/the-cultural-revolution-50-years-on-all-you-need-to-know -about-chinas-political-convulsion.

17   **sixteen million young people**   "China's Cultural Revolution, Explained," *New York Times*.

17   **integrate these young people**   "China's 'Sent-Down' Youth," *Financial Times*, September 20, 2013, https://www.ft.com/content/3d2ba75c-1fdf-11e3-8861 -00144feab7de.

17   **Cultural Revolution killed millions**   "Who Killed More: Hitler, Stalin, or Mao?" *New York Review of Books*, February 5, 2018, https://www.nybooks.com/daily /2018/02/05/who-killed-more-hitler-stalin-or-mao/.

17   **mangled China's economy**   "The Cost of the Cultural Revolution, Fifty Years Later," *New Yorker*, May 6, 2016, https://www.newyorker.com/news/daily -comment/the-cost-of-the-cultural-revolution-fifty-years-later.

17   **higher value on social stability than human rights**   Thomas Lum, *Human Rights in China and U.S. Policy*, Congressional Research Service, July 18, 2011, 29, https://fas.org/sgp/crs/row/RL34729.pdf.

17   **sweeping social and economic reforms**   "Where to Now? 40 Years after the Big Economic Experiment That Changed China," *South China Morning Post*, November 13, 2018, https://www.scmp.com/news/china/politics/article/2172934 /where-now-40-years-after-big-economic-experiment-changed-china.

17   **relegalizing private business**   Ibid.

17   **reopening China to foreign trade**   Ibid.

17   **world's second-largest economy**   "China's Economy Became No. 2 by Defying No. 1," *New York Times*, November 25, 2018, https://www.nytimes.com /interactive/2018/11/25/world/asia/china-economy-strategy.html.

17   **lifted the ban on religion**   "Freedom of Religion in China: A Historical Perspective," Berkley Center for Religion, Peace & World Affairs, Georgetown University, October 1, 2014, https://berkleycenter.georgetown.edu/essays /freedom-of-religion-in-china-a-historical-perspective.

17   **Thousands of practices**   "Banned in China, Thriving in New York; A Mystical Exercise Regimen Draws Immigrants and the Deeply Curious," *New York Times*, October 29, 1999, https://www.nytimes.com/1999/10/29/nyregion/banned-china -thriving-new-york-mystical-exercise-regimen-draws-immigrants-deeply.html.

17   **throughout the 1980s and '90s**   Ian Johnson, *The Souls of China: The Return of Religion after Mao* (New York: Vintage Books, 2018), 213.

17   **filling China's spiritual void**   "Culture : Filling a Void with 'Qigong' in China : Millions Have Turned to the Practice, Which Mixes Exercise and Meditation. Officials Fear Unpredictable Political Consequences," *Los Angeles Times*, October 16, 1990, https://www.latimes.com/archives/la-xpm-1990-10-16-wr-2703-story.html.

17   **attracting seventy million followers**   "Tension over a Parade: Falun Gong Adherents Aim to Join Despite Security Concerns," *Wall Street Journal*, January 25, 2012, https://www.wsj.com/articles/SB10001424052970203718504577181270747465002.

17   **Chinese embassy in Paris**   David Ownby, *Falun Gong and the Future of China* (Oxford: Oxford University Press, 2008), 127.

17   **state-run China Qigong**   "The Origins and Long-Term Consequences of the Communist Party's Campaign against Falun Gong," Freedom House, December 18, 2012, https://freedomhouse.org/article/China-communist-party -campaign-against-falun-gong#_ftn6.

17   **goal of the society**   Ownby, *Falun Gong*, 61.

18   **co-opt strategy**   Takashi Suzuki, "China's United Front Work in the Xi Jinping Era—Institutional Developments and Activities," *Journal of Contemporary East Asia Studies* 8, no. 1 (2019), https://www.tandfonline.com/doi/full/10.1080 /24761028.2019.1627714.

18   **"evil cult"**   "Origins and Long-Term Consequences," Freedom House.

18   **The modern Chinese political system**   "How China Stays Stable Despite 500 Protests Every Day," *Atlantic*, January 5, 2012, https://www.theatlantic.com /international/archive/2012/01/how-china-stays-stable-despite-500-protests -every-day/250940/.

18   **portion of the Chinese population**   "'Corruption and Elitism' Fueling Inequality in China," *Deutsche Welle*, July 28, 2014 , https://www.dw.com/en/corruption-and -elitism-fueling-inequality-in-china/a-17813952.

18   **aggrieved college students, workers, and intellectuals**   "Remembering Tiananmen," Transnational Institute, June 27, 2007, https://www.tni.org/es /node/13850.

18   **democratic elections and freedom of the press**   "How Today's China Was Shaped by the Events in Tiananmen Square 30 Years Ago," *Washington Post*, June 1, 2019, https://www.washingtonpost.com/world/asia_pacific/how-todays -china-was-shaped-by-the-events-in-tiananmen-square-30-years-ago/2019/06/01 /21119780-7708-11e9-a7bf-c8a43b84ee31_story.html.

18   **as many as one million people**   "1989 Tiananmen Square Protests," Amnesty International, May 31, 2019, https://www.amnesty.org.uk/china-1989-tiananmen -square-protests-demonstration-massacre.

18   **ended the six-week protest with a massacre**   "Timeline: Tiananmen Protests," BBC, June 2, 2014, https://www.bbc.com/news/world-asia-china-27404764.

18   **steadily increasing its domestic security**   "How Has Tiananmen Changed China?" *Washington Post*, June 3, 2019, https://www.washingtonpost.com/politics /2019/06/03/how-has-tiananmen-changed-china/.

19   **a third to almost 100 percent**   "'Changing the Soup but Not the Medicine?' Abolishing Re-Education through Labour in China," Amnesty International, 2013, https://www.amnesty.org/download/Documents/12000/asa170422013en.pdf.

21   **60 percent of all clothing**   "The Price of Fast Fashion," *Nature Climate Change* 8, no. 1 (January 2, 2018), https://www.nature.com/articles/s41558-017-0058-9.

21   **one garbage truck full**   "One Garbage Truck of Textiles Wasted Every Second: Report Creates Vision for Change," Ellen MacArthur Foundation, November 28, 2017, https://www.ellenmacarthurfoundation.org/news/one-garbage-truck-of -textiles-wasted-every-second-report-creates-vision-for-change.

21   **can take decades**   "In the Sea, Not All Plastic Lasts Forever," *New York Times*, October 11, 2019, https://www.nytimes.com/2019/10/11/science/plastics-ocean -degrade.html.

21   **hundreds of years to decompose**   "What Happens to All That Plastic?" Earth Institute, Columbia University, January 31, 2012, https://blogs.ei.columbia.edu /2012/01/31/what-happens-to-all-that-plastic/.

21   **size of one hundred soccer fields**   "China's Largest Dump Fills Up 20 Years Ahead of Schedule," Sixth Tone, November 13, 2019, https://www.sixthtone.com /news/1004838/chinas-largest-dump-fills-up-20-years-ahead-of-schedule.

21   **quarter of a century ahead of schedule**   "A Rubbish Story: China's Mega-Dump Full 25 Years Ahead of Schedule," BBC, November 15, 2019, https://www.bbc.com /news/world-asia-50429119.

21   **Landfills release an enormous amount of emissions**   "Basic Information about Landfill Gas," US Environmental Protection Agency, https://www.epa.gov/lmop /basic-information-about-landfill-gas.

21   **largest producer of greenhouse gases**   "China Is Surprisingly Carbon-Efficient— but Still the World's Biggest Emitter," *Economist*, May 25, 2019, https://www .economist.com/graphic-detail/2019/05/25/china-is-surprisingly-carbon-efficient -but-still-the-worlds-biggest-emitter.

21   **25 percent of those emissions**   Robert Harriss and Bin Shui, "Implications of Offshoring Carbon Emissions for Climate Policy," James A. Baker III Institute for Public Policy, Rice University, September 2010, 10, https://www.bakerinstitute.org /files/615/.

22   **accurate tracking**   "Tracking Greenhouse Gas Emissions—A Move towards Real-Time Emissions Data," Harvard University, https://green.harvard.edu/tools -resources/case-study/tracking-greenhouse-gas-emissions.

22   **S&P 500 index**   "Sustainable Corporations Perform Better Financially, Report Finds," *Guardian*, September 23, 2014, https://www.theguardian.com/sustainable -business/2014/sep/23/business-companies-profit-cdp-report-climate-change -sustainability.

22   **18 percent higher return on investment**   Ibid.

22   **67 percent higher return**   Ibid.

23   **first labor camps opened in the 1930s**   Harry Wu, *Laogai: The Chinese Gulag* (Boulder, CO: Westfield Press, 1992) 54–5.

23   **sentences of up to four years**   *2008 Annual Report*, Congressional-Executive Commission on China, https://www.cecc.gov/publications/annual-reports/2008 -annual-report.

23   **first opened in the late 1950s**   *Laogai Handbook: 2007–2008*, Laogai Research Foundation, 342, https://laogai.org/system/files/u1/handbook2008-all.pdf.

23   **expanded in 1999**   "'Changing the Soup but Not the Medicine?'" Amnesty International.

24   **25 percent of the US manufacturing sector**   "Got Skills? Think Manufacturing," June 2014, Bureau of Labor Statistics, US Department of Labor, https://www.bls .gov/careeroutlook/2014/article/manufacturing.htm.

24   **three to five million people**   "Laogai Museum in D.C. Focuses on Human Rights Abuses in China," *Washington Post*, June 27, 2011, https://www.washingtonpost .com/local/dc-museum-focuses-on-human-rights-in-china/2011/06/15/AGsW wznH_story.html.

24   **1.5 to 3 million people alone**   "U.S. Steps Up Criticism of China for Detentions in Xinjiang," *New York Times*, March 13, 2019, https://www.nytimes.com/2019/03 /13/world/asia/china-muslim-xinjiang.html; "Transcript: Assistant Secretary of Defense for Indo-Pacific Security Affairs Schriver Press Briefing on the 2019 Report on Military and Security Developments in China," US Department of Defense, May 3, 2019, https://www.defense.gov/Newsroom/Transcripts/Transcript /Article/1837011/assistant-secretary-of-defense-for-indo-pacific-security-affairs -schriver-press/.

Chapter Two

28   **Roman Empire**   Walter Scheidel, ed., *The Cambridge Companion to the Roman Economy* (Cambridge: Cambridge University Press, 2012), 89.

28   **West Indies**   "Britain and the Caribbean," BBC, https://www.bbc.co.uk/bitesize /guides/zjyqtfr/revision/3; "Slavery in the Caribbean," National Museums Liverpool, https://www.liverpoolmuseums.org.uk/slavery-caribbean.

28   **slave-produced cotton industry**   "How Slavery Became America's First Big
Business," *Vox*, August 16, 2019, https://www.vox.com/identities/2019/8/16
/20806069/slavery-economy-capitalism-violence-cotton-edward-baptist.

28   **"most important raw material"**   Edward E. Baptist, *The Half Has Never Been
Told: Slavery and the Making of American Capitalism* (New York: Basic Books,
2016), 113.

28   **Great Wall**   "A Chinese Plea: Bring Back the Great Wall," *New York Times*,
July 24, 1984, https://www.nytimes.com/1984/07/24/world/a-chinese-plea-bring
-back-the-great-wall.html.

28   **Grand Canal**   Scott Tong , *A Village with My Name: A Family History of China's
Opening to the World* (Chicago: University of Chicago Press, 2017), 128.

28   **system of national roads**   *To Abolish Forced Labor through ILO, Hearings before
the Subcommittee on Labor of the Committee on Labor and Public Welfare*, US
Senate, 84th Congress, second session, on S.J. Res. 117 (April 25 and 27, 1956), 272.

28   **first half of the Ming dynasty**   James W. Tong, *Disorder under Heaven: Collective
Violence in the Ming Dynasty* (Stanford, CA, Stanford University Press, 1992), 142.

28   **final imperial dynasty collapsed**   "Is China Ripe for a Revolution?" opinion
piece, *New York Times*, February 9, 2012, https://www.nytimes.com/2012/02/12
/opinion/sunday/is-china-ripe-for-a-revolution.html.

28   **regional warlords fought**   Hsi-Sheng Ch'I, *Warlord Politics in China: 1916–1928*
(Stanford: Stanford University Press, 1976), 1–4.

29   **political party in the early 1920s**   Donald Treadgold, *The West in Russia
and China: Religious and Secular Thought in Modern Times. Volume 2, China
1582–1949* (Cambridge: Cambridge University Press, 1973), 148.

29   **military alliance**   "Mao Zedong (1893–1976)," BBC, https://www.bbc.co.uk
/history/historic_figures/mao_zedong.shtml.

29   **betrayed the Communists** Ibid.

29   **purging . . . and killing thousands**   "In Taiwan, the Towering Chiang Image Is
Losing Its Luster," *New York Times*, May 20, 1988, https://www.nytimes.com
/1988/05/20/world/in-taiwan-the-towering-chiang-image-is-losing-its-luster.html.

29   **Chiang Kai-shek reunified**   "Before the East Was Red," *New York Times*,
February 29, 2004, https://www.nytimes.com/2004/02/29/books/before-the-east
-was-red.html.

29   **civil war against the Nationalists**   "The Long March: For Communist China,
It Is the Central Epic," *New York Times*, February 22, 1972, https://www.nytimes
.com/1972/02/22/archives/the-long-march-for-communist-china-it-is-the-central
-epic.html.

29   **military bases in rural regions**   Wu, *Laogai*, 54.

29   **goods for the CCP's military**   Ibid., 55.

29   **Japan invaded China in 1937**   "Introduction to China's Modern History,"
Asia for Educators, Weatherland East Asian Institute, Columbia University,
http://afe.easia.columbia.edu/timelines/china_modern_timeline.htm.

29   **stabilize and recruit new members**   "The CCP Didn't Fight Imperial Japan;
the KMT Did," *Diplomat*, September 4, 2014, https://thediplomat.com/2014/09
/the-ccp-didnt-fight-imperial-japan-the-kmt-did/.

29   **Japanese surrendered in 1945**   "Introduction to China's Modern History," Asia for Educators.

29   **civil war . . . resumed**   Ibid.

29   **Communist Party was much larger**   "The Chinese Revolution of 1949," Office of the Historian, US Department of State, https://history.state.gov/milestones /1945-1952/chinese-rev.

29   **Nationalists suffered a military defeat**   Ibid.

29   **retreat to the island of Taiwan**   Ibid.

30   **wool and textile plants**   Wu, *Laogai*, 58.

30   **Liu Shaoqi**   Third National Public Security Meeting, May 11, 1951, Laogai Museum, Washington, DC, https://www.laogai.org/sites/default/files/pdf /DigitizedArchives.pdf.

30   **over six hundred laogai farms**   Wu, *Laogai*, 60.

30   **Hundred Flowers Campaign**   Weijian Shan, *Out of the Gobi: My Story of China and America* (Hoboken, NJ: Wiley, 2019), 35–36.

30   **millions of disapproving letters**   "The Silence that Preceded China's Great Leap into Famine," *Smithsonian*, September 26, 2012, https://www.smithsonianmag .com/history/the-silence-that-preceded-chinas-great-leap-into-famine-51898077/.

31   **Anti-Rightist Campaign**   Ibid.

31   **sent hundreds and thousands of intellectuals**   Ibid.

31   **Ai Qing**   Ibid.

31   *hashar*   "Discrimination, Mistreatment and Coercion: Severe Labor Rights Abuses Faced by Uyghurs in China and East Turkestan," Uyghur Human Rights Project, April 5, 2017, https://uhrp.org/docs/Discrimination_Mistreatment _Coercion.pdf.

31   **began in preindustrial China**   Frederick de Jong, *Uyghur Texts in Context: Life in Shinjang Documented from Public Spaces* (Boston: Brill, 2017), 83.

31   **eighteen and sixty-five**   "Forced Labour in East Turkestan: State-Sanctioned Hashar System," World Uyghur Congress, November 2016, https://www.uyghur congress.org/en/wp-content/uploads/2016/11/Forced_Labour_in_East_Turkestan -WUC.pdf.

31   **weeks at a time**   Ibid.

31   **pay a fine**   Ibid.

31   **Nikita Khrushchev . . . began dismantling**   Anne Applebaum, *Gulag: A History* (New York: Anchor Books, 2004), xvii.

31   **successors built more laogai camps**   Wu, *Laogai*, 61.

32   **formal diplomatic relations**   "China Policy," Office of the Historian, US Department of State, https://history.state.gov/milestones/1977-1980/china-policy.

32   **United States initially refused to acknowledge it**   Ibid.

32   **Nationalist government in Taiwan**   Ibid.

32   **President Jimmy Carter**   Ibid.

32   **US trade with mainland China**   "Foreign Relations of the United States 1951, Korea and China, Volume VII, Part 2," Office of the Historian, US Department of State, https://history.state.gov/historicaldocuments/frus1951v07p2/d280.

32   **giving North Korea military assistance**   "Q&A: China-North Korea Relationship," *New York Times*, July 13, 2006, https://archive.nytimes.com /www.nytimes.com/cfr/world/slot2_071306.html.

32   **China's second-largest importer**   Philip Wik, *How to Do Business with the People's Republic of China* (New York: Simon & Schuster, 1983), 57.

32   **1.7 billion yuan**   Wu, *Laogai*, 61.

32   **Peng Daiming**   "Chinese Labor Camp Inmate Tells of True Horror of Halloween 'SOS,'" CNN, November 7, 2013, http://www.cnn.com/2013/11/06/world/asia /china-labor-camp-halloween-sos/index.html; "Walking Out of Masanjia," Human Rights in China, April 7, 2013, https://www.hrichina.org/en/content/6631

32   **new waves of laboring dissidents**   Wu, *Laogai*, 61.

33   **highest number of journalists behind bars**   "China: RSF Demands the Release of Uyghur Citizen Journalist, 2019 Václav Havel Prize Laureate," Reporters without Borders, October 1, 2019, https://rsf.org/en/news/china-rsf-demands-release -uyghur-citizen-journalist-2019-vaclav-havel-prize-laureate.

33   **cofounded in 1992**   "Harry Wu, Who Told World of Abuses in China, Dies at 79," *New York Times*, April 27, 2016, https://www.nytimes.com/2016/04/28/world /asia/harry-wu-who-told-world-of-abuses-in-china-dies-at-79.html.

33   **survived nineteen years**   Ibid.

33   **posing as prospective buyers of laogai products**   "Harry Wu's Legacy," opinion piece, *Wall Street Journal*, April 28, 2016, https://www.wsj.com/articles/harry -wus-legacy-1461885877.

33   **tracked their online advertisements**   "Not for Sale: Advertising Forced Labor Products for Illegal Export," Laogai Research Foundation, February 2010, https://www.laogai.org/reports/not-sale-advertising-forced-labor-products-illegal -export.

33   **identified more than fourteen hundred operating camps**   *Laogai Handbook*, 3.

34   **expected to be 2.76 billion by 2022**   "Inside China Tech: How Facial Recognition Technology Facilitates China's Surveillance," *South China Morning Post*, May 17, 2019, https://www.scmp.com/podcasts/article/3010673/inside-china-tech-how -facial-recognition-technology-facilitates-chinas

35   **three hundred thousand juveniles**   *Forced Labor in China, Roundtable before the Congressional-Executive Commission on China*, 109th Congress, first session, June 22, 2005, https://www.govinfo.gov/content/pkg/CHRG-109hhrg22613/html /CHRG-109hhrg22613.htm.

35   **radio parts, toys, and electronic components**   *Laogai Handbook*, 411.

36   **Bordering Afghanistan and Pakistan**   "For Them, Afghanistan Is Safer Than China," *Foreign Policy*, November 1, 2018, https://foreignpolicy.com/2018/11/01 /for-them-afghanistan-is-safer-than-china/.

36   **Uyghurs, followed by Kazakhs**   "China's Expanding War on Islam: Now They're Coming for the Kazakhs," *Washington Post*, March 1, 2019, https://www.washingtonpost.com/outlook/chinas-expanding-war-on-islam -now-theyre-coming-for-the-kazakhs/2019/03/01/16ebbe76-38ff-11e9-a2cd- 307b06d0257b_story.html.

36   **"the only area"**   "China: Uighur Ethnic Identity under Threat in China," Amnesty International UK, July 6, 2009, https://www.amnesty.org.uk/press -releases/china-uighur-ethnic-identity-under-threat-china.

36   **system's persistence**   "Authorities in Xinjiang Use Pledge System to Exert Control over Village Life," Congressional-Executive Commission on China, December 10, 2010, https://www.cecc.gov/publications/commission-analysis /authorities-in-xinjiang-use-pledge-system-to-exert-control-over.

36   **second-class citizens**   "China's Repression of Uighurs in Xinjiang," Council on Foreign Relations, November 25, 2019, https://www.cfr.org/backgrounder/chinas -repression-uighurs-xinjiang.

36   **unprecedented high-tech police state**   ""Eradicating Ideological Viruses": China's Campaign of Repression Against Xinjiang's Muslims," Human Rights Watch, September 9, 2018, https://www.hrw.org/report/2018/09/09/eradicating -ideological-viruses/chinas-campaign-repression-against-xinjiangs.

36   **from 30.05 billion yuan to 57.95 billion yuan**   Adrian Zenz, "China's Domestic Security Spending: An Analysis of Available Data," *China Brief* 18, no. 4 (March 12, 2018), https://jamestown.org/program/chinas-domestic-security -spending-analysis-available-data/.

36   **1,000 percent higher**   Ibid.

37   **three million central Asian Muslims**   "2019 Report on Military and Security Developments in China," US Department of Defense.

37   **Turkic population . . . twelve million**   "Securitization and Mass Detentions in Xinjiang: How Uyghurs Became Quarantined from the Outside World," Quartz, September 4, 2018, https://qz.com/1377394/securitization-and-mass-detentions -in-xinjiang-how-uyghurs-became-quarantined-from-the-outside-world/. Some sources state ten million, but that is inaccurate. There are ten million Uyghurs in Xinjiang. Although Uyghurs are the majority ethnic population there, Uyghurs are not the only Turkic group that is targeted for reeducation camps.

37   **In October 2018, a state-run news channel**   "Worker Rights Consortium Factory Assessment, Hetian Taida Apparel Co., LTD. (China), Findings, Recommendations, and Status," Worker Rights Consortium, June 24, 2019, https://www.workersrights.org/wp-content/uploads/2019/06/WRC-Report-on -Hetian-Taida-China-June-2019.pdf; original CCTV article and video of camp's vocational training: http://tv.cctv.com/2018/10/16/VIDEVvr9aq34SsDMrB6I RGnh181016.shtml.

37   **broke the story that Badger Sportswear**   "US Sportswear Traced to Factory in China's Internment Camps," Associated Press, December 19, 2018, https://apnews.com/99016849cddb4b99a048b863b52c28cb.

37   **"We're making our contribution to eradicating poverty"**   Ibid.

37   **more than thirty facilities**   Ibid.

37   **After the exposé, Badger**   "Sourcing Update," Founder Sport Group, https://www.foundersport.com/service/sourcing-update/; *Staff Research Report*, Congressional-Executive Commission on China, March 2020, https://www.cecc.gov/sites/chinacommission.house.gov/files/documents /CECC%20Staff%20Report%20March%202020%20-%20Global%20Supply%20 Chains%2C%20Forced%20Labor%2C%20and%20the%20Xinjiang%20Uyghur%20 Autonomous%20Region.pdf.

37   **disposable chopsticks**   *Prison Labor Exports*, US-China Commission.

37   **children's toys**   *Forced Labor in China*, CECC, June 22, 2005.

38   **journalist Yuan Yang**   "Supply Chains: The Dirty Secret of China's Prisons," *Financial Times*, August 29, 2018, https://www.ft.com/content/1416a056-833b -11e7-94e2-c5b903247afd.

38   **19 factories in Shanghai**   "Our Supplier Factory List," H&M, https://sustainability .hm.com/en/sustainability/downloads-resources/resources/supplier-list.html#.

38   **American Girl boxes**   Picture of Red American Girl packaging on Meizhou government website, November 7, 2016, https://www.meizhou.gov.cn/intensivism /jds/gzdt/t20161107_1946.htm; https://www.meipian.cn/9oyq8t2.

39   **"The issue is not the size of the system"**   Author interview with Jeffrey Fiedler, commissioner with the US-China Economic and Security Review Commission and cofounder of Laogai Research Foundation, March 2019.

Chapter Three

41   **communes, left over from one of Mao's**   "China's Communes Shock Some Reds," *New York Times*, October 21, 1958, http://movies2.nytimes.com/library/world/asia /102158communes-shock.html.

43   **imperial capital**   "China's Ancient Capital Rises Again," BBC, December 8, 2013, http://www.bbc.com/travel/story/20131025-chinas-ancient-capital-rises-again.

43   **three thousand inscribed stone slabs**   "Forest of Stone Steles Museum," Beijing Tours Guide, http://www.beijingtoursguide.com/attractions/forest-of-stone-steles -museum.html.

43   **handwriting of Emperor Kangxi**   Details of the Confucian temple are drawn from "Stele Forest—Beilin Museum," Travel China Guide, June 24, 2019, https://www.travelchinaguide.com/attraction/shaanxi/xian/stone_stele/.

44   **assigned quotas for majors**   "Education in China: A Snapshot," Organisation for Economic Co-Operation and Development, 2016, https://www.oecd.org/china /Education-in-China-a-snapshot.pdf.

46   **defense industrial base**   "Chongqing Turns Its Dilapidated Factories, Arsenals into Fashion and Arts Centers," *Global Times*, November 7, 2017, http://www .globaltimes.cn/content/1073984.shtml; Joshua H. Howard, *Workers at War: Labor in China's Arsenals, 1937–1953* (Stanford: Stanford University Press, 2004), 131.

46   **ammunition plants and arsenals**   Ibid.

49   **her hometown, Baoji**   "Wei River and Chinese Earliest Civilization," FollowCN, March 12, 2017, https://history.followcn.com/2017/03/12/wei-river-chinese -earliest-civilization/.

50   *hukou*   "China's Middle Class Chafes against Maze of Red Tape," *New York Times*, March 13, 2015, https://www.nytimes.com/2015/03/14/world/asia/chinas -growing-middle-class-chafes-against-red-tape.html.

52   **"To get rich is glorious"**   "Horatio Alger Multiplied by 1.3 Billion," *New York Times*, April 26, 2008, https://www.nytimes.com/2008/04/26/business/26nocera.html.

52   **China's so-called "economic miracle"**   "China Anniversary: How the Country Became the World's 'Economic Miracle,'" BBC, October 1, 2019, https://www.bbc .com/news/business-49806247.

52   **around three hundred demonstrations**   Ownby, *Falun Gong,* 169.

52   **Ministry of Public Security conducted two studies**   Ibid., 168.

Chapter Four

54   **"Everything can be taken from a man"**   Viktor E. Frankl, *Man's Search for Meaning* (New York: Pocket Books, 1985), 86.

54   **people began assembling at seven**   Ownby, *Falun Gong*, 172 (see chap. 1 notes).

54   **Throughout the next sixteen hours**   Ibid., 171.

54   **fifteen-hundred-acre rectangular compound**   "Zhongnanhai—the Political Center of China," Travel China Guide, July 18, 2019, https://www.travelchinaguide.com/attraction/beijing/zhongnanhai.htm.

54   **gunned down in one night**   "Tiananmen Square Protest Death Toll 'Was 10,000,'" BBC, December 23, 2017, https://www.bbc.com/news/world-asia-china-42465516.

54   **elderly folks in tennis shoes**   Ownby, *Falun Gong*, 3.

54   **yuppies in suits** Details of the protestors and the surrounding environment are drawn from photographs at "Peaceful Protest of April 25, 1999," Minghui, http://en.minghui.org/cc/86/.

55   **arrests of practitioners in Tianjin**   Ownby, *Falun Gong*, 171 (see chap. 1 notes); He Zuoxiu, "I Do Not Approve of Teenagers Practicing *Qigong*," *Chinese Law and Government* 32, no. 5 (1999), https://doi.org/10.2753/CLG0009-4609320595.

55   **city seventy-five miles away**   "The Chinese Professor Who Started a Ruckus," *New York Times*, February 5, 2001, https://www.nytimes.com/2001/02/05/world/the-chinese-professor-who-started-a-ruckus.html.

55   **theoretical physicist named He Zuoxiu**   Ownby, *Falun Gong*, 171 (see chap. 1 notes).

55   **student to develop schizophrenia**   "An Interview with He Zuoxiu: How He Exposes and Fights against Falun Gong," Facts.org.cn, http://www.facts.org.cn/Views/200801/02/t20080102_775326.htm.

55   **brother-in-law of one of the top . . . officials**   "An Occurrence on Fuyou Street," *National Review*, July 2, 2009, https://www.nationalreview.com/magazine/2009/07/20/occurrence-fuyou-street/.

55   **six thousand Falun Gong adherents**   Ownby, *Falun Gong*, 171 (see chap. 1 notes).

55   **arresting forty-five practitioners**   Ibid.

56   **resting after breakfast**   James W. Tong, *Revenge of the Forbidden City: The Suppression of the Falungong in China, 1999–2005* (Oxford: Oxford University Press, 2009), 3.

56   **must have been shocked**   Ibid., 5.

56   **Premier Zhu Rongji**   Ownby, *Falun Gong*, 172.

56   **met with the deputy director**   Tong, *Revenge*, 5.

56   **dialogue carried on for six hours**   Ibid.

56   **"We demand the release"**   Ibid. Since the original dialogue was in Chinese, I edited the English slightly for readability.

56   **outside the compound until eleven o'clock**   Ownby, *Falun Gong*, 172.

56   **avoid inundating public restrooms**   Ibid., 171.

56   **leaving the street litter-free**   Tong, *Revenge*, 6.

57   **agency called the 610 Office**   Ownby, *Falun Gong*, 175.

57   **Arrests began two days before**   Ibid.

57   **organizers in twenty-two cities**   Tong, *Revenge*, 27.

57   **labor camps across China expanded**   *Forced Labor in China*, CECC, June 22, 2005.

57   **Pulitzer Prize–winning journalist Ian Johnson**   "Practicing Falun Gong Was a Right, Ms. Chen Said, up to Her Last Day," *Wall Street Journal*, April 20, 2000, https://www.wsj.com/articles/SB956186343489597132.

58   **software called Freegate**   "Freegate Opens a Door to Asia," Voice of America, https://projects.voanews.com/circumvention/freegate; "FreeGate," Global Internet Freedom Consortium, http://www.internetfreedom.org/FreeGate.html.

58   **North Korea**   "Freegate 7.73," TechSpot, https://www.techspot.com/downloads /6243-freegate.html.

58   **Syria**   "Syria's Internet Hijack," Voice of America, May 12, 2011, https://blogs .voanews.com/digital-frontiers/2011/05/12/syrias-internet-hijack/.

58   **Vietnam**   "Freegate Opens a Door to Asia," Voice of America, https://projects .voanews.com/circumvention/freegate.

58   **Falun Gong's proxy service**   "Social Networks Spread Defiance Online," *New York Times*, June 15, 2009, https://www.nytimes.com/2009/06/16/world /middleeast/16media.html; "Tear Down This Cyberwall!" *New York Times*.

58   **woman and her twelve-year-old daughter**   "Girl Who Immolated Herself in Beijing Dies," *New York Times*, March 19, 2001, https://www.nytimes.com /2001/03/19/world/girl-who-immolated-herself-in-beijing-dies.html.

58   **exotic dancer at a nightclub**   "Human Fire Ignites Chinese Mystery," *Washington Post*, February 4, 2001, https://www.washingtonpost.com/archive/politics /2001/02/04/human-fire-ignites-chinese-mystery/e27303e3-6117-4ec3-b6cf -58f03cdb4773/.

59   **underground initiative called Tuidang**   "Communism, China and Tuidang, the 'Quit the Party' Movement," Tuidang, May 6, 2018, https://en.tuidang.org /news/tuidang-news/2018/05/communism-china-and-tuidang-the-quit-the-party -movement.html.

59   **renunciations . . . from three hundred million**   "300 Million Withdrawals from Chinese Communist Party: Historic Milestone Marked in Ottawa," *Epoch Times*, May 7, 2018, https://www.theepochtimes.com/300-million -withdrawals-from-chinese-communist-party-historic-milestone-marked-in- ottawa_2516319.html.

60   **cumbersome the yearlong application**   "The Long, Arduous Process to Joining China's Communist Party," *South China Morning Post*, July 1, 2016, https://www.scmp.com/news/china/policies-politics/article/1984044/long -arduous-process-joining-chinas-communist-party.

60   **China Anti-Cult Association**   Stephen Noakes and Caylan Ford, "Managing Political Opposition Groups in China: Explaining the Continuing Anti-Falun Gong Campaign," *China Quarterly* (Cambridge: Cambridge University Press, July 23, 2015), 675, https://doi.org/10.1017/S030574101500078.

61   **Sixteenth National Congress**   Accounts of detainees.

61   **police did not need arrest warrants**   Wu, *Laogai*, 64.

62   **business name was Chini Stone Quarry**   *Laogai Handbook*, 111.

62   **"The state paid the labor camp"**   *Above the Ghosts' Heads: The Women of Masanjia Labor Camp*, Chinese Human Rights Defenders, 2013 https://www .youtube.com/watch?v=VhoVrg3lvGA; "Petitioners Reveal Brutalities in Masanjia Forced Labor Camp," *Epoch Times*, June 26, 2010, https://www.theepochtimes .com/petitioners-reveal-brutalities-in-masanjia-forced-labor-camp_1511671.html.

64   **interrupted all eight channels**   Yuezhi Zhao, "Falun Gong, Identity, and the Struggle over Meaning Inside and Outside China," *Contesting Media Power: Alternative Media in a Networked World*, eds. Nick Couldry and James Curran (New York: Rowman & Littlefield, 2003), 209, https://www.sfu.ca/cmns/faculty /zhao_y/assets/14_03-168_Ch13.pdf; "Falun Gong 'Hijacks' Chinese Airwaves," CNN, March 7, 2002, http://www.cnn.com/2002/WORLD/asiapcf/east/03/07 /china.fgong/index.html.

64   **three hundred thousand households**   Zhao, "Falun Gong," 209.

64   **tortured to death**   "Into Thin Airwaves," Ethan Gutmann, *Weekly Standard*, December 6, 2010, https://www.weeklystandard.com/ethan-gutmann/into-thin -airwaves.

64   **Christmas lights and Homer Simpson slippers**   "Tuesdays with Jay: Prisoner of the PRC," *National Review*, December 11, 2007, https://www.nationalreview .com/2007/12/tuesdays-jay-prisoner-prc-jay-nordlinger/.

66   **underground printing houses**   Caylan Ford, *Tradition and Dissent in China: The Tuidang Movement and Its Challenge to the Communist Party* (Ann Arbor, MI: ProQuest, 2012), 51.

67   **800 yuan (about $120) per prisoner**   This is according to accounts from Masanjia survivors.

Chapter Five

68   **remote verdant grassland**   Descriptions of what Masanjia looked like from the outside are drawn from photos that Sun Yi sent me, as well as from "True Horror of Halloween 'SOS,'" CNN.

68   **eleven hundred acres**   "Background Information on Masanjia Labor Camp," Minghui, June 1, 2001, http://en.minghui.org/html/articles/2001/6/1/zip.html.

68   **orchards and fields**   *Laogai Handbook*, 342.

68   **Masanjia Xinsheng Farm**   Ibid.

72   **Dun & Bradstreet**   Ibid., 2.

73   **Fortune 500 companies**   Dun & Bradstreet, https://www.dnb.com/about-us.html.

73   **Dow Chemical**   "Probing Dow's *Laogai* Links," *Multinational Monitor*, October 1995, https://www.multinationalmonitor.org/hyper/issues/1995/10/mm1095_08.html.

73   **"didn't think anybody read Chinese"**   Author interview with Jeffrey Fiedler.

73   **scented soaps**   *Laogai Handbook*, 334.

73   **waterproof paint and insulated pipes**   Ibid., 332.

73   **Prison Administration Bureau**   Nicole Kempton and Nan Richardson, eds., *Laogai: The Machinery of Repression in China* (New York: Umbrage Editions, 2009), 68; "Minister of Justice Discusses Prison Reform: Prisons Say Goodbye to Profits," South CN, December 5, 2003, December 5, 2003, http://news.southcn.com /community/shzt/prison/outline/200405101067.htm.

73   **cutting taxes for prisons**   Kempton and Richardson, *Laogai*, 68; "Notice Issued by Ministry of Finance and National Revenue Board Regarding Value-Added Tax Collection Policy" for prison enterprises and laojiao (reeducation through labor), effective as of April 20, 1998 (translation of the original document can be found in *Laogai Handbook*, 552).

73   **began offering subsidies**   Kempton and Richardson, *Laogai*, 68.

74   **saved by extensive funding**   "Masanjia Labor Camp," Chinascope, http://china scope.org/archives/6443; "Shenyang Great North Prison Relocates to New Place," Xinhua, October 28, 2003, https://chinatribunal.com/wp-content/uploads/2019/08 /MagnitskySubmission_OfficialsSurgeons_Final.pdf; "Shenyang Builds the First Green Prison Town of the Country," *China News*, July 2003, http://www.china.com .cn/chinese/2003/Jul/357977.htm; "Advance toward Modern Prisons—A Report on the Prison Overhaul in Liaoning Province," South CN, November 27, 2002, https://chinatribunal.com/wp-content/uploads/2019/08/MagnitskySubmission _OfficialsSurgeons_Final.pdf.

74   **down clothing for children**   "Down Coats Made by Slave Labor in Masanjia Forced Labor Camp," Minghui, January 21, 2013, http://en.minghui.org/html /articles/2013/1/21/137196.html.

74   **cooling filters, oil pumps**   *Laogai Handbook*, 342.

74   **lungs ached from inhaling feather**   Descriptions of forced down-coat manufacturing are drawn from accounts from survivors published on Minghui, including "Down Coats Made by Slave Labor in Masanjia Forced Labor Camp," January 21, 2013, http://en.minghui.org/html/articles/2013/1/21/137196.html.

74   **one hundred to two hundred down coats**   Ibid.

74   **Masanjia earned hundreds of dollars a day**   From accounts of former prisoners.

77   **Beijing residents lost their homes**   Hyun Bang Shin and Bingqin Li, "Whose Games? The Costs of Being 'Olympic Citizens' in Beijing," *Environment and Urbanization* 25, no. 2 (September 11, 2013), https://doi.org/10.1177/0956247813501139.

Chapter Six

82   **China director of Human Rights Watch**   "Haunting Message," *Oregonian*.

82   **Sears Holdings . . . statement**   Emailed to author by a Sears Holdings media representative.

82   **three thousand audits**   "California Transparency Act," Sears, https://www.sears .com/en_us/customer-service/policies/california-transparencyact.html.

82   **killed more than one thousand workers**   "Bangladeshi Garment Maker Shuts 3 Factories," *Wall Street Journal*, May 9, 2013, https://www.wsj.com/articles /SB10001424127887324059704578472221438165096.

82   **two of the factories in that complex**   "Collapsed Factory Was Built without Permit," *Wall Street Journal*, April 25, 2013, https://www.wsj.com/articles/SB10001 4241278873237897045784444280661545310.

82   **means a cursory inspection**   "Fast and Flawed Inspections of Factories Abroad," *New York Times*, September 1, 2013, https://www.nytimes.com/2013/09/02 /business/global/superficial-visits-and-trickery-undermine-foreign-factory -inspections.html.

82   **might check the cleanliness of a factory**   "5 Different Types of Audits to Evaluate Your Supplier," InTouch, July 23, 2019, https://www.intouch-quality.com/blog/the -3-most-common-types-of-factory-audits.

83   **social compliance audit**   Ibid.

83   **costs $1,000 or more**   "Fast and Flawed," *New York Times*.

83   **"I personally could not prove"**   Author interview with social compliance auditor.

83   **more extensive five-day audit**   "Fast and Flawed," *New York Times*.

83   **cross-analyze wage documents**   I have interviewed auditors who described this process and scenario.

83   **one hundred thousand suppliers at the first level**   "Supply Chain Audits Work for Corporations, but Not the Planet, Says New Report," *Forbes*, January 16, 2017, https://www.forbes.com/sites/jwebb/2017/01/16/supply-chain-audits-work-for -corporations-but-not-the-planet-says-new-report/.

84   **"A brand says, 'We want to know'"**   Author interview with auditor in China.

84   **payroll records for "at least one year"**   "Sears Holdings Global Compliance Program, Guidebook to Program Requirements," April 2018, https://searsholdings .com/docs/corporate-responsibility/Global_Compliance_Program_Guidebook _0518_v3.pdf.

84   **Sears Holdings filed for bankruptcy**   "Sears Gets $4.4 Billion Bid to Buy Company Out of Bankruptcy from Lampert," *USA Today*, December 28, 2018, https://www.usatoday.com/story/money/2018/12/28/sears-bankruptcy-filing -deadline-buy-retailer-today/2426912002/.

84   **in February 2019 a new corporation**   "Privacy Policy," Transformco, https://transformco.com/privacy.

84   **Transform Holdco still requires**   "Guidebook for Program Requirements," Global Compliance Program, Transform SR Holding Management LLC, October 2019, https://transformco.com/docs/corporate-responsibility/Global_Compliance _Program_Guidebook.pdf.

85   **Nike's reliance on child workers**   "Nike Chronology," Center for Communication & Civic Engagement, University of Washington, https://depts.washington.edu/ccce /polcommcampaigns/NikeChronology.htm.

85   **Nike initially denied responsibility**   "Sarah Soule: How Activism Can Fuel Corporate Social Responsibility," Stanford Graduate School of Business, October 10, 2014, https://www.gsb.stanford.edu/insights/sarah-soule-how -activism-can-fuel-corporate-social-responsibility.

85   **more than forty universities**   Ibid.

85   **audit of one of its Vietnam factories**   Charles Hill and Gareth Jones, *Strategic Management Theory: An Integrated Approach,* 9th ed. (Boston: Cenage Learning, 2009), 366.

85   **77 percent . . . suffered from respiratory ailments**   Ibid.

85   **surpassed the local legal limit by 177 percent**   Ibid.

85   **consumers . . . stopped buying Nike products**   "Sarah Soule," Stanford Graduate School of Business; "How Activism Forced Nike to Change Its Ethical Game," *Guardian*, July 6, 2012, https://www.theguardian.com/environment/green-living -blog/2012/jul/06/activism-nike.

85   **shared many of the reports with the public**   "Nike, Inc.," Fair Labor Association, https://www.fairlabor.org/affiliate/nike-inc?page=3.

86   **Gap, Reebok, and Timberland**   Alexandra Harney, *The China Price: The True Cost of Chinese Competitive Advantage* (New York: Penguin Books, 2008), 195.

86   **"monitoring does not bring about sustainable change"**   "Ethical Audits and the Supply Chains of Global Corporations," SPERI Global Political Economy Brief No. 1, University of Sheffield, January 2016, http://un-act.org/wp-content/uploads/2016/04/Ethical_Audits_and_Supply_Chains.pdf.

86   **can create fictitious production data**   Harney, *China Price*, 202.

86   **"irregular attendance records"**   "A Look at How Some Chinese Factories Lie to Pass Audits," China Labor Watch, April 30, 2012, http://www.chinalaborwatch.org/newscast/168.

86   **"They get trained by auditing firms"**   Author interview with auditor in China.

86   **Rushan Alice Garments Company**   "The Failure of Target's Audit System in Its Chinese Supplier Factories," China Labor Watch, September 28, 2011, http://www.chinalaborwatch.org/report/54.

87   **mixing outsourced products**   Ibid.

87   **China Labor Watch's undercover workers**   "Hua Haifeng's Wife: My Husband Is Arrested for Investigating Ivanka Trump's Supplier Factory, and I Become the Main Monitored Subject," China Labor Watch, June 15, 2017, http://www.chinalaborwatch.org/newscast/624.

87   **travel restrictions and police surveillance**   "Men Who Investigated Ivanka Trump's China Suppliers Off Bail," Associated Press, June 26, 2018, https://apnews.com/49172bf85c8a484599b8aa5b98fdc3df/Men-who-investigated-Ivanka-Trump-China-suppliers-off-bail.

87   **the world's largest manufacturer**   "Still Made in China: Chinese Manufacturing Remains Second to None," *Economist*, September 10, 2015, https://www.economist.com/special-report/2015/09/10/still-made-in-china.

87   **Factories with paper-thin margins**   Harney, *China Price*, 40.

87   **factory owner using the alias Glory**   "How Some Chinese Factories Lie," China Labor Watch.

88   **Since the early 2000s, fast-fashion**   "Why Fast Fashion Is Slow Death for the Planet," *Guardian*, May 7, 2011, https://www.theguardian.com/lifeandstyle/2011/may/08/fast-fashion-death-for-planet; Elizabeth L. Cline, *Overdressed: The Shockingly High Cost of Cheap Fashion* (New York: Portfolio, 2012) 95–6; "Polka Dots Are In? Polka Dots It Is!" *Slate*, June 21, 2012, https://slate.com/culture/2012/06/zaras-fast-fashion-how-the-company-gets-new-styles-to-stores-so-quickly.html.

88   **one hundred new items every day**   "Become an Affiliate," Boohoo, https://us.boohoo.com/page/affiliate.html.

88   **a thousand new styles every week**   "Fashion Nova's Secret: Underpaid Workers in Los Angeles Factories," *New York Times*, December 16, 2019, https://www.nytimes.com/2019/12/16/business/fashion-nova-underpaid-workers.html.

88   **"came to mind Sunday night"**   Ibid.

88   **"They want new and they want it now"**   *Fashion Retail: New Measures of Success*, WSGN, https://lp.wgsn.com/rs/948-BWZ-312/images/fashion-retail-new-measures -of-success-by-wgsn-analytics.pdf; "The Biggest Difference between Zara and H&M Explains Why One Is Thriving While the Other Is Flailing," *Business Insider*, June 21, 2018, https://www.businessinsider.fr/us/zara-is-beating-hm-in-fast-fashion-2018-6.

88   **logistics management company**   "7 Characteristics of a Best in Class Supply Chain," Cerasis, https://cerasis.com/best-in-class-supply-chain/.

89   **by air, at much higher costs**   "Hidden Subcontracting," SOMO.

89   **give the brand a 5 percent discount**   "Why Retailers Don't Know Who Sews Their Clothing: Poorly Regulated Subcontractors Are a Factor in Garment Trade's Deadly Accidents," *Wall Street Journal*, July 24, 2013, https://www.wsj.com/articles /why-retailers-donapost-know-who-sews-their-clothing-1390822042.

89   **if there is "reasonable" evidence**   "Forced Labor," US Customs and Border Protection, https://www.cbp.gov/trade/programs-administration/forced-labor.

89   **up to ninety days**   Author phone conversation with CBP official.

89   **eyewitness accounts**   "Not for Sale," Laogai Research Foundation.

90   **three special agents in Hong Kong**   *U.S. Exposure to Forced Labor Exports from China*, US-China Economic and Security Review Commission, August 8, 2017, https://www.uscc.gov/sites/default/files/Research/Forced%20Labor%20Report.pdf.

90   **five in mainland China**   Ibid.

90   **stretched too thin**   Testimony of James Ink of ICE, *Memoranda of Understanding between the U.S. and China Regarding Prison Labor, Hearing before the US-China Economic and Security Review Commission*, June 19, 2008, 39. http://www.uscc.gov /sites/default/files/transcripts/6.19.08HearingTranscript.pdf.

90   **twenty-six active detention orders**   "Withhold Release Orders and Findings," US Customs and Border Protection, accessed July 2020, https://www.cbp.gov/trade /trade-community/programs-outreach/convict-importations/detention-orders; Kempton and Richardson, *Laogai*, 82.

90   **US Tariff Act of 1930**   "Forced Labor," CBP.

90   **struggles during the Great Depression**   "Congress Bans Import of Forced Labor Products," *Chicago Tribune*, February 12, 2016, https://www.chicagotribune.com /news/nationworld/ct-congress-bans-forced-labor-products-20160212-story.html.

90   **loophole was closed in 2016**   "Forced Labor," CBP.

90   **"a defense that importers could raise"** Author interview with US Customs and Border Protection official.

90   **Transparency in Supply Chains Act**   "The California Transparency in Supply Chains Act: A Resource Guide," California Department of Justice, 2015, https://oag.ca.gov/sites/all/files/agweb/pdfs/sb657/resource-guide.pdf.

91   **nonbinding legislation**   Ibid.: for examples of a binding agreement, see "The Accord on Fire and Building Safety in Bangladesh," Business & Human Rights Resource Centre, https://www.business-humanrights.org/en/the -accord-on-fire-and-building-safety-in-bangladesh, and Fair Food Program, http://www.fairfoodprogram.org/.

91   **"terminate a supplier"**   "California Transparency Act," Sears, https://www .sears.com/en_us/customer-service/policies/california-transparencyact.html; "California Transparency Act," Transformco, https://transformco.com/site /california-transparency-act.

Chapter Seven

92   **surpassing half a million views**   "Plea for Help from Labor Camp Gets International Attention," *Oregonian,* December 28, 2012, https://www.oregonlive.com/happy-valley/2012/12/plea_for_help_from_labor_camp.html.

92   **seven hundred comments**   Ibid.

92   **"It shouldn't take a letter tucked"**   zluruc, December 2012 comment in "Halloween decorations carry haunting message of forced labor" thread, Reddit, https://www.reddit.com/r/Portland/comments/15fsi9/halloween_decorations_carry_haunting_message_of/.

92   **"Ethical people don't"**   "pdxtone," ibid.

92   **Brazilian government inspectors**   "Hidden Subcontracting," SOMO.

93   *Telegraph* "Company behind Zara Investigated for 'Slave Labour,'" *Telegraph,* August 18, 2011, https://www.telegraph.co.uk/news/worldnews/southamerica/brazil/8710023/Company-behind-Zara-investigated-for-slave-labour.html.

93   **Reuters**   "Zara Supplier Accused of Slave Labor in Brazil," Reuters, August 18, 2011, https://uk.reuters.com/article/zara-brazil/zara-supplier-accused-of-slave-labor-in-brazil-idUKN1E77G18N20110817.

93   **BBC**   "Fashion Chain Zara Acts on Brazil Sweatshop Conditions," BBC, August 18, 2011, https://www.bbc.com/news/world-latin-america-14570564.

93   **Refinery29**   "H&M's Factories in Myanmar Employ Workers as Young as 14," Refinery29, August 21, 2016, https://www.refinery29.com/en-us/2016/08/120742/hm-myanmar-factories-child-labor.

93   *New York Times* "Retailers like H&M and Walmart Fall Short of Pledges to Overseas Workers," *New York Times,* May 31, 2016, https://www.nytimes.com/2016/05/31/business/international/top-retailers-fall-short-of-commitments-to-overseas-workers.html.

93   **Cambodia**   "'Exploitation': Clothing Labels Accused of Cambodia Worker Discrimination, Child Labor," RT, March 12, 2015, https://www.rt.com/news/240069-discrimination-workers-cambodia-retailers/.

93   **"When 14- to 18-year-olds are working"**   "H&M Factories in Myanmar Employed 14-Year-Old Workers," Guardian, August 21, 2016, https://www.theguardian.com/business/2016/aug/21/hm-factories-myanmar-employed-14-year-old-workers.

93   **Amancio Ortega**   "#6 Amancio Ortega," *Forbes,* accessed March 2020, https://www.forbes.com/profile/amancio-ortega/#27c183f116cf.

93   **Stefan Persson**   "#71 Stefan Persson," *Forbes,* accessed March 2020, https://www.forbes.com/profile/stefan-persson/#6ccc75645dbe.

93   **Futerra**   "88% of Consumers Want You to Help Them Make a Difference," *Forbes,* November 21, 2018, https://www.forbes.com/sites/solitairetownsend/2018/11/21/consumers-want-you-to-help-them-make-a-difference/.

94   **"decoupling one side of a decision problem"**   Author interview with Ulrich Orth of the University of Bern, August 2019.

94   **In a 2019 study, Orth**   Ulrich R. Orth, Stefan Hoffmann, and Kristina Nickel, "Moral Decoupling Feels Good and Makes Buying Counterfeits Easy," *Journal of Business Research* 98 (May 2019): 117–125, https://doi.org/10.1016/j.jbusres.2019.01.001.

95   **"The sophisticated allocation of attention"**   Daniel Kahneman, *Thinking, Fast and Slow,* (New York: Farrar Straus & Giroux, 2011), 35.

95   **hypothetical scenario**   Ibid.

95   **Stanford, MIT, and Carnegie Mellon**   "Spend 'Til It Hurts: Researching the Pain of Paying," Carnegie Mellon University, 2007, https://www.cmu.edu/homepage /practical/2007/winter/spending-til-it-hurts.shtml.

95   **their 2007 study**   Brian Knutson et al. "Neural Predictors of Purchases," *Neuron* 53, no. 1 (January 4, 2007): 147–156, https://doi.org/10.1016/j.neuron.2006.11.010.

97   **Ikea fans expressed outrage**   Sebastian Schmalz and Ulrich R. Orth, "Brand Attachment and Consumer Emotional Response to Unethical Firm Behavior," *Psychology & Marketing* 29, no. 11 (November 2012): 869–884, https://doi.org /10.1002/mar.20570.

97   **After the scandal**   "Ikea Drops Live-Plucked Chinese Down Bedding from Shops," *Digital Journal*, February 17, 2009, http://www.digitaljournal.com/article/267439.

97   **study recruited 365 consumers**   Orth, Hoffmann, and Nickel, "Moral Decoupling."

97   **"If you alert people"**   Author interview with Ulrich Orth.

97   **"Maybe minutes."**   Ibid.

98   **"when consumers are forced to make"**   "Choosing the Right Green-Marketing Strategy," *MIT Sloan Management Review*, October 14, 2004, https://sloanreview .mit.edu/article/choosing-the-right-greenmarketing-strategy/.

98   **87 percent of consumers**   Sheila M. J. Bonini and Jeremy M. Oppenheim, "Helping 'Green' Products Grow," *McKinsey Quarterly*, October 2008, http://actrees.org/files/Research/mckinsey_greenproductsgrow.pdf.

98   **only 33 percent said**   Ibid.

98   **65 percent of consumers**   "The Elusive Green Consumer," *Harvard Business Review*, July–August 2019, https://hbr.org/2019/07/the-elusive-green-consumer.

98   **only 26 percent actually buy**   Ibid.

98   **Marie Kondo**   "The Origin Story of Marie Kondo's Decluttering Empire," *New Yorker*, December 8, 2015, https://www.newyorker.com/books/page-turner /the-origin-story-of-marie-kondos-decluttering-empire.

98   **treat the environment**   "Millennials Drive Big Growth in Sustainable Products," *Business Journals*, December 28, 2018, https://www.bizjournals.com/bizwomen /news/latest-news/2018/12/millennials-drive-big-growth-in-sustainable.html; "Want to Win Gen Z's Respect? Show Some Respect for the Environment," Gen Z Insights, April 22, 2019, https://www.genzinsights.com/to-win-gen-z-show -some-respect-for-the-environment.

98   **and their workers well**   "Millennials: Ethics and Morals Become Identity Markers for Brands," MediaPost, July 16, 2018, https://www.mediapost.com/publications /article/322250/millennials-ethics-and-morals-become-identity-mar.html; "Purpose over Profit: How Generation Z Is Redefining Business," *Nikkei Asian Review*, September 18, 2019, https://asia.nikkei.com/Spotlight/Cover-Story /Purpose-over-profit-How-Generation-Z-is-redefining-business.

98   **born from 1981 to 1996**   "Millennials Projected to Overtake Baby Boomers as America's Largest Generation," Pew Research Center, March 1, 2018, https://www.pewresearch.org/fact-tank/2018/03/01/millennials-overtake-baby -boomers/.

98   **like companies with a purpose**   "Millennials Call for Values-Driven Companies, but They're Not the Only Ones Interested," *Forbes*, May 23, 2018, https://www .forbes.com/sites/forrester/2018/05/23/millennials-call-for-values-driven-companies -but-theyre-not-the-only-ones-interested/; "Gen-Z and the Three Elements of Purpose Brands," *Forbes*, July 26, 2019, https://www.forbes.com/sites/jefffromm /2019/07/26/gen-z-and-the-three-elements-of-purpose-brands/.

98   **buy-one, give-one business model**   "96.5 Million Lives Impacted—and Counting," Toms Shoes, https://www.toms.com/impact.

99   **a third of its annual net profits**   "Toms Shoes Creditors to Take Over the Company," CNBC, December 30, 2019, https://www.cnbc.com/2019/12/30 /toms-shoes-creditors-to-take-over-the-company.html.

99   **multimillion-dollar brand's**   "What's Next for Toms, the $400 Million For-Profit Built on Karmic Capital," *Inc.*, May 2016, https://www.inc.com/magazine/201605 /leigh-buchanan/toms-founder-blake-mycoskie-social-entrepreneurship.html.

99   **main consumer demographic is millennial women**   "TOMS—Marketing to Millennials One Step at a Time," Reach Smarter, May 31, 2012, http://www.reach smarter.com/blog/index.php/2012/05/31/toms-marketing-to-millennials-one-step -at-a-time/.

99   **largest demographic of consumers**   "The Millennial Generation: A Demographic Bridge to America's Diverse Future," Brookings Institution, January 2018, https://www.brookings.edu/research/millennials/.

99   **largest generation in US history**   Ibid.

99   **40 percent of all retail purchases by 2020**   "What Is Generation Z, and What Does It Want?" *Fast Company*, May 4, 2015, https://www.fastcompany.com /3045317/what-is-generation-z-and-what-does-it-want.

99   **more environmentally and socially conscious**   "Want to Win Gen Z's Respect?" Gen Z Insights; "Gen Z Believes In Its Own Power to Make Change, but That Companies Must Lead the Way," Sustainable Brands, October 23, 2019, https://sustainablebrands.com/read/marketing-and-comms/gen-z-believes -in-its-own-power-to-make-change-but-that-companies-must-lead-the-way.

99   **"serious concern about the environment and factories"**   Author interview with marketing consultant Nancy Nessel, November 2019.

100   **"one recycled sweater from Patagonia"**   Ibid.

100   **"haul video" phenomenon**   "Hauling: Material Girls Flaunt Their Purchases on YouTube," *Guardian*, August 21, 2011, available online at https://www.theguardian .com/technology/2011/aug/21/hauling-youtube-teenagers-showing-shopping.

100   **considerably less brand loyalty**   "How Loyalty Marketing Can Survive in a Gen Z World," *Adweek*, March 1, 2018, https://www.adweek.com/brand-marketing/ how-loyalty-marketing-can-survive-in-a-gen-z-world/; "Marketing to Gen Z: Death of Brand Loyalty?" opinion piece, *Marketing Insider*, February 5, 2019, https://www.mediapost.com/publications/article/331541/marketing-to-gen-z -death-of-brand-loyalty.html; "Gen Zers Are Redefining Brand Loyalty," American Marketing Association Toronto, December 14, 2017, https://www.ama-toronto .com/blog/gen-zers-are-redefining-brand-loyalty.

100   **"Sustainability is becoming an expectation"**   Author interview with consultant Jonah Stillman of Gen Z Guru.

100   **bankruptcy of Forever 21**   "Forever 21 Bankruptcy Signals a Shift in Consumer Tastes," *New York Times*, September 29, 2019, https://www.nytimes.com/2019/09 /29/business/forever-21-bankruptcy.html.

100   **H&M's record loss in 2018**   "H&M's Pile of Unsold Garments Grows as Earnings Plunge," Bloomberg, March 27, 2018, https://www.bloomberg.com/news/articles /2018-03-27/h-m-profit-plunges-to-16-year-low-as-clothing-chain-loses-allure.

100   **H&M began listing the names**   "H&M's Different Kind of Clickbait," *New York Times*, December 18, 2019, https://www.nytimes.com/2019/12/18/fashion/hms -supply-chain-transparency.html.

100   **"Product Sustainability" section of its website**   H&M, https://www2.hm.com /en_us/customer-service/product-and-quality/product-sustainability.html.

101   **carbon-neutral since 2015**   "Carbon Is Canceled," Reformation, https://www.thereformation.com/pages/carbon-is-canceled.

101   **summaries of its factories' audit scores**   "Factories," Reformation, https://www.thereformation.com/pages/factories.

101   **doesn't reveal the comprehensiveness**   "CA Supply Chain," Reformation, https://www.thereformation.com/pages/sub-footer-ca-supply-chain.

101   **outerwear made from plastic bottles**   "The Future of Fashion in One Word: Plastics," *Wired*, November 21, 2018, https://www.wired.com/story/plastics-in -fashion-everlane-renew/.

101   **audit scores of only a select few**   "The Heel Factory," Everlane, https://www.everlane.com/factories/heel.

Chapter Eight

102   **"Masanjia used to be a graveyard"**   *Above the Ghosts' Heads.*

104   **jam and twist toothbrushes**   "The Chinese Communist Party Is the Source of All the Atrocities during the Persecution of Falun Gong (Photos)," Minghui, February 15, 2006, http://en.minghui.org/html/articles/2006/2/15/69968.html; Du Bin, *Vagina in Coma* (Taiwan: Zhang Huitan, 2011); *Above the Ghosts' Heads*; "Petitioners Reveal Brutalities," *Epoch Times.*

105   **Yin Liping described her sexual assault**   Author's translation of the Chinese version of Yin Liping's account. "'I Still Tremble When I Think about It—I Was Locked Up in a Men's Cell at Masanjia Forced Labor Camp' (Part 1)," Minghui, October 13, 2013, http://en.minghui.org/html/articles/2013/10/13/142691.html.

105   **women made uniforms**   According to Lin Hua, Masanjia survivor, in *Above the Ghosts' Heads*; corroborated by accounts from other female Masanjia survivors, including "A Personal Account of Torture at the Masanjia Forced Labor Camp," Minghui, October 1, 2013, http://en.minghui.org/html/articles/2013/10/1/142473p .html.

105   **shirts for a South Korean company**   Hua in *Above the Ghosts' Heads*; in addition to her account, an online company profile of the Xinyu Garment Company states that "we welcome all new and old customers to visit . . . Our specific address is: Shenyang City, Yuhong District, Masanjia North Township (Liaoning Province Reeducation through Labor Facility)." Translation by US-China Economic and Security Review Commission staff researchers; original available at http://3533576 .czvv.com/about.

105 **down coats for an Italian brand** Hua, *Above the Ghosts' Heads*; "Down Coats Made by Slave Labor in Masanjia Forced Labor Camp," Minghui, January 21, 2013, http://en.minghui.org/html/articles/2013/1/21/137196.html.

105 **women did not even have protective masks** Hua, *Above the Ghosts' Heads*.

105 **Xinyu Clothing Company** *Prison Labor Exports*, US-China Commission.

106 **"Our faces were covered with tiny feathers"** Hua, *Above the Ghosts' Heads*.

106 **Liu, a nanny** *Prison Labor Exports*, US-China Commission.

106 **embezzlement by the party secretary** *Above the Ghosts' Heads*.

106 **"so hungry that our bodies shook"** Ibid.

107 **menstrual blood seeped across her bottom** Ibid.

107 **"three hundred forty pants every day"** Ibid.

107 **promptly arrested Du Bin and Liu Hua** "Chinese Labor Camp Whistleblower Escapes, Vows to Pursue Lawsuit," Radio Free Asia, April 22, 2014, https://www.rfa.org/english/news/china/masanjia-04222014154057.html; "China Detains Photographer Who Exposed Labour Camp Abuses," Amnesty International, June 14, 2013, https://www.amnesty.org/en/latest/news/2013/06/china-detains-photographer-who-exposed-labour-camp-abuses/.

107 **detained for thirty-seven days** "Chinese Journalist Released but Restrictions Remain," Committee to Protect Journalists, July 11, 2013, https://cpj.org/2013/07/chinese-journalist-released-but-restrictions-remai.php.

107 **conditions were no better at other camps** Author interview with Yu Zhenjie, female forced-labor-camp survivor, May 2018.

107 **"more painful than when I gave birth"** Ibid.

108 **Ma Chunmei . . . experienced similar tortures** Author interview with Ma Chunmei, female forced-labor-camp survivor, August 2018.

108 **Changchun City Arts and Crafts Factory** "Products Made by Detainees at Jilin Province Women's Labor Camp," Minghui, April 25, 2013, http://en.minghui.org/html/articles/2013/4/25/139054.html.

108 **"These are the exact birds"** Text message from Ma Chunmei to author, November 2018.

Chapter Nine

109 **culture of self-mutilation** Yun Zhao's interview with Masanjia survivors, October 2017.

109 **Little Sichuan stabbed himself in the stomach** Ibid.

109 **If the workshops had lye** Ibid.

110 **man in his thirties named Meng** Ibid.

110 **"If I slashed my wrist"** Ibid.

111 **refute some of the defining features** "Three Ways Chinese Christians Are Responding to Persecution in China," Advancing Native Missions, November 7, 2018, https://advancingnativemissions.com/persecution-in-china-three-ways-the-church-is-responding/; "Assisting the Church in China," *Decision*, June 19, 2008, Billy Graham Evangelistic Association, https://billygraham.org/decision-magazine/june-2008/assisting-the-church-in-china/.

111   **Three-Self Patriotic Movement**   "Church-State Clash in China Coalesces around a Toppled Spire," *New York Times*, May 29, 2014, https://www.nytimes.com/2014/05/30 /world/asia/church-state-clash-in-china-coalesces-around-a-toppled-spire.html.

111   **worship in informal house churches**   "Why Many Christians in China Have Turned to Underground Churches," BBC, March 26, 2016, https://www.bbc.com /news/world-asia-china-35900242.

111   **human rights lawyers are Christians**   "In China, They're Closing Churches, Jailing Pastors—and Even Rewriting Scripture," *Guardian*, January 13, 2019, https://www.theguardian.com/world/2019/jan/13/china-christians-religious -persecution-translation-bible.

Chapter Ten

117   **paper had green lines**   "Haunting Message," *Oregonian*.

119   **Heizuizi Women's Labor Camp**   "A Film Reminded Me of Abuses in a Changchun Forced Labor Camp," Minghui, September 21, 2018, http://en.minghui .org/html/articles/2018/9/21/171990.html.

Chapter Eleven

122   **the quarry at Guangdong No. 1**   "Bloodstained Flowers," Laogai Research Foundation.

122   **"It tasted awful"**   Author interview with Chen Pokong, pro-democracy organizer and former prisoner, March 2019.

123   **"I did not have a trial"**   Ibid.

123   **"the trademarks and prices were in English"**   Ibid.

123   **Chen started writing a secret letter**   "Bloodstained Flowers," Laogai Research Foundation. Full English translation of his letter:

> To: United Nations International Human Rights Organization
> Voice of America
> Asian Watch
>
> From: Chen Jingsong, Guangdong, China
>
> I am Chen Jingsong, alias Chen Pokong, formerly teacher, department of economics, Zhongshan University, Guangzhou. I was arrested as a "culprit" for participating in, and leading, the pro-democracy movement in Guangdong area in 1989, and sentenced to 3-year imprisonment on charges of "counterrevolutionary propaganda and instigation."
> In July 1992, upon completing my term, I was released. However, I continued engaging in political activities—disseminating ideas of

democracy, creating progressive publications, and disseminating them.

In August 1993, I was again wanted by the authorities. I fled to Hong Kong and applied to the Hong Kong government for political asylum, but to no avail. On Sept. 1, 1993, I was again arrested in Zhengcheng, Guangdong. Two months later, I was sent to reeducation through labor for a duration of two years.

To vent their bitter hatred, the Guangdong authorities sent me to a most vicious RTL—Guangdong No. 1 RTL, Quarry 1, Company 9, in Chini Town, Hua County, Guangdong Province, where I am engaged in long hours and high-intensity slave labor.

Reeducation through labor is the darkest part of China's current political system. Ironically, RTL policy and regulations worked out by the Chinese government itself have been altered beyond recognition in their practical implementation. According to the RTL policy and regulations, RTL is lighter than LR (labor reform): inmates get their pay, have their benefits and holidays, enjoy the right of correspondence, cultural, recreational and sports activities, do not labor more than 8 hours daily, can visit their families on holidays, can be bailed out for medical treatment, etc. In reality, RTL is hell.

Here, we labor 14 hours daily. In daytime, we transport stone materials on a wharf and load them in boats. At night, we make handicrafts, artificial flowers. On Sundays and holidays, we labor as usual (except for three days during the Spring Festival). We labor rain or shine. Inmates are just tools of labor, by no means "trainees," as we are called.

Here, labor intensity is extremely high. "Production" quotas are heavy. Those who fail to complete have their "points" reduced (i.e., their RTL duration lengthened). To complete our quotas, we must often labor overtime, sometimes even through the night. Without the discreet assistance from my fellow inmates, I would have to labor almost always through the night.

Inmates who labor slightly slower are brutally beaten and misused [sic] by supervisors and team leaders (themselves inmates). Inmates are often beaten until they are bloodstained all over, collapse or lose consciousness (shortly before I was sent there, one inmate was beaten to death). Nobody would believe such cruelty and barbarity, should he not see all this with his own eyes. Though discreetly taken care of by the company commander, several times I was beaten by the team leader. I am constantly exposed to terror.

Living conditions here are harsh. Every meal consists of coarse rice and rotten vegetable leaves. Hardly can we see any grease. We have a little bit of meat only on major holidays (Spring Festival, for instance). We make our own daily arrangements: bedding, clothing, daily necessities, even medical treatment, which is a great burden for us.

Inmates are seldom given leave when they are injured on the job or sick, to say nothing of being bailed for medical treatment. Still, they have to labor. Many inmates, including myself, our hands and feet having been squashed by big stones, stained with blood and pus, have to labor as usual. As a consequence, many inmates were crippled for life.

There are almost no cultural, recreational, and sports facilities. The only entertainment is watching TV series for ½ to 1 hour in the evening when production quotas are not too heavy. No books at all. Very few newspapers. No broadcasts to listen to. Complete cultural and press blockade. For me, there is something more: correspondence blockade, as I receive and mail almost no letters.

The artificial flowers we make are for export. The trademarks are in English, the prices in USD. Even the company commander and the quarry director said the flowers are made in cooperation with a Hong Kong company that exports them. This is in serious violation of international human rights norms, international law, even the Chinese government's law.

As a matter of fact, in the recent decade and more, all products produced by LR, RTL, and detention facilities in Guangdong Province are almost exclusively for export (usually in cooperation with Hong Kong and Taiwanese companies). For instance, Huanghua Detention Center in Guangzhou, at least since 1989, when I was there and experienced everything myself, has been forcing detainees to make artificial flowers, necklaces, jewelry (trademarks in English, prices in USD). This can be testified by anybody who was there, including Hong Kongers.

What I testify to above is wanton trampling, not only on international human rights norms, but upon basic humanitarian norms as well. Here in RTL, the concept of human rights is zero!

I am thrown into this hell because the Guangdong authorities want to crush me spiritually and physically. This is political retaliation and persecution.

Being in this critical situation, I have no choice but to appeal to you. I strongly urge all expressive forces the world over to

[help] the Chinese people who are in an abyss of misery. I strongly appeal to international progressive organizations to urge the Guangdong authorities to cease persecuting me politically!

I understand that once my letter is published, I might be persecuted even more harshly. I might even be killed. But I have no choice!

Thank you!
Chen Pokong

124 **California home of Harry Wu** Harry Wu and George Vecsey, *Troublemaker: One Man's Crusade against China's Cruelty* (New York: Times Books, 1996), 12–15.

124 **survivor of forced labor himself** "Harry Wu, Dissident and Activist Who Endured 19 Years in Chinese Labor Camps, Dies at 79," *Washington Post*, April 27, 2016, https://www.washingtonpost.com/world/asia_pacific/harry-wu -dissident-and-activist-who-endured-19-years-in-chinese-labor-camps-dies-at -79/2016/04/27/294f2734-0c83-11e6-bfa1-4efa856caf2a_story.html.

124 **attempted to sneak out a similar message** Wu and Vecsey, *Troublemaker*, 15.

124 **caught and placed in solitary confinement** Ibid.

124 **Nancy Pelosi** "Chinese Forced Labor," *Congressional Record* 140, no. 143.

125 **detention order for artificial flowers from Kwong Ngai** "Withhold Release Orders and Findings: China," CBP, *https://www.cbp.gov/trade/trade-communit y/programs-outreach/convict-importations/detention-orders*.

125 **"Theoretically, you can have an importer"** Author interview with US Customs and Border Protection official.

125 **Ngai Kwong Industrial Company** Bloomberg, https://www.bloomberg.com /profiles/companies/NGAIKZ:HK-ngai-kwong-industrial-co-ltd. It is also known as Ngai Kwong International Ltd., at the same address: http://www.nki.cc/contact .php. There is a precedent for industry-wide bans. In 2018, the United States banned all cotton goods from Turkmenistan—a country known for state-sanctioned forced labor: "U.S. Bans Imports of Slave-Picked Cotton from Turkmenistan," Reuters, May 24, 2018, https://www.reuters.com/article/us-usa-trafficking-turkmenistan /u-s-bans-imports-of-slave-picked-cotton-from-turkmenistan-idUSKCN1IP3UB.

125 **"It's a bit meaningless"** Author interview with Jeffrey Fiedler.

126 **undercover with CBS journalist Ed Bradley** "Made in China," *60 Minutes*, CBS, September 1991, https://www.youtube.com/watch?v=DHVZO5PlFTM.

126 **visited more than twenty laogai facilities** "The Hidden World of China's Gulag," *Washington Post*, July 15, 1993, https://www.washingtonpost.com/archive /lifestyle/1993/07/15/the-hidden-world-of-chinas-gulag/292161c5-3d69-400d -b2d7-3720e8fcd1c6/.

126 **dropped to seventy-two pounds** Ibid.

126 **"Our products are never exported directly"** "Made in China," *60 Minutes*.

126 **"hiding behind a vat of chemicals"** Wu and Vecsey, *Troublemaker*, 116.

127 **Qinghai Hide and Garment Works** Ibid., 115.

127 **framed exporting license** Ibid., 116.

127   **advanced collective for suppressing rebellion**   Ibid.

127   **Ned Hall, an audio engineer**   Ibid., 125–126.

127   **"experience with this type of labor"**   Ned Hall's dialogue with the trading company from "Made in China," *60 Minutes.*

127   **first-ever hearing on laogai**   *One Year after the Nobel Peace Prize Award to Liu Xiaobo: Conditions for Political Prisoners and Prospects for Political Reform, Hearing before the Congressional-Executive Commission on China,* 112th Congress, first session, December 6, 2011, https://www.govinfo.gov/content/pkg/CHRG -112hhrg73764/html/CHRG-112hhrg73764.htm.

127   **$300 million and $1 billion**   *U.S Implementation of Prison Labor Agreements with China, Hearing Before the Committee on Foreign Relations, US Senate,* 105th Congress, first session, May 21, 1997, https://www.govinfo.gov/content/pkg/CHRG -105shrg47725/html/CHRG-105shrg47725.htm.

127   **George H. W. Bush signed**   Statement of Jeffrey L. Fiedler, *Forced Labor in China,* CECC, June 22, 2005.

128   **air purification equipment**   "UNICOR Schedule of Products by FSC Code," Unicor, https://www.unicor.gov/SopFscList.aspx.

128   **textile fabrics to office supplies**   Ibid.

128   **wages as low as twenty-three cents an hour** "Inmate Pay Rates," Unicor, https://www.unicor.gov/FAQ_General.aspx.

128   **as problematic as the US prison system is**   Michelle Alexander, *The New Jim Crow: Mass Incarceration in the Age of Colorblindness* (New York: The New Press, 2010).

128   **"as a consequence of a conviction"**   "International Labour Standards on Forced Labour," International Labour Organization, https://www.ilo.org/global/standards /subjects-covered-by-international-labour-standards/forced-labour/lang--en/index .htm.

128   **convict in 99.9 percent of all cases**   "No Sign of Change in China's Deeply Flawed Criminal Justice System," opinion piece, *South China Morning Post,* December 14, 2016, https://www.scmp.com/comment/insight-opinion/article/2054456/no-sign -change-chinas-deeply-flawed-criminal-justice-system; "China: State Security, Terrorism Convictions Double," Human Rights Watch, March 16, 2016, https://www .hrw.org/news/2016/03/16/china-state-security-terrorism-convictions-double.

128   **Jesse Helms**   *U.S. Implementation of Prison Labor Agreements,* May 21, 1997.

129   **"visit" instead of "inspect"**   *Prison Labor Exports,* US-China Commission.

129   **"'inspect' has a rigorous connotation"**   Author interview with Jeffrey Fiedler.

129   **"within 60 days"**   *Prison Labor Exports,* US-China Commission.

129   **rudely rebuffed**   *U.S. Implementation of Prison Labor Agreements.*

129   **Fuyang General Machinery Factory**   Kempton and Richardson, *Laogai,* 77.

129   **knew about Soviet gulags**   This was drawn from a panel at the Laogai Museum in Washington, DC, January 2019.

130   **returning to China in 1995**   "Remembering Harry Wu, 'Troublemaker' for the Chinese Communist Party," *Fresh Air,* NPR, April 29, 2016, https://www.npr.org /2016/04/29/476153483/remembering-harry-wu-troublemaker-for-the-chinese -communist-party.

130   **"People remember Anne Frank"**   Wu and Vecsey, *Troublemaker,* 187.

130   **charged him with espionage**   "Harry Wu's Journey," *New Yorker*, July 24, 1995, https://www.newyorker.com/magazine/1995/07/24/harry-wus-journey.

130   **letting Wu go after sixty-six days**   "Remembering Harry Wu," *Fresh Air*, NPR.

130   **bespectacled man**   Peter Levy's physical descriptions are drawn from the video footage he took in Nanjing: *Nightline*, ABC News, May 21, 1997, as seen on the Laogai Research Foundation's YouTube channel, https://www.youtube.com/watch?v=egCfMLjeIDw.

130   **descendant of Holocaust survivors**   *U.S. Implementation of Prison Labor Agreements*.

130   **owner of Labelon/Noesting**   Ibid.

130   **employed twenty people**   Ibid.

131   **"We are all looking for a competitive advantage"** Ibid.

131   **dominate one-third of the US market**   "Chinese Firm Pleads Guilty in Labor Case," *New York Times*, March 1, 2001, https://www.nytimes.com/2001/03/01/nyregion/chinese-firm-pleads-guilty-in-labor-case.html.

131   **largest spring-clip factory in the world**   Ibid.

131   **"not in any position to effectively investigate"**   *U.S. Implementation of Prison Labor Agreements*.

132   **thirty-six hundred clips a day**   "Chinese Firm Pleads Guilty," *New York Times*.

132   **fingers bled**   Ibid.

132   **ALLIED NANJING on the door**   *Nightline*, ABC News, May 21, 1997.

132   **Chinese officials never cooperated**   "Chinese Firm Pleads Guilty," *New York Times*.

132   **Allied International pleaded guilty**   Ibid.

132   **"came under pressure from its primary customer"**   Ibid

132   **seized twenty-four million Officemate binder clips**   Ibid.

132   **only US corporation to have ever been prosecuted**   *Laogai Handbook*, 15.

132   **Gary Marck, a US ceramics importer**   "A Case Study of Alleged Chinese Prison Labor Imports: The Case of Marck & Associates, Inc. v. Photo USA Corporation," *2008 Report to Congress*, US-China Economic and Security Review Commission https://www.uscc.gov/sites/default/files/annual_reports/2008-Report-to-Congress-_0.pdf.

133   **lowered the prices . . . by sixteen cents**   Ibid., 328.

133   **Photo USA was reportedly sourcing from**   Ibid., 327.

133   **partially owned a ceramics factory in the same area**   Ibid., 328.

133   **ability to meet high-volume orders**   Ibid., 327.

133   **only one kiln**   Ibid.

133   **located just outside a known labor camp**   Ibid.

133   **seventy million ceramic products a year**   *Laogai Handbook*, 385.

133   **produced over 50 percent of US ceramic imports**   Edmund Macriowski, written submission to the US International Trade Commission in regard to Investigation #332–491, *China: Government Policies Affecting U.S. Trade in Selected Sectors*, February 1, 2008.

133   **"mugs made at Luzhong"**   Testimony of Gary G. Marck, *Memoranda of Understanding*, US-China Commission, June 19, 2008, https://www.uscc.gov/sites/default/files/6.19.08Marck.pdf.

133   **Marck filed a lawsuit against Photo USA**   "A Case Study," US-China Commission, 328.

133   **He gave eyewitness testimony**   Ibid.

133   **court ruled**   Ibid.

133   **production at Luzhong Prison had stopped**   Ibid.

134   **allowed US officials to inspect**   *Prison Labor Exports*, US-China Commission.

134   **could not find evidence**   Ibid.

134   **suspected forced-labor facilities since 2009**   *U.S. Exposure to Forced Labor Exports*, US-China Commission.

134   **"those requests are pending."**   Author interview with official with the US Department of Homeland Security, March 2019.

134   **SOS message inside a box of Christmas cards**   "6-Year-Old Finds Message Alleging Chinese Prison Labor in Box of Christmas Cards," NPR, December 23, 2019, https://www.npr.org/2019/12/23/790832681/6-year-old-finds-message-alleging -chinese-prison-labor-in-box-of-christmas-cards.

135   **most favored nation (MFN) trading status**   "Human Rights in China," Brookings Institution, June 1, 1999, https://www.brookings.edu/research/human-rights-in -china/.

135   **decision to reverse his previous position**   "China Called Clinton's Bluff on Human Rights," *Los Angeles Times*, September 10, 1996, https://www.latimes.com /archives/la-xpm-1996-09-10-mn-42270-story.html; *Prison Labor Exports*, US-China Commission.

135   **"Clinton's conciliatory approach"**   "What We Did in China," *National Journal*, July 18, 1998, Clinton Digital Library, https://clinton.presidentiallibraries.us/items /show/11244.

135   **In 2001, the issue of forced-labor exports**   *Prison Labor Exports*, US-China Commission.

135   **Despite growing evidence**   Between 1992, when the MOU was signed, and 2001, when China joined the WTO, twenty CBP detention orders were issued for Chinese prison products, according to "Withhold Release Orders and Findings: China," CPB.

135   **permitted to join the World Trade Organization**   "China and the WTO," World Trade Organization, https://www.wto.org/english/thewto_e/countries_e/china_e .htm.

136   **help China transition to a democracy**   "Future Shock: The WTO and Political Change in China," *Policy Brief* 1, no. 3 (February 2001), Carnegie Endowment for International Peace, https://carnegieendowment.org/files/dem.PolBrief3.pdf.

136   **never happened**   "The Broken Promises of China's WTO Accession: Reprioritizing Human Rights," Congressional-Executive Commission on China, March 1, 2017, https://www.cecc.gov/events/hearings/the-broken-promises-of- chinas-wto-accession-reprioritizing-human-rights.

136   **lose 3.4 million factory jobs**   "The Growing Trade Deficit with China Cost 3.4 Million U.S. Jobs between 2001 and 2015," Economic Policy Institute, January 31, 2017, https://www.epi.org/press/the-growing-trade-deficit-with-china-cost-3-4 -million-u-s-jobs-between-2001-and-2015/.

136   **immigrated to New York City**   "17 Prominent Chinese Dissidents Living in Exile in the U.S.—Demand the Right to Return to China," Human Rights in China, October 21, 1997, https://www.hrichina.org/en/content/2797.

136   **"I thought . . . China would transition"**   Author interview with Chen Pokong.

136   **his official YouTube channel**   Official Channel of Chen Pokong," https://www
.youtube.com/channel/UCwb7avxK-L5vPjMC1ZIGayw.

137   **demanding democratic reforms**   "The Hong Kong Protests Explained in 100 and
500 Words," BBC, November 28, 2019, https://www.bbc.com/news/world-asia-china
-49317695.

137   **former British colony**   Ibid.

137   **"After so many disappointments"**   Author interview with Chen Pokong.

Chapter Twelve

138   **"very close to dying then"**   Author interview with Ma Chunmei.

138   **estimated to be worth a billion dollars**   "China Forcefully Harvests Organs from
Detainees, Tribunal Concludes," NBC, June 18, 2019, https://www.nbcnews.com
/news/world/china-forcefully-harvests-organs-detainees-tribunal-concludes
-n1018646.

139   **In 2016, both the US House**   Expressing Concern Regarding Persistent and
Credible Reports of Systematic, State-Sanctioned Organ Harvesting from Non-
Consenting Prisoners of Conscience in the People's Republic of China, Including
from Large Numbers of Falun Gong Practitioners and Members of Other Religious
and Ethnic Minority Groups," H.R. Res. 343, 114th Congress (2015), https://www
.congress.gov/bill/114th-congress/house-resolution/343.

139   **European Parliament**   Written Declaration Submitted under Rule 136 of the
Rules of Procedure on Stopping Organ Harvesting from Prisoners of Conscience
in China, European Parliament (April 27, 2016), http://www.europarl.europa.eu
/sides/getDoc.do?type=WDECL&reference=P8-DCL-2016-0048&format=PDF&
language=EN.

139   **"systematic, state-sanctioned organ harvesting"**   Ibid.

139   **first came to light in 2006**   David Matas and David Kilgour, *Bloody Harvest:
Organ Harvesting of Falun Gong Practitioners in China* (Niagara Falls, ON:
Seraphim Editions, 2009), 203, http://www.organharvestinvestigation.net/report
0701/report20070131.htm#_Toc158023107.

139   **41,500 organ donations**   Matas and Kilgour, *Bloody Harvest*.

139   **"a full explanation of the source of organ transplants"**   *2009 Annual Report*,
Congressional-Executive Commission on China, https://www.cecc.gov/publications
/annual-reports/2009-annual-report#1613a.

139   **Gutmann interviewed over one hundred witnesses**   "Face *the Slaughter*,"
National Review, August 25, 2014, http://live-national-review.pantheonsite.io
/sites/default/files/nordlinger_gutmann08-25-14.html.

139   **doctors who had been pressured**   Ethan Gutmann, *The Slaughter: Mass Killings,
Organ Harvesting, and China's Secret Solution to Its Dissident Problem* (New York:
Prometheus Books, 2014), 9–10; 17–19.

139   **as early as the 1990s**   *Organ Harvesting of Religious and Political Dissidents by
the Chinese Communist Party, Joint Hearing before the Subcommittee on Oversight
and Investigations and the Subcommittee on Africa, Global Health, and Human
Rights, of the Committee on Foreign Affairs*, US House of Representatives, 112th
Congress, second session, September 12, 2012, https://www.govinfo.gov/content
/pkg/CHRG-112hhrg75859/pdf/CHRG-112hhrg75859.pdf.

140   **spread beyond Xinjiang**   Ibid.

140   **sixty thousand to one hundred thousand organs a year**   David Kilgour, Ethan Gutmann, and David Matas, *An Update to Bloody Harvest & The Slaughter*, June 22, 2016, https://endtransplantabuse.org/wp-content/uploads/2017/05/Bloody _Harvest-The_Slaughter-2016-Update-V3-and-Addendum-20170430.pdf.

140   **inexplicable blood and urine tests**   "What Is the Evidence of 'Forced Organ Harvesting' in China?" *Journal of Political Risk* 7 (July 2019), http://www.jpolrisk .com/what-is-the-evidence-of-forced-organ-harvesting-in-china/.

140   **consistent with tests that evaluate organ quality**   Ibid.

140   **ninety-one hospitals performing organ transplants**   Ibid.

140   **six years later, there were one thousand**   Ibid.

140   **no functioning voluntary organ donation system**   Ibid.

140   **between 2006 and 2018**   *A WOIPFG Investigation Report on the Chinese Communist Party's Ongoing Crime of Live Organ Harvesting against Falun Dafa Practitioners (VI): New Evidence of the CCP's Crime of Live Organ Harvesting from Falun Gong Practitioners*, World Organization to Investigate the Persecution of Falun Gong, December 2, 2018, https://www.upholdjustice.org/node/404.

141   **Huang Jiefu admitted**   *2006 Annual Report*, Congressional-Executive Commission on China, https://www.cecc.gov/publications/annual-reports/2006-annual-report #397a.

141   **World Medical Association**   WMA Council Resolution on Organ Donation in China, May 2005, https://web.archive.org/web/20101204232011/http://www.wma .net/en/30publications/10policies/30council/cr_5/index.html.

141   **China International Transplantation Assistance Center's**   "Final Judgement Report," China Tribunal, June 17, 2019, https://chinatribunal.com/final-judgement-report/.

141   **average wait time . . . is 3.6 years**   "Organ Donation and Transplantation Statistics," National Kidney Foundation, https://www.kidney.org/news/newsroom/factsheets /Organ-Donation-and-Transplantation-Stats.

141   **In 2006, Kirk Allison**   *Falun Gong: Organ Harvesting and China's Ongoing War on Human Rights, Hearing before the Subcommittee on Oversight and Investigations of the Committee on International Relations*, US House of Representatives, 109th Congress, second session, September 29, 2006, https://www.govinfo.gov/content/pkg/CHRG-109hhrg30146/pdf/CHRG-109hhrg 30146.pdf.

142   **tribunal consisted of**   "Who We Are," China Tribunal, https://chinatribunal.com /who-we-are/.

142   **spent a year reviewing academic papers**   "Reading Material," China Tribunal, https://chinatribunal.com/reading-material/.

142   **"proof beyond reasonable doubt"**   "Final Judgement Report, China Tribunal; "'Crimes against Humanity': Is China Killing Political Prisoners for Their Organs?" *Sydney Morning Herald*, November 9, 2019, https://www.smh.com.au /lifestyle/health-and-wellness/crimes-against-humanity-is-china-killing-political -prisoners-for-their-organs-20191105-p537md.html.

142   **major inconsistencies**   "Final Judgement Report," China Tribunal.

143   **suggested systemic falsification of data**   Matthew P. Robertson, Raymond L. Hinde, and Jacob Lavee, "Analysis of Official Deceased Organ Donation Data Casts Doubt on the Credibility of China's Organ Transplant Reform," *BMC Medical Ethics* 20, no. 79 (November 14, 2019), https://doi.org/10.1186/s12910-019-0406-6.

143   **"Falun Gong practitioners have been one"**   "Final Judgement Report," China Tribunal.

143   **Turkic people in Xinjiang**   Ibid.

Chapter Thirteen

144   **thirteen-foot concrete wall**   As estimated by Sun and other Masanjia survivors.

145   **the Chinese phrase *xinao***   Aminda M. Smith, *Thought Reform and China's Dangerous Classes: Reeducation, Resistance, and the People* (New York: Rowman & Littlefield, 2012), 4.

145   **multiple-choice survey**   Described from memory by survivors.

146   **Masanjia learned from other camps**   Survivors heard guards explain.

149   **"he has a lot of backbone"**   *Letter from Masanjia*, directed by Leon Lee (2018).

Chapter Fourteen

152   **in his late thirties**   "Lawyers Pay High Price for Coming to Aid of Tibetans," *Star*, June 17, 2008, https://www.thestar.com/news/2008/06/17/lawyers_pay_high _price_for_coming_to_aid_of_tibetans.html.

152   **had a lot to lose**   Description of Jiang Tianyong's daughter drawn from an Amnesty International photo, https://www.amnesty.org/en/latest/campaigns /2017/07/china-lawyers-crackdown-two-years-torment-continues/.

152   **praying and singing hymns**   Jiang Tianyong's testimony, "Chinese Human Rights Attorneys Testify before the Tom Lantos Human Rights Commission," *Congressional Record* 155, no. 159 (October 29, 2009), https://www.congress.gov /congressional-record/2009/10/29/extensions-of-remarks-section/article/E2671-2.

153   **"Stop your illegal activities"**   Ibid.

153   **a few hundred lawyers in China**   Kempton and Richardson, *Laogai*, 37.

153   **Beijing implemented reforms**   Elizabeth C. Economy, *The Third Revolution* (Oxford: Oxford University Press, 2018), 7.

153   **Law was the fastest-growing major**   *China Statistical Year Book 2015*, National Bureau of Statistics of China, http://www.stats.gov.cn/tjsj/ndsj/2015/indexeh.htm; "China Now Produces Twice as Many Graduates a Year as the US," World Economic Forum, April 13, 2017, https://www.weforum.org/agenda/2017/04/higher-education -in-china-has-boomed-in-the-last-decade.

153   **disbarred, placed under house arrest**   "Third Anniversary of the Lawyers Crackdown in China," Amnesty International, July 9, 2018, https://www.amnesty .org/en/latest/campaigns/2018/07/china-human-rights-lawyers-crackdown-third -anniversary/.

153   **defended nearly twenty Falun Gong followers**   Jiang's testimony, "Chinese Human Rights Attorneys Testify."

153   **petitioners, HIV/AIDS victims**   "Jiang Tianyong," Front Line Defenders, https://www.frontlinedefenders.org/en/profile/jiang-tianyong.

154   **anniversary of the 1959 Tibetan uprising**   "Tibet Protests," *Guardian*, March 14, 2008, https://www.theguardian.com/world/gallery/2008/mar/14/1.

154   **cursing the Dalai Lama**   Jiang's testimony, "Chinese Human Rights Attorneys Testify."

154   **between eighty and two hundred nuns**   *The New York Times* initially reported eighty: "Senior Tibetan Cleric Faces Prison in China," *New York Times*, April 24, 2009, https://www.nytimes.com/2009/04/25/world/asia/25tibet.html. Jiang Tianyong reported two hundred: "Chinese Human Rights Attorneys Testify."

154   **one of eighteen lawyers**   "China Disbars Lawyers Who Offered to Defend Tibetans," *New York Times*, June 3, 2008, https://www.nytimes.com/2008/06/03 /world/asia/03iht-04tibet.13432270.html.

154   **defended Phurbu Tsering Rinpoche**   "Senior Tibetan Cleric Faces Prison in China," *New York Times*, April 24, 2009, https://www.nytimes.com/2009/04/25 /world/asia/25tibet.html.

154   **Tibetan abbot**   "Tibetan 'Living Buddha' Phurbu Tsering Jailed by China," BBC, January 1, 2010, http://news.bbc.co.uk/2/hi/asia-pacific/8436865.stm.

154   **sentenced to eight and a half years**   "Phurbu Tsering Rinpoche," Chinese Human Rights Defenders, April 10, 2017, https://www.nchrd.org/2017/04/phurbu -tsering-rinpoche/.

154   **put under house arrest**   "Chinese Rights Defense Lawyers under All-Out Attack by the Authorities," Human Rights in China, June 4, 2009, https://www.hrichina .org/en/content/300.

154   **sentenced to life**   "Senior Tibetan Cleric," *New York Times*.

154   **Several were executed**   "China Executes Tibetan Protestors," *Guardian*, October 22, 2009, https://www.theguardian.com/world/2009/oct/22/china -executes-tibet-protesters.

155   **Torture was illegal in China**   *2008 Annual Report*, CECC.

155   **Yu Jiang began making preparations**   Yun Zhao's interview with a former Masanjia inmate-guard, August 2017.

Chapter Fifteen

164   **Since as early on as 2004**   "The Great Firewall of China: Xi Jinping's Internet Shutdown," *Guardian*, June 29, 2018, https://www.theguardian.com/news/2018 /jun/29/the-great-firewall-of-china-xi-jinpings-internet-shutdown.

164   **one hundred thousand human censors**   "Learning China's Forbidden History, So They Can Censor It," *New York Times*, January 2, 2019, https://www.nytimes .com/2019/01/02/business/china-internet-censor.html; "Cat and Mouse: How China Makes Sure Its Internet Abides By the Rules," *Economist*, April 6, 2013, https://www.economist.com/special-report/2013/04/06/cat-and-mouse.

164   **state propaganda departments**   "Great Firewall," *Guardian*.

164   **companies that have privatized censorship**   Ibid.

164   **commenters, who are paid**   Ibid.

164   **Harvard study estimated that 448 million**   Gary King, Jennifer Pan, and Margaret E. Roberts, "How the Chinese Government Fabricates Social Media Posts for Strategic Distraction, Not Engaged Argument," *American Political Science Review* 111, no. 3 (2017), 484–501, https://gking.harvard.edu/50C.

165   **human rights lawyer Pu Zhiqiang**   "Surviving Bo Xilai's Reign of Red Terror," *South China Morning Post*, December 22, 2012, https://www.scmp.com/news /china/article/1110213/surviving-bo-xilais-reign-red-terror.

165   **then–party secretary, Bo Xilai**   "Timeline: The Chongqing Scandal," *South China Morning Post*, September 24, 2012, https://www.scmp.com/news/china/article /1046068/timeline-chongqing-scandal.

165   **series of political campaigns**   "Surviving Bo Xilai's Reign," *South China Morning Post*.

165   **merely posted online comments**   Ibid.

165   **In August 2011** "Prospects for Reforming China's Reeducation through Labor System," Congressional-Executive Commission on China, https://www.cecc.gov /publications/issue-papers/prospects-for-reforming-chinas-reeducation-through -labor-system.

165   **Ren Jianyu**   "Opposition to Labor Camps Widens in China," *New York Times*, December 14, 2012, https://www.nytimes.com/2012/12/15/world/asia/opposition -to-labor-camps-widens-in-china.html.

165   **informally sentenced**   Ibid.

165   **two years in a labor camp**   "Prospects for Reforming," CECC.

165   **"spreading negative comments and information online"**   Ibid.

165   **Ren's two-year sentence was ultimately reduced**   *The End of Reeducation through Labor? Recent Developments and Prospects for Reform, Roundtable before the Congressional-Executive Commission on China*, 113th Congress, first session, May 9, 2013, https://www.govinfo.gov/content/pkg/CHRG-113hhrg81853/html /CHRG-113hhrg81853.htm.

165   **eleven-year-old girl . . . was kidnapped**   Ibid.

165   **Tang Hui, spent six years petitioning**   "Mother Seeks Justice, Gets 18 Months in Labor Center," *Global Times*, August 7, 2012, http://www.globaltimes.cn/content /725545.shtml.

165   **sentenced the girl's mother**   "Prospects for Reforming," CECC.

165   **"disturbing social order"**   "Chinese Mother Loses Compensation Bid over Labor for Rape Protest," Reuters, April 12, 2013, https://www.reuters.com/article/us -china-labourcamp/chinese-mother-loses-compensation-bid-over-labor-for-rape -protest-idUSBRE93B0FA20130412.

165   **1.6 million posts in solidarity**   "Mother of Underage Rape Victim Freed," *Global Times*, August 11, 2012, www.globaltimes.cn/content/726336.shtml.

165   **three hundred million Sina Weibo users**   "China Records 300 Million Registered Microblog Users," Reuters, November 21, 2011, https://www.reuters .com/article/us-china-microblogs/china-records-300-million-registered-micro blog-users-idUSTRE7AK1Q720111121.

165   **almost equivalent to the entire US population**   "U.S. and World Population Clock," US Census Bureau, https://www.census.gov/popclock/.

165   **online signature campaign**   "Prospects for Reforming," CECC.

166   **more than one hundred thousand signatures**   Ibid; "Re-Education to Be Reformed," *Global Times*, January 8, 2013, http://www.globaltimes.cn/content/754403.shtml.

166   **reform was on the table**   "Officials' Statements on Reform," CECC.

166   **the Xinhua news agency**   *Prison Labor Exports*, US-China Commission.

167   **trying to visit another human rights lawyer**   "Jiang Tianyong," Chinese Human Rights Defenders, February 20, 2017, https://www.nchrd.org/2017/02/jiang-tianyong/.

167   **lost hearing in his left ear**   Ibid.

167   **forced Jiang to return to his hometown**   "Rights Group Slams Crackdown,"
      Radio Free Asia, November 19, 2012, https://www.rfa.org/english/news/crackdown
      -11192012150954.html.

168   **"I feel so proud that I participated in this"**   Yun Zhao interview, March 2017.

168   **"I'm one of the witnesses"**   The original article that Laopo left a comment on:
      "US Government Launches Investigation of SOS Letter Hidden in Halloween
      Product from Masanjia Re-Education through Labor Camp," *Epoch Times*,
      December 26, 2012, http://www.epochtimes.com/gb/12/12/26/n3761422.htm.

Chapter Sixteen

170   **virtual private networks (VPNs)**   "What's Really Happening with China's Great
      Firewall," ProPublica, February 2, 2015, https://www.propublica.org/article/whats
      -really-happening-with-chinas-great-firewall.

170   **journalist named Yuan Ling**   "Story of Women's Labor Camp Abuse Unnerves
      Even China," *New York Times*, April 15, 2013, https://cn.nytimes.com/china
      /20130415/c15abuse/en-us/.

170   **interviewing a dozen female Masanjia survivors**   "True Horror of Halloween
      'SOS,'" CNN.

171   **five thousand forced laborers at its peak**   Ibid.

171   **annual revenue was nearly 100 million yuan**   Ibid.

171   **ceased publication for several months**   Ibid.

171   **abolishing the reeducation through labor system**   "China: Fully Abolish
      Re-Education through Labor," Human Rights Watch, January 8, 2013, https://www
      .hrw.org/news/2013/01/08/china-fully-abolish-re-education-through-labor.

171   **99.9 percent conviction rate**   "No Sign of Change," *South China Morning Post*.

171   **world knew very little about him**   "Xi Jinping: Chinese Ruler Who's a Riddle to
      the World," *Guardian*, November 30, 2013, https://www.theguardian.com/the
      observer/2013/dec/01/xi-jinping-china-leader.

171   **Western academics hoped**   "Can Xi Jinping's Governing Strategy Succeed?"
      Brookings Institution, September 26, 2013, https://www.brookings.edu/articles
      /can-xi-jinpings-governing-strategy-succeed/.

171   **"compulsory isolation drug detox centers"**   "A Jail by Another Name: China
      Labor Camps Now Drug Detox Centers," Reuters, December 2, 2013, https://www
      .reuters.com/article/us-china-camps/a-jail-by-another-name-china-labor-camps-
      now-drug-detox-centers-idUSBRE9B10CQ20131202; "China Ends One Notorious
      Form of Detention, but Keeps Others," NPR, February 5, 2014, https://www.npr
      .org/sections/parallels/2014/02/05/271412045/china-ends-one-notorious-form-
      of-detention-but-keeps-others; *Annual Report 2018*, Congressional-Executive
      Commission on China, https://www.cecc.gov/sites/chinacommission.house.gov/
      files/Annual%20Report%202018.pdf.

172   **de facto labor camps**   This has been independently confirmed by Human Rights
      Watch and news organizations such as the *New York Times*: "China Turns Drug
      Rehab into a Punishing Ordeal," *New York Times*, January 7, 2010, https://www.ny
      times.com/2010/01/08/world/asia/08china.html; "'Where Darkness Knows No
      Limits': Incarceration, Ill-Treatment and Forced Labor as Drug Rehabilitation
      in China," Human Rights Watch, January 7, 2010, https://www.hrw.org/report
      /2010/01/07/where-darkness-knows-no-limits/incarceration-ill-treatment-and
      -forced-labor-drug.

172   **dissidents with no history of drug addiction**   "Torture Camp Rebranded in China," *Epoch Times*, June 17, 2014, https://www.theepochtimes.com/torture -camp-rebranded-in-china_743777.html. Earlier accounts showed that Falun Gong detainees were arbitrarily held in drug detox centers, suggesting that these facilities served as de facto forced labor camps even before the abolition of RTL camps: "Announcement: 'Coalition to Investigate the Persecution' Announces the First Group of Facilities Targeted for Investigation and Evidence Collection," Minghui, April 12, 2006, http://en.minghui.org/html/articles/2006/4/12/71889.html.

172   **half a million people across China were held**   "China Turns Drug Rehab into a Punishing Ordeal," *New York Times*.

173   **"I saw the packaging"**   "True Horror of Halloween 'SOS,'" CNN.

173   **Sun gave an interview to the *New York Times***   "Behind Cry for Help," *New York Times*.

174   **"Case Closed"**   US Immigration and Customs Enforcement, August 2019.

174   **"As China's technology becomes more sophisticated"**   Leon Lee interview of Sun Yi.

175   **"the most organized group in China"**   Author interview with Chen Pokong, October 2019.

176   **showing even more authoritarian tendencies**   "Born Red," *New Yorker*, March 30, 2015, https://www.newyorker.com/magazine/2015/04/06/born-red; "Five Ways China Has Become More Repressive under President Xi Jinping," *Time*, October 6, 2016, https://time.com/4519160/china-xi-jinping-cecc-human-rights-rule-of-law/.

176   **Since the 1980s**   Deyong Yin, "China's Attitude toward Foreign NGOs," *Washington University Global Studies Law Review* 8, no. 3 (January 2009): 525, https://openscholarship.wustl.edu/cgi/viewcontent.cgi?article=1090&context =law_globalstudies.

176   **domestic and foreign NGOs had helped expand**   Chen Jie, "The NGO Community in China," *China Perspectives* 68 (November–December 2006), 29–40, https://doi.org/10.4000/chinaperspectives.3083.

176   **NGOs from abroad were necessary**   Economy, *The Third Revolution*, x.

176   **severely restricted these groups**   "China Passes Law Imposing Security Controls on Foreign NGOs," *Guardian*, April 28, 2016, https://www.theguardian.com/world /2016/apr/28/china-passes-law-imposing-security-controls-on-foreign-ngos.

176   **"hostile foreign forces"**   Economy, *The Third Revolution*, x.

176   **On July 1, 2015**   "The Truth about China's New National Security Law," *Diplomat*, July 1, 2015; https://thediplomat.com/2015/07/the-truth-about-chinas -new-national-security-law/; "The Implications of China's New Security Law," Deutsche Welle, July 2, 2015, https://www.dw.com/en/the-implications-of-chinas -new-security-law/a-18557771.

176   **"other major national interests"**   Ibid.

176   **over three hundred lawyers and activists**   Economy, *The Third Revolution*, 46.

176   **709 Crackdown**   Ibid.

176   **At one law firm alone**   Ibid.

176   **trials took place behind closed doors**   Ibid.

176   **seven-year sentence**   "China Verdict: Lawyer Zhou Shifeng Sentenced," Al Jazeera, August 4, 2016, https://www.aljazeera.com/news/2016/08/china -verdict-lawyer-zhou-shifeng-sentenced-160804081833785.html.

176   **represented activist artist Ai Weiwei**   Ibid.

177   **tainted baby formula**   "Chinese Lawyer Who Exposed Baby Milk Scandal Jailed for Subversion," *Guardian*, August 4, 2016, https://www.theguardian.com /world/2016/aug/04/chinese-lawyer-who-exposed-baby-milk-scandal-jailed-for -subversion.

177   **made confessions on state television**   "China Verdict," Al Jazeera.

177   *Southern Weekly*   Economy, *The Third Revolution*, 48.

177   *Yanhuang Chunqiu*, **a monthly journal**   Ibid.

177   **unprecedented high-tech predictive policing**   "China's Algorithms of Repression," Human Rights Watch, May 1, 2019, https://www.hrw.org/report /2019/05/01/chinas-algorithms-repression/reverse-engineering-xinjiang-police-mass-surveillance; "Eradicating Ideological Viruses," Human Rights Watch.

177   **"suspicious people"**   "Eradicating Ideological Viruses," Human Rights Watch.

177   **China Electronics Technology Group**   "China's Algorithms of Repression," Human Rights Watch.

177   **open-air prison**   "Security Clampdown Bites in China's Xinjiang Region," *Financial Times*, November 13, 2017, https://www.ft.com/content/ee28e156-992e -11e7-a652-cde3f882dd7b.

178   **administering "health checks"**   "China's Hi-Tech War on Its Muslim Minority," *Guardian*, April 11, 2019, https://www.theguardian.com/news/2019/apr/11/china-hi -tech-war-on-muslim-minority-xinjiang-uighurs-surveillance-face-recognition.

178   **Integrated Joint Operations Platform**   Ibid.

178   **computer program generates lists of people**   "China: Big Data Fuels Crackdown in Minority Region," Human Rights Watch, February 26, 2018, https://www.hrw .org/news/2018/02/26/china-big-data-fuels-crackdown-minority-region.

178   **nationalistic flag-raising ceremonies**   Ibid.

178   **missing phone bill payments**   Ibid.

178   **using too much electricity**   Ibid; "China's Xinjiang Citizens Monitored with Police App, Says Rights Group," BBC, May 2, 2019, https://www.bbc.com/news /world-asia-china-48130048.

178   **trillion-dollar economic development strategy**   "One Belt One Road Could Be China's Trillion-Dollar Mistake," opinion piece, *Washington Post*, April 9, 2018, https://www.washingtonpost.com/news/theworldpost/wp/2018/04/09/one-belt -one-road/.

178   **Bordering eight countries**   "Xinjiang Territory Profile," BBC, October 12, 2018, https://www.bbc.com/news/world-asia-pacific-16860974.

178   **strategic intersection on the Silk Road**   Damodar Panda, "Xinjiang and Central Asia: China's Problems and Policy Implications," *Indian Journal of Asian Affairs* 19, no. 2 (December 2006): 29–44, https://www.jstor.org/stable/41950474.

178   **more than seventy nations**   "This Map Shows a Trillion-Dollar Reason Why China Is Oppressing More Than a Million Muslims," *Business Insider*, February 23, 2019, https://www.businessinsider.com/map-explains-china-crackdown-on -uighur-muslims-in-xinjiang-2019-2.

178   **Schools, parks, hospitals**   "Being Tracked While Reporting in China, Where 'There Are No Whys,'" *New York Times*, April 16, 2019, https://www.nytimes.com /2019/04/16/insider/china-xinjiang-reporting-surveillance-uighur.html.

178   **New passbook systems**   "China's Hi-Tech War," *Guardian*.

179   **Uyghur intellectuals** "Imprisoned Chinese Uygur Scholar Ilham Tohti Given Top Human Rights Award," *South China Morning Post*, October 11, 2016, https://www.scmp.com/news/china/policies-politics/article/2027106/imprisoned -chinese-uygur-scholar-ilham-tohti-given-top.

179   **"What's really driving the incarceration"**   Author interview with Anna Hayes, lecturer at James Cook University, April 2019.

Chapter Seventeen

185   **Wang Zhiwen whose passport was canceled**   *Annual Report 2016*, Congressional-Executive Commission on China, 171, https://www.cecc.gov /publications/annual-reports/2016-annual-report.

Chapter Eighteen

189   **unable to legally work**   "'Open Prison': The Growing Despair of Refugees Stuck in Indonesia," Al Jazeera, March 3, 2019, https://www.aljazeera.com/news/2019/02 /prison-growing-despair-refugees-stuck-indonesia-190225055714272.html.

189   **about 13,800 refugees**   "Suicide, Depression and Poverty: Indonesia's Refugees' Bleak Future Now There's Almost No Chance of Being Resettled," *South China Morning Post*, March 21, 2018, https://www.scmp.com/lifestyle/article/2137993 /suicide-depression-and-poverty-indonesias-refugees-bleak-future-now-theres.

189   **Afghanistan, and Myanmar**   Ibid.

189   **forbids permanent refugee resettlement**   Ibid.

189   **tens of millions of people displaced**   "Figures at a Glance," UN Refugee Agency (UNHCR), https://www.unhcr.org/en-us/figures-at-a-glance.html.

189   **not many slots opening up**   "Suicide, Depression and Poverty," *South China Morning Post*.

189   **met with Philip Alston**   "Free Jiang Tianyong & End Suppression on Lawyers," Chinese Human Rights Defenders, November 21, 2017, https://www.nchrd.org /2017/11/free-jiang-tianyong-end-suppression-on-lawyers/.

189   **secret detention center for more than nine months**   "'709 Trials' Facts of the Alleged Crime in the Trial of Jiang Tianyong," China Human Rights Lawyers Concern Group, September 5, 2017, http://www.chrlawyers.hk/en/content/709 -trials-facts-alleged-crime-trial-jiang-tianyong.

189   **"inciting subversion of the state"**   "Jailed Chinese Human Rights Lawyer Jiang Tianyong Back Home after Going Missing on Release Day," *South China Morning Post*, March 2, 2019, https://www.scmp.com/news/china/politics/article/2188374 /jailed-chinese-human-rights-lawyer-jiang-tianyong-back-home.

189   **"doesn't even remember how old his kid is"**   "Third Anniversary of the Lawyers Crackdown," Amnesty International.

190   **borrowed from the Soviet Union**   "Psychiatric Abuse in Soviet Assailed," *New York Times*, May 14, 1987, https://www.nytimes.com/1987/05/14/us /psychiatric-abuse-in-soviet-assailed.html.

190   **Jiang was ultimately released in February 2019**   "Restrictions on Released Human Rights Lawyer," Amnesty International, March 15, 2019, https://www.amnesty.org/download/Documents/ASA1700212019ENGLISH.pdf.

190   **His safety remains tenuous**   "Wife of Lawyer under House Arrest Pens Appeal to Merkel Ahead of China Trip," Radio Free Asia, September 5, 2019, https://www.rfa.org/english/news/china/jiang-tianyong-09052019145211.html.

190   **closed the "consumptive demand clause" loophole**   Trade Facilitation and Trade Enforcement Act of 2015, CPB.

190   **then-representative Bernie Sanders**   *Congressional Record* 153, no. 7 (April 19, 2007), https://www.govinfo.gov/content/pkg/CRECB-2007-pt7/pdf/CRECB-2007-pt7-issue-2007-04-19.pdf; Paul C. Rosenthal and Anne E. Hawkins, "Applying the Law of Child Labor in Agricultural Supply Chains: A Realistic Approach," UC Davis, 2015, https://jilp.law.ucdavis.edu/issues/volume-21-1/Rosenthal.pdf.

190   **Senators Sherrod Brown and Ron Wyden**   "Brown, Wyden Urge Customs and Border Protection to Initiate Its Own Investigations into Products Made with Child and Forced Labor," Sherrod Brown, Senator for Ohio, July 15, 2016, https://www.brown.senate.gov/newsroom/press/release/brown-wyden-urge-customs-and-border-protection-to-initiate-its-own-investigations-into-products-made-with-child-and-forced-labor.

190   **75–20 vote**   "All Information (Except Text) for H.R.644—Trade Facilitation and Trade Enforcement Act of 2015," US Congress, https://www.congress.gov/bill/114th-congress/house-bill/644/all-info; "Senate Sends Sweeping Trade Enforcement Bill to Obama," *New York Times*, February 11, 2016, https://www.nytimes.com/2016/02/12/business/international/sweeping-trade-enforcement-law-gets-final-senate-approval.html.

192   **revealing his identity to the international press**   "A Firm and Resolute Chinese Hero," *Epoch Times*, September 11, 2018, https://www.theepochtimes.com/a-firm-and-resolute-chinese-hero_2658168.html.

193   **Hello Sun Yi**   Original email forwarded to author.

193   **"I'm just curious to hear his story"**   Author interview with Julie Keith.

194   **"You come here so long distance"**   Dialogue between Sun Yi and Julie Keith is drawn from transcripts shared by Leon Lee, director of *Letter From Masanjia*.

Chapter Nineteen

197   **some 160,000 detainees**   "China: Fully Abolish Re-Education through Labor," Human Rights Watch.

197   **informal, unregulated detention centers**   *Annual Report 2018*, CECC, 179.

197   **"there are 'black jails'"**   Author interview with Teng Biao, human rights lawyer.

198   **number of detainees . . . increased by sixfold**   "What Is a 'Legal Education Center' in China," China Change, April 3, 2014, https://chinachange.org/2014/04/03/what-is-a-legal-education-center-in-china/.

198   **thousands had already been tortured to death**   Ibid

198   **considered a state secret**   "2016 Human Rights Report: China (includes Tibet, Hong Kong, and Macau)," US Department of State, March 3, 2017, https://www.state.gov/reports/2016-country-reports-on-human-rights-practices/china-includes-tibet-hong-kong-and-macau/.

198   **guards have physically attacked . . . foreign journalists**   "'An Alleyway in Hell': China's Abusive Black Jails" Human Rights Watch, November 12, 2009, https://www.hrw.org/report/2009/11/12/alleyway-hell/chinas-abusive-black-jails.

198   **abolished custody and education centers**   "China Ends Forced Labour for Sex Workers," BBC, December 28, 2019, https://www.bbc.com/news/world-asia-china -50934305.

198   **run by the police**   "America's Hand in Chinese Drug Detox Prisons," *Atlantic*, August 7, 2012, https://www.theatlantic.com/health/archive/2012/08/americas -hand-in-chinese-drug-detox-prisons/260809/; "'Where Darkness Knows No Limits,'" Human Rights Watch; "China's Drug 'Rehabilitation' Centers Deny Treatment Allow Forced Labor," Human Rights Watch, January 6, 2010, https://www.hrw.org/news/2010/01/06/china-drug-rehabilitation-centers-deny -treatment-allow-forced-labor; "Shanghai's Struggle to Rehabilitate Rehab," Sixth Tone, September 28, 2016, http://www.sixthtone.com/news/1394/shanghais -struggle-to-rehabilitate-rehab.

199   **"There is absolutely no support"**   "'Where Darkness Knows No Limits,'" Human Rights Watch.

199   **pail of cold water in the face**   "China Turns Drug Rehab into a Punishing Ordeal," *New York Times*.

199   **Masanjia Women's Reeducation Through Labor Camp**   *Annual Report 2014*, Congressional-Executive Commission on China, https://www.cecc.gov/sites /chinacommission.house.gov/files/2014%20annual%20report_0.PDF.

199   **continue to manufacture products**   "Does the Masanjia Women's Detoxification Center in Shenyang Do Farm Work?" Baidu, June 15, 2016, https://zhidao.baidu .com/question/755556719227992404.html?qbl=relate_question_6.

199   **"a drug detox center or a prison?"**   Author discussion with employees of drug detox center in Shanghai.

200   **brand name Ruffin' It**   Westminster Pet Products, http://www.westminsterpet .com.

200   **Kmart, Walmart, Amazon, and Target**   "Ruffin' It Toss 'N Floss Rope Ball Dog Toy, Assorted Colors, 3/Pack," Kmart, https://www.kmart.com/ruffin-it-18213-toss -n-floss-rope-ball/p-SPM13694557610; "Westminster Pet Ruffin' It Durabone 4.75 in. Chew Dental Dog Toy 80506," Walmart, https://www.walmart.com/ip /Westminster-Pet-Ruffin-it-Durabone-4-75-In-Chew-Dental-Dog-Toy-80506 /38473849; "Westminster Pet 19315 Ruffin It Pet Waste Bags and Dispenser 2 Rolls of 15 Bags Each Assorted Colors," https://www.amazon.com/Westminster-Pet -Ruffin-Dispenser-Assorted/dp/B0051WTHLU/ref=sr_1_fkmrnull_2; "Ruffin'it Captain Jack Rubber Chicken Dog Toy - Large (17")," Target, https://www.target .com/p/ruffin-it-captain-jack-rubber-chicken-dog-toy-large-17/-/A-50700960#.

200   **large US retailers sell Kikkerland school supplies**   "Kikkerland T-Rex Eraser," Amazon, https://www.amazon.com/Kikkerland-ER19-T-Rex-Eraser/dp/B007EBA TKO; "Tiger Eraser KIKKERLAND DESIGN," Nordstrom, https://shop.nordstrom .com/s/kikkerland-design-tiger-eraser/3881252; Set of 3 Erasers, Heads, Kikkerland," Walmart, https://www.walmart.com/ip/ SET-OF-3-ERASERS-HEADS-KIKKERLAND-ER44/119347586.

200   **"don't have any information about the factories"**   Author discussion with a Kikkerland marketing director.

200   **"aspires" to audit its manufacturers**   "California Supply Chain Transparency Act Statement," Amazon, https://www.amazon.com/gp/help/customer/display .html?nodeId=GXYZF9M33FRJ5TMA.

200   **Apple's official 2018 supplier list**   I followed the detox center truck to the Primax Electronics facility located at No. 2688, Tong Xin Road, Yu Shan Town, Kunshan, Jiangsu, China, which is listed on Apple's website, https://www.apple.com/supplier -responsibility/pdf/Apple-Supplier-List.pdf#.

201   **Apple "strictly prohibits" any "involuntary labor"**   Author discussion with Apple spokesperson, March 2019.

201   **trained 17.3 million supplier employees**   *Supplier Responsibility: 2019 Progress Report*, Apple, https://www.apple.com/supplier-responsibility/pdf/Apple_SR_2019 _Progress_Report.pdf.

201   **reimburse $616,000 to workers**   *2018 Statement on Efforts to Combat Human Trafficking and Slavery in Our Business and Supply Chains*, Apple, https://www .apple.com/supplier-responsibility/pdf/Apple-Combat-Human-Trafficking-and -Slavery-in-Supply-Chain-2018.pdf.

201   **something akin to concentration camps**   "China Putting Minority Muslims in 'Concentration Camps,' U.S. Says," Reuters, May 3, 2019, https://fr.reuters.com /article/topNews/idUSKCN1S925K.

201   **a quarter of the twelve million Turkics**   "Securitization and Mass Detentions in Xinjiang: How Uyghurs Became Quarantined from the Outside World," Quartz, September 4, 2018, https://qz.com/1377394/securitization-and-mass-detentions -in-xinjiang-how-uyghurs-became-quarantined-from-the-outside-world/. Some sources state ten million, but that is inaccurate. There are ten million Uyghurs in Xinjiang. Although Uyghurs are the majority ethnic population in Xinjiang, they are not the only Turkic group that is being targeted for reeducation camps.

201   **erase an entire racial identity**   "China Is Detaining Muslims in Vast Numbers. The Goal: 'Transformation,'" *New York Times*, September 8, 2018, https://www .nytimes.com/2018/09/08/world/asia/china-uighur-muslim-detention-camp.html.

202   **daily indoctrination classes**   "China Is Treating Islam Like a Mental Illness," *Atlantic*, August 28, 2018, https://www.theatlantic.com/international/archive/2018 /08/china-pathologizing-uighur-muslims-mental-illness/568525/; "Data Leak Reveals How China 'Brainwashes' Uighurs in Prison Camps," BBC, November 24, 2019, https://www.bbc.com/news/world-asia-china-50511063; "Tens of Thousands of Xinjiang's Kuchar County Residents Held in Political 'Re-Education Camps,'" Radio Free Asia, August 9, 2018, https://www.rfa.org/english/news/uyghur/kuchar -08092018124248.html.

202   **sterilizing Turkic women**   "China's Attacks on Uighur Women Are Crimes against Humanity," opinion piece, *Washington Post*, October 21, 2019, https://www.washingtonpost.com/opinions/2019/10/21/chinas-attacks-uighur -women-are-crimes-against-humanity/.

202   **children are stolen from their parents**   "China's Jaw-Dropping Family Separation Policy," *Atlantic*, September 4, 2018, https://www.theatlantic.com/international/ archive/2018/09/china-internment-camps-uighur-muslim-children/569062/.

202   **Jamestown Foundation**   Adrian Zenz, "Sterilizations, IUDs, and Mandatory Birth Control: The CCP's Campaign to Suppress Uyghur Birthrates in Xinjiang," Jamestown Foundation, July 21, 2020, https://jamestown.org/wp-content/uploads/2020/06/Zenz -Internment-Sterilizations-and-IUDs-UPDATED-July-21-Rev2.pdf?x53419.

202   **84 percent**   Ibid

202   **Nearly zero**   Ibid

202   **initially denied the existence**   "China Changes Law to Recognise 'Re-Education Camps' in Xinjiang," *South China Morning Post*, October 10, 2018, https://www .scmp.com/news/china/politics/article/2167893/china-legalises-use-re-education -camps-religious-extremists.

202   **researchers used satellite imagery**   "What Satellite Images Can Show Us about 'Re-Education' Camps in Xinjiang," opinion piece, ChinaFile, August 23, 2018, http://www.chinafile.com/reporting-opinion/features/what-satellite-images-can -show-us-about-re-education-camps-xinjiang.

202   **condemnation from the UN**   "U.N. Calls on China to Free Uighurs from Alleged Re-Education Camps," Reuters, August 30, 2018, https://www.reuters.com/article /us-china-rights-un/u-n-calls-on-china-to-free-uighurs-from-re-education-camps -idUSKCN1LF1D6.

202   **conflicting narratives**   "You Can't Force People to Assimilate. So Why Is China At It Again?" opinion piece, *New York Times*, July 16, 2019, https://www.nytimes.com /2019/07/16/opinion/china-xinjiang-repression-uighurs-minorities-backfire.html.

202   **435 Uyghur intellectuals**   "UHRP Update: 435 Intellectuals Detained and Disappeared in the Uyghur Homeland," Uyghur Human Rights Project, May 21, 2019, https://uhrp.org/press-release/uhrp-update-435-intellectuals-detained-and -disappeared-uyghur-homeland.html.

203   **"The scope of this campaign"**   "China's Policy of Mass Detentions in Xinjiang 'Has Nothing to Do with Terrorism': US Anti-Terror Czar," Radio Free Asia, July 11, 2019, https://www.rfa.org/english/news/uyghur/czar-07112019155502.html.

203   **"complete ideological supremacy"**   "You Can't Force People to Assimilate." *New York Times*.

203   **annexed East Turkestan**   "Xinjiang, China's Restive Northwest," Human Rights Watch, https://www.hrw.org/legacy/campaigns/china-98/sj_xnj2.htm.

203   **"new frontier"**   Ibid.

203   **several Uyghur uprisings**   "East Turkestan," World Uyghur Congress, https://www.uyghurcongress.org/en/?page_id=29681.

203   **teeming with minerals**   "The Human Costs of Controlling Xinjiang," *Diplomat*, October 10, 2017, https://thediplomat.com/2017/10/the-human-costs-of-controlling -xinjiang/.

203   **oil, and natural gas**   "China Invests in Region Rich in Oil, Coal and Also Strife," *New York Times*, December 20, 2014, https://www.nytimes.com/2014/12/21/world /asia/china-invests-in-xinjiang-region-rich-in-oil-coal-and-also-strife.html.

204   **surged to 40 percent**   Anthony Howell and C. Cindy Fan, "Migration and Inequality in Xinjiang: A Survey of Han and Uyghur Migrants in Urumqi," *Eurasian Geography and Economics* 52, no. 1 (January 2011): 119–139, https://www.geog.ucla .edu/sites/default/files/users/fan/403.pdf; "Uighurs and China's Xinjiang Region," Council on Foreign Relations, May 29, 2012, https://www.cfr.org/backgrounder /uighurs-and-chinas-xinjiang-region.

204   **earmarked for the Chinese**   "Resentment Simmers in Western Chinese Region," *New York Times*, September 4, 2010, https://www.nytimes.com/2010/09/05/world /asia/05uighur.html

204   **language began disappearing from schools**   "China: Uighur Ethnic Identity under Threat in China," Amnesty International, July 6, 2009, https://www.amnesty .org.uk/press-releases/china-uighur-ethnic-identity-under-threat-china.

204   **fines for speaking Uyghur**   Ibid.

204   **primary language taught in Xinjiang preschools**   Ibid.

204   **"ethnic harmony" campaigns**   "Uyghur Leaflets Prompt Crackdown," Radio Free Asia, July 11, 2011, https://www.rfa.org/english/news/china/leaflets-071120111 13203.html.

204   **relatively secular**   "Forced Labour in East Turkestan," World Uyghur Congress.

204   **knife attack**   "Four Sentenced in China over Kunming Station Attack," BBC, September 12, 2014, https://www.bbc.com/news/world-asia-china-29170238/.

204   **large amount of food at home**   "Eradicating Ideological Viruses," Human Rights Watch.

204   **quit drinking and smoking**   Ibid.

205   **Rebiya Kadeer**   "Face of the Uighur Movement Is an Unlikely One," NPR, July 9, 2009, https://www.npr.org/templates/transcript/transcript.php?storyId =106437889.

205   **Ilham Tohti**   "Hundreds of Academics Urge China's President to Free Professor Ilham Tohti," Amnesty International, January 15, 2016, https://www.amnesty.org /en/latest/news/2016/01/hundreds-of-academics-urge-chinas-president-to-free -professor-ilham-tohti/.

205   **charged with separatism**   Ibid.

205   **Mihrigul Tursun**   For details regarding electric chair torture, see transcript of Tursun's congressional testimony. "Video: In Full—Ex-Xinjiang Detainee Mihrigul Tursun's Full Testimony at the US Congressional Hearing," *Hong Kong Free Press*, December 8, 2018, https://www.hongkongfp.com/2018/12/08/video-full-ex-xinjiang -detainee-mihrigul-tursuns-full-testimony-us-congressional-hearing/.

205   **"Long live Xi Jinping"**   Ibid.

206   **ten months in various reeducation camps**   Ibid. Details regarding Tursun's children and how she left Xinjiang are also from here.

206   **"I never thought"**   Ibid.

206   **"government made it clear"**   Ibid.

206   **"these men could be our fathers"**   Ibid.

206   **nine deaths in her cell**   Ibid.

206   **woman named Patemhan**   Ibid.

207   **woman named Gulnisa**   Ibid.

207   **claims of releasing . . . Muslim detainees**   "China Said It Closed Muslim Detention Camps. There's Reason to Doubt That," *New York Times*, August 9, 2019, https://www .nytimes.com/2019/08/09/world/asia/china-xinjiang-muslim-detention.html.

207   **pop up on satellite images**   Ibid; East Turkistan National Awakening Movement, https://nationalawakening.org/coordinates/.

207   **leaked a series of internal documents**   "'Absolutely No Mercy': Leaked Files Expose How China Organized Mass Detentions of Muslims," *New York Times*, November 16, 2019, https://www.nytimes.com/interactive/2019/11/16/world/asia/china-xinjiang -documents.html; "Leaked China Files Show Internment Camps Are Ruled by Secrecy and Spying," *New York Times*, November 24, 2019, https://www.nytimes.com/2019 /11/24/world/asia/leak-chinas-internment-camps.html; "Watched, Judged, Detained," CNN, February 2020, https://edition.cnn.com/interactive/2020/02/asia/xinjiang -china-karakax-document-intl-hnk/.

207   **extend the crackdown on Islam**   "'Absolutely No Mercy,'" *New York Times*.

207   **did not deny the authenticity**   "China Defends Crackdown on Muslims, and
Criticizes Times Article," *New York Times*, November 18, 2019, https://www
.nytimes.com/2019/11/18/world/asia/china-xinjiang-muslims-leak.html.

207   **economic incentives . . . to open factories**   "China's Detention Camps
for Muslims Turn to Forced Labor," *New York Times*, December 16, 2018,
https://www.nytimes.com/2018/12/16/world/asia/xinjiang-china-forced-labor
-camps-uighurs.html.

208   **Australian Strategic Policy Institute**   "Uyghurs For Sale," Australian Strategic
Policy Institute, March 1, 2020, https://www.aspi.org.au/report/uyghurs-sale.

208   **policies forbid forced labor**   "Human Rights and Labor Compliance Standards,"
Nike, https://purpose.nike.com/human-rights; "Supplier Responsibility," Apple,
https://www.apple.com/supplier-responsibility/; "BMW Group Code on Human
Rights and Working Conditions," BMW, https://www.bmwgroup.com/content
/dam/grpw/websites/bmwgroup_com/responsibility/downloads/en/2019/2019
-BMW-Group-Code-on-human-rights.pdf.

209   **"seen things like this since the 1930s"**   "Pompeo: Human Rights Abuses in
China Worst 'Since the 1930s,'" *Hill*, March 13, 2019, https://thehill.com/home
news/administration/433891-pompeo-human-rights-abuses-in-china-worst-since
-the-1930s.

209   **did not start off building death camps**   "From Citizens to Outcasts,
1933–1938," US Holocaust Memorial Museum, https://www.ushmm.org/
learn/introduction-to-the-holocaust/path-to-nazi-genocide/chapter-3/
from-citizens-to-outcasts-1933-1938.

209   **drive Jews and other "undesirable"**   "Holocaust Expert Counters Myths about
the Holocaust," Northwestern University, November 18, 2009, https://www
.northwestern.edu/newscenter/stories/2009/11/hayes.html.

209   **Final Solution**   Christopher R. Browning, "The Nazi Decision to Commit Mass
Murder: Three Interpretations: The Euphoria of Victory and the Final Solution":
Summer-Fall 1941, *German Studies Review* 17, no. 3 (October 1994): 473–81,
https://www.jstor.org/stable/1431894.

209   **"Goals can change"**   "Uncovering China's Secret Internment Camps with Rian
Thum: Podcast & Transcript," opinion piece, *Why Is This Happening?* NBC,
April 24, 2019, https://www.nbcnews.com/think/opinion/uncovering-china-s
-secret-internment-camps-rian-thum-podcast-transcript-ncna998116.

209   **Turkic population's biometric data**   "Chinese Authorities Collecting DNA
from All Residents of Xinjiang," *Guardian*, December 12, 2017, https://www.the
guardian.com/world/2017/dec/13/chinese-authorities-collecting-dna-residents
-xinjiang.

209   **ensuring accurate organ matching**   "What Is the Evidence?" *Journal of Political
Risk*.

209   **more than seventy countries**   "China's Belt and Road Initiative: Why the Price
Is Too High," Wharton School, University of Pennsylvania, April 30, 2019,
https://knowledge.wharton.upenn.edu/article/chinas-belt-and-road-initiative-
why-the-price-is-too-high/.

209   **Pakistan initially criticized Beijing**   "Pakistan Abruptly Stopped Calling Out
China's Mass Oppression of Muslims. Critics Say Beijing Bought Its Silence,"
Business Insider, January 13, 2019, https://www.businessinsider.my/pakistan-wont
-call-out-china-uighur-oppression-shows-power-of-money-2019-1/.

209   **Imran Khan later backtracked**   "PM 'Doesn't Know Much' about Condition of Uighurs in China," *Express Tribune*, January 8, 2019, https://tribune.com.pk/story/1883992/1-pm-doesnt-know-much-condition-uighurs-china/.

210   **blacklisted Xinjiang's entire public security bureau**   "U.S. Department of Commerce Adds 28 Chinese Organizations to Its Entity List," US Department of Commerce, October 7, 2019, https://www.commerce.gov/news/press-releases/2019/10/us-department-commerce-adds-28-chinese-organizations-its-entity-list.

210   **eight Chinese tech companies**   Ibid.

210   **"Manufacturing using forced labor"**   "Xinjiang: CECC Commissioners Seek Import Restrictions on Forced Labor Made Goods," Congressional-Executive Commission on China, November 5, 2019, https://www.cecc.gov/media-center/press-releases/xinjiang-cecc-commissioners-seek-import-restrictions-on-forced-labor.

210   **Uyghur Forced Labor Prevention Act**   "Sens. Cruz, Rubio Introduce Bipartisan Uyghur Forced Labor Prevention Act," Ted Cruz, US Senator for Texas, March 21, 2020, https://www.cruz.senate.gov/?p=press_release&id=4980.

210   **detention order for Hetian Taida**   "Withhold Release Orders and Findings: China," CBP.

210   **first detention order . . . in more than a year**   Ibid.

210   **Hetian Haolin Hair Accessories**   "Withhold Release Orders and Findings: China," CBP.

210   **Uyghur Human Rights Policy Act**   "S.3744 - Uyghur Human Rights Policy Act of 2020," US Congress, May 14, 2020, https://www.congress.gov/bill/116th-congress/senate-bill/3744.

211   **introduced the bill**   "House sends Uyghur human rights bill to Trump's desk," *CNN*, May 27, 2020, https://www.cnn.com/2020/05/27/politics/house-uyghur-bill-passage/index.html.

211   **more than fifty senators**   Ibid.

211   **CEO of Volkswagen**   "VW Boss 'Not Aware' of China's Detention Camps," BBC, April 16, 2019, https://www.bbc.com/news/av/business-47944767/vw-boss-not-aware-of-china-s-detention-camps.

211   **Muji and Uniqlo**   "Cotton and Corporate Responsibility: Fighting Forced Labor in Xinjiang and Uzbekistan," *Diplomat*, November 14, 2019, https://thediplomat.com/2019/11/cotton-and-corporate-responsibility-fighting-forced-labor-in-xinjiang-and-uzbekistan/.

211   **six million Jews had died**   "Americans and the Holocaust," US Holocaust Memorial Museum, https://exhibitions.ushmm.org/americans-and-the-holocaust/main; "Red Cross Admits Knowing of the Holocaust during the War," New York Times, December 19, 1996, https://www.nytimes.com/1996/12/19/us/red-cross-admits-knowing-of-the-holocaust-during-the-war.html; "Vatican Opens Archives of World War II-Era Pope Pius XII," NPR, March 2, 2020, https://www.npr.org/2020/03/02/811170588/vatican-opens-archives-of-world-war-ii-era-pope-pius-xii.

Epilogue

213   **acclaimed Uyghur singer**   "China Retaliates after Turkey's Claims about Abdurehim Heyit," BBC, February 11, 2019, https://www.bbc.com/news/world-asia-47196528.

213   **"That kind of pushback matters"**   Author interview with Anna Hayes.

214   **Raphaël Glucksmann**   "The EU's fight against fashion's forced labour supply chain," *Vogue Business*, August 3, 2020, https://www.voguebusiness.com/sustainability/eu-mandatory-due-diligence-legislation-uyghur-forced-labour-supply-chain.

214   **In the summer of 2020**   Raphaël Glucksmann, June 16 post on Instagram, "We won't give up," https://www.instagram.com/p/CBds3uPjgIQ/.

214   **eighty-two major corporations**   "Uyghurs for Sale," Australian Strategic Policy Institute.

216   **fairtrade label**   "What Is Fairtrade?" Fairtrade America, http://fairtradeamerica.org/About-Us/FAQs.

216   **inspired by a sustainable shopping post**   "Hold That Cardigan! A List of Questions to Ask Yourself Before You Shop," Man Repeller, November 26, 2019, https://www.manrepeller.com/2019/11/questions-to-ask-before-you-shop.html.

Bibliography

Allen, Michael Thad. *The Business of Genocide: The SS, Slave Labor, and the Concentration Camps*. Chapel Hill: University of North Carolina Press, 2005.

Applebaum, Anne. *Gulag: A History*. New York: Anchor Books, 2004.

Baptist, Edward. *The Half Has Never Been Told: Slavery and the Making of American Capitalism*. New York: Basic Books, 2016.

Bin, Du. *Vagina in Coma*. Taiwan: Zhang Huitan, 2011.

Ch'I, Hsi-Sheng. *Warlord Politics in China: 1916–1928*. Stanford, CA: Stanford University Press, 1976.

Chang, Jung. *Wild Swans: Three Daughters of China*. New York: Simon & Schuster, 2003.

Chang, Jung, and Jon Halliday. *Mao: The Unknown Story*. New York: Anchor Books, 2006.

Chang, Leslie T. *Factory Girls: From Village to City in a Changing China*. New York: Spiegel & Grau, 2009.

de Jong, Frederick. *Uyghur Texts in Context: Life in Shinjang Documented from Public Spaces*. Boston: Brill, 2017.

Doig, Will. *High-Speed Empire: Chinese Expansion and the Future of Southeast Asia*. New York: Columbia Global Reports, 2018.

Economy, Elizabeth. *The Third Revolution: Xi Jinping and the New Chinese State*. Oxford: Oxford University Press, 2018.

Elkins, Caroline. *Imperial Reckoning: The Untold Story of Britain's Gulag in Kenya*. New York: Holt, 2005.

Guangcheng, Chen. *The Barefoot Lawyer: A Blind Man's Fight for Justice and Freedom in China*. New York: Picador, 2016.

Gutmann, Ethan. *The Slaughter: Mass Killings, Organ Harvesting, and China's Secret Solution to Its Dissident Problem*. New York: Prometheus Books, 2014.

Harney, Alexandra. *The China Price: The True Cost of Chinese Competitive Advantage*. New York: Penguin Books, 2008.

Hessler, Peter. *Country Driving: A Journey through China from Farm to Factory*. New York: Harper, 2010.

Hongci, Xu. *No Wall Too High: One Man's Daring Escape from Mao's Darkest Prison*, trans. Erling Hoh. New York: Sarah Crichton Books, 2017.

Howard, Joshua H. *Workers at War: Labor in China's Arsenals, 1937–1953*. Stanford, CA: Stanford University Press, 2004.

Jingsheng, Wei. *The Courage to Stand Alone: Letters from Prison and Other Writings*. New York: Penguin Books, 1998.

Johnson, Ian. *The Souls of China: The Return of Religion after Mao*. New York: Vintage Books, 2018. Johnson, Ian. *Wild Grass: Three Portraits of Change in Modern China*. New York: Vintage, 2005.

Kadeer, Rebiya. *Dragon Fighter: One Woman's Epic Struggle for Peace with China*. Carlsbad, CA: Kales Press, 2011.

Laogai: The Machinery of Repression in China, edited by Nicole Kempton and Nan Richardson, New York: Umbrage Editions, 2009.

Li, Xiaobing, and Qiang Fang. *Modern Chinese Legal Reform: New Perspectives*. Lexington: University Press of Kentucky, 2013.

Lian, Xi. *Redeemed by Fire: The Rise of Popular Christianity in Modern China*. New Haven, CT: Yale University Press, 2010.

Lifton, Robert Jay. *Thought Reform and the Psychology of Totalism: A Study of 'Brainwashing' in China*. Chapel Hill: University of North Carolina Press, 1989.

Macy, Beth. *Factory Man: How One Furniture Maker Battled Offshoring, Stayed Local—and Helped Save an American Town*. New York: Little, Brown, 2014.

Moskowitz, Marc L. *Cries of Joy, Songs of Sorrow: Chinese Pop Music and Its Cultural Connotations*. Honolulu: University of Hawai'i Press, 2009.

Osnos, Evan. *Age of Ambition: Chasing Fortune, Truth, and Faith in the New China*. New York: Farrar, Straus and Giroux, 2014.

Ownby, David. *Falun Gong and the Future of China*. Oxford: Oxford University Press, 2008.

Palmer, David. *Qigong Fever: Body, Science, and Utopia in China*. New York: Columbia University Press, 2007.

Penny, Benjamin. *The Religion of Falun Gong*. Chicago: University of Chicago Press, 2012.

Pomfret, John. *Chinese Lessons: Five Classmates and the Story of the New China*. New York: Holt, 2006.

Saunders, Kate. *Eighteen Layers of Hell: Stories from the Chinese Gulag*. London: Cassell, 1996.

Schechter, Danny. *Falun Gong's Challenge to China: Spiritual Practice or "Evil Cult"?* New York: Akashic Books, 2001.

Shan, Weijian. *Out of the Gobi: My Story of China and America*. Hoboken, NJ: Wiley , 2019.

Smith, Aminda M. *Thought Reform and China's Dangerous Classes: Reeducation, Resistance, and the People*. New York: Rowman & Littlefield, 2012.

Solzhenitsyn, Aleksandr. *The Gulag Archipelago*, vols. 1–3. New York: HarperCollins, 2007.

Thum, Rian. *The Sacred Routes of Uyghur History*. Cambridge, MA: Harvard University Press, 2014.

Tong, James W. *Revenge of the Forbidden City: The Suppression of the Falungong in China, 1999–2005*. Oxford: Oxford University Press, 2009.

Tong, Scott. *A Village with My Name: A Family History of China's Opening to the World*. Chicago: University of Chicago Press, 2017.

Treadgold, Donald. *The West in Russia and China: Religious and Secular Thought in Modern Times: Volume 2, China 1582–1949*. Cambridge: Cambridge University Press, 1973.

Wu, Hongda Harry. *Laogai: The Chinese Gulag*. Boulder, CO: Westview Press, 1992.

Wu, Harry, and Carolyn Wakeman. *Bitter Winds: A Memoir of My Years in China's Gulag*. Hoboken, NJ: Wiley, 1995.

Wu, Harry, and George Vecsey. *Troublemaker: One Man's Crusade against China's Cruelty*. New York: Times Books, 1996.

Yang, Xianhui. *Woman from Shanghai: Tales of Survival from a Chinese Labor Camp*. New York: Anchor Books, 2010.